2015 NIAN WAIYU JIAOXUE YU YANJIU LUNWENJI

2015年外语教学与研究

论文集

主 编◎刘明宇

副主编◎马 蓉 卢丹军

知识产权出版社

全国百佳图书出版单位

图书在版编目(CIP)数据

2015年外语教学与研究论文集 / 刘明宇主编. —北京:知识产权出版社,2015.11
ISBN 978-7-5130-3897-3

Ⅰ.①2… Ⅱ.①刘… Ⅲ.①外语教学—教学研究—文集 Ⅳ.①H09-53

中国版本图书馆CIP数据核字(2015)第270400号

内容提要

本书收录了北京工商大学外国语学院教师2015年度的论文。论文类型涉及翻译、语言学与教学、外国文学与文化、教学管理与实验教学等研究领域。论文作者中有教授、副教授、讲师，有博士、硕士、海归学者，他们具有多年的教学经验，并且都工作在外语教学的第一线。经典的教研理论和亲身体会，使论文形成了独特的文风，和对实践有切实指导的观点。汇编出版本书，不仅有助于作者之间相互交流、共同提高，也可供其他学校的广大同行参考。

责任编辑：安耀东

2015年外语教学与研究论文集
刘明宇 主编
马 蓉 卢丹军 副主编

出版发行：知识产权出版社有限责任公司	网 址：http：//www.ipph.cn
电 话：010-82004826	http：//www.laichushu.com
社 址：北京市海淀区马甸南村1号	邮 编：100088
责编电话：010-82000860转8534	责编邮箱：an569@qq. com
发行电话：010-82000860转8101/8029	发行传真：010-82000893/82003279
印 刷：北京中献拓方科技发展有限公司	经 销：各大网上书店、新华书店及相关专业书店
开 本：720mm×1000mm 1/16	印 张：20.25
版 次：2015年11月第1版	印 次：2015年11月第1次印刷
字 数：323千字	定 价：61.00元

ISBN 978-7-5130-3897-3

目 录
CONTENTS

翻译研究

语言学与教学研究

外国文学与文化研究

教育、教学探讨与实验教学研究

翻译研究 ☜

语言学与教学研究

外国文学与文化研究

教育、教学探讨与实验教学研究

Reflections on Translation of Chinese University Mottos into English

张艳华

摘　要：校训，作为大学精神实质的表述、治学育人的理念、培养模式和智慧结晶的体现，有着深刻的内涵和鲜明的特色。它不仅形式独特、含义隽永，而且具有强烈的节奏感和视觉、审美效果，历来备受各个学校重视。随着中外高校交流和合作的加强，我国高校要走向世界，校训的英译已成为对外宣传的焦点和核心之一，校训译文质量的高低也直接影响对外宣传的效果，影响学校的办学特色、办学思想和教育模式。

中国有着历史悠久的教育传统和许多优秀的教育思想，这些在校训中都有体现。如何忠实、通达、雅致地把校训翻译成英语并非是一件容易的事情。本文探索中国高校校训的来源、特色、历史渊源等，并重点论述校训英译的有效策略和技巧。

关键词：高校校训；特点；挑战；策略

With the economic globalization proceeding ever faster and China's entry to the WTO, exchanges in every aspect have come up into a new phase, and cultural exchanges have definitely become a major part of the current flow. Sino-foreign co-operative education is growing into a new education style receiving more and more

---

项目/基金：本文得到2015年北京工商大学教育教学改革研究项目的资助，项目编号JG155217。

作者简介：张艳华，女，北京工商大学副教授，主要研究方向为英语语言学、翻译理论与实践、英语教学等。

popularity. Universities are going global. The intensification of international educational exchanges and co-operations gives rise to the importance of University publicity. In this sense, introduction of universities has become a very urgent business that all universities have to put on the agenda. University mottos, as expressions of the spirit essence of universities and the soul of campus culture, are the banners that convey the value and the guiding principles of each university, encouraging students and universities alike to pursue the common ideal. Thus the importance of translating university mottos is becoming greater than ever before. However, motto translation is still a relatively new subject in China that lacks sophisticated guiding theories or principles, and the unique characteristics and cultural peculiarities of the language of Chinese university mottos provide further obstacles to motto translation into English.

1 Definition of Motto

According to *Longman Dictionary of Contemporary English*, motto means:

1) A short sentence or a few words taken as the guiding principle of a person, of a school, etc;

2) Esp. BrE, an amusing clever short printed phrase put esp. inside a Christmas cracker;

3) A few words, or a short musical phrase, placed at the beginning of a book, or of a piece of music.

According to *The American Heritage Dictionary of the English Language* (*Fourth Edition*):

1) A brief statement used to express a principle, goal, or ideal;

2) A sentence, phrase, or word of appropriate character inscribed on or attached to an object;

3) A maxim adopted as a guide to one's conduct.

Definition from *Wikipedia*:

"A motto is a phrase or collection of words intended to describe the motivation or intention of a sociological grouping or organization."

From the definitions given above, we can conclude the meaning of university mottos as "A brief statement intended to express the guiding principles, motivation, goal or ideal of a university."

2 Features of Chinese University Mottos

University mottos retain some special features, which make it striking to the eye as well as stimulating to the mind, both in content and form.

2.1 Origins of Chinese University Mottos

2.1.1 Ancient Classical Works

China enjoys a long and profound literary and philosophical tradition. As early as 2000 years ago, a lot of great works were produced, and left us with a rich cultural tradition and abundant philosophical thoughts on education. A good number of the Chinese university mottos take their origin from some classical works by the great scholars of ancient China. Thus, these university mottos are bestowed with rich and profound cultural and philosophical meanings.

① Tsinghua University: Self-discipline and Social Commitment, from *Book of Changes.*

（清华大学：自强不息，厚德载物）

② The Hong Kong Polytechnic University:

To Learn and to Apply for the Benefit of Mankind, from *Book of Changes* and *On Balance*（《论衡》）.

（香港理工大学：开物成务，励学利民）

③ JiNan University: Loyalty, Credibility, Sincerity, and Piety, from *The Analects of Confucius.*

（暨南大学：忠信笃敬）

④ Southeast University: Strive for Perfection, from *The Analects of Confucius.*

（东南大学：止于至善）

⑤ Huazhong University of Science & Technology（HUST）:

Commend Morals, Advocate Knowledge, Seek Truth and Make Innovations, from *The Great Learning*.

（华中科技大学：明德、厚学、求是、创新）

2.1.2 Famous Historical Figures

Some university mottos have their own stories with some famous historical figures, and these mottos might as well have been part of the personal mottos of those important figures. For example, the motto of China Ocean University（青岛海洋大学校训：海纳百川，至人至德）take form the personal motto of the great hero and famous official of the Qing Dynasty, Lin Zexu（林则徐）. He used to hang a scroll in the main hall of his house, with the motto "海纳百川，有容乃大；壁立千刃，无欲则刚."

2.1.3 President or Founder of the University

Still some university mottos have evolved from the educational philosophy or thinking of the president of the universities. University mottos, in this case, are often changed so that they can keep up with the contemporary society, and at the same time guide the university and students to meet the needs of the real world. The current motto of Peking University offers a vivid example of this kind. The motto "爱国、进步、民主、科学"（Patriotism, Advancement, Democracy and Science）was put forward by Mr. Cai Yuanpei, President of Peking University who played an active role in the reform and development of the university. As an educationist and democratic revolutionary, Mr. Cai fixed a new motto for Peking University, the center of the Chinese New-Culture Movement and the earliest base for the dissemination of Marxism in China, and gave the university a new guideline to match its glorious revolutionary tradition.

2.1.4 Contemporary or Other Sources

A few university mottos comply with the state government's policy, or even are directly taken from the remarks or ideas of some government leaders. When the former premier Zhu Rongji visited Shanghai National Accounting Institute in

April，2001，he expressed his hope for accountants in China- "Making No Fake Accounts"（不做假账），and later this wish became the current motto of the school. About six month later，this principle was included in the motto of Beijing National Accounting Institute. University mottos borrowed this way often reflect colors of the modern society，as well as the needs of the country.

2.2 Traditional Philosophies of Education in China

China has a long and profound tradition of education，and some great educationists had put forward many philosophies of education either through their personal experience or their practices in education. The principles are many，but only some most familiar ones are listed here.

(1) Educational philosophies initiated by Lao Zi（老子）:

· Make progress gradually in due course.（循序渐进）

· Self-transform in accordance with objective principles.（无为自化）

(2) Educational philosophies initiated by Confucius（孔子）:

· Educate according to the student's characteristics.（因材施教）

· Inspire and guide.（启发诱导）

· Emphasize both learning and reflecting.（学思并重）

· Keep persistent interest in learning.（学而不厌）

· Put what you learn into practice.（学以致用）

· Give prominence to education on virtues.（突出德育）

· To attain new knowledge through reviewing the old.（温故知新）

(3) Educational philosophies initiated by Mencius（孟子）:

· Pursue excellence and make progress.（深造自得）

· Perseverance and concentration.（专心有恒）

(4) Educational philosophies initiated by Mo Zi（墨子）:

· Be initiative to learn.（主动性原则）

· To learn through examples and classifications.（察类明故）

(5) Educational philosophies initiated by Xun Zi（荀子）:

· Value perseverance in learning.（学贵有恒）

· Make good use of tools.（善假于物）

· Practice with earnestness.（力行）

3 Strategies of Translating Chinese University Mottos into English

3.1 Literal Translation

Literal translation is a way in which the grammatical constructions of the source language are converted into its nearest equivalents of the target language but the lexical words are translated singly, out of context. This method is usually employed for the original text with few or no connotations, such as:

① Peking University: Patriotism, Advancement, Democracy and Science.

（北京大学：爱国、进步、民主、科学）

② Zhejiang University: Seek Truth and Be Creative.

（浙江大学：求是、创新）

③ National University of Defense Technology: Dedication and Practicality.

（国防科技大学：奉献、求实）

Literal translation can retain as much as possible the foreign flavor of the original text and at the same time introduces fresh expressions into the target language. But due to the vast discrepancies between languages and cultures, literal translation is not always feasible, thus various methods of accommodation and compensation are recommended.

3.2 Literal Translation Combined With Free Translation

Literal translation is the best means of sticking to the principle of "be faithful to the source," and free translation is a good choice resulting from sufficient consideration of the need or status of target readers. This tells us an ideal translation should be faithful to the SL text as well as understandable to the target readers. In this sense, it is very necessary and significant to combine literal translation and free translation in certain cases. As for some Chinese university mottos, translators render the original mottos literally in the former part to keep their national features and then paraphrase them in the latter part so that the readers can grasp them without any trouble. For some other mottos, translators employ literal translation for the parts that are easy to understand for target readers while free translation for the difficult parts.

(1) The motto of Beijing University of Aeronautics and Astronautics (北京航空航天大学：德才兼备，知行合一) is translated as "Having Both Ability and Integrity, Seeking and Acting for Truth."

The first part of the motto is easy to understand, so literal translation is acceptable, but for the second part, the meaning is different from what can be seen on the surface: here "知" means "seeking for truth" rather than "knowledge", so it's necessary to employ free translation to make up for what free translation can't achieve in this part.

(2) Harbin Institute of Technology: Strict Standard and Sufficient Effort.

(哈尔滨工业大学：规格严格，功夫到家)

To translate the first part "规格严格" as "Strict Standard" literally not only retain the feature in Chinese and the cherished quality of this university, but also makes the translation brief and concise as the original text. But for the latter part, it'll cause serious confusion and misunderstanding if we continue to adopt literal translation and translate it as "Martial Arts Go Home." While the version "Sufficient Effort" coming from free translation can bring to light to the target readers the exact meaning of the original Chinese phrase. There are more examples of this kind.

(3) The Chinese University of Hong Kong : Broaden One's Intellectual Horizon and Keep It Within The Bounds of Propriety.

(香港中文大学：博文、约礼)

(4) Fudan University: Rich in Knowledge and Tenacious of Purpose; Inquiring with Earnestness and Reflecting with Self-practice.

(复旦大学：博学而笃志，切问而近思)

(5) Sichuan University: Persist Devotion and Perseverance in Learning; Make Progress Everyday.

(四川大学：精韧不怠，日进有功)

3.3 Cultural Compensation

Taking roots in the rich soil of Chinese culture, Chinese university mottos usually bear strong national flavors, and are featured with their profound cultural background. In order to avoid cultural loss and retain in the translation the same level of impact and appeal as the original motto text has had in Chinese culture, the translator should rewrite rather than translate the motto text rigidly word for word, with the basic idea or message retained and the cultural context compensated. Let's take an example from the translation of the motto of University of Science and Technology of China——"红专并进，理实交融." The word "红专并进" is transformed from the slogan "又红又专." If we fail to note the cultural connotation of "红" in this slogan, and translate it word for word as "both red and professional", the target readers would in no way understand the exact meaning of the original phrase. In Chinese, "red" is sometimes associated with advanced performances and revolution. But this connotation is not commonly known to native English Speakers. Therefore, it's best we contain it into the translation and translate it as "Socialist-Minded and Professionally Proficient."

More examples of this kind:

① Beijing Normal University: Learn to be an Excellent Teacher; Act as an Exemplary Person.

(北京师范大学：学为人师，行为世范)

② Beijing University of Aeronautics and Astronautics: Having Both Ability and Integrity, Seeking and Acting for Truth.

(北京航空航天大学：德才兼备，知行合一)

3.4 Converting and Restructuring

To maintain the aesthetic properties of the style and content of Chinese university mottos, we often have to make some conversion between words and rearrange the word order as well as structure in translation. In many cases, there are some words or sentence structures, which are unique for the Chinese university mottos. It's impossible to successfully reappear the full content and same structure of the original mottos in the target language by literal translation or free translation. At this time, we need the method of converting and restructuring, of words and structure.

① The motto of Hong Kong Polytechnic University: To Learn and to Apply for the Benefit of Mankind.

（香港理工大学：开物成务，励学利民）

② The motto of Tsinghua University: Self-discipline and Social Commitment.

（清华大学：自强不息，厚德载物）

This translation is a good example of this kind. The Chinese motto text is translated as "Self- discipline and Social Commitment", which successfully reappeared the profound meaning and concise structure of the original text.

3.5 Imitation or Substitution

The approach of imitation or substitution is not commonly employed to translating Chinese university mottos so far, and only two of the examples of this kind both come from Hong Kong, and are both translated in Latin, as most university mottos in America and the UK do. This kind of translations meets the target readers' idiomatic way of speaking. In this sense, this strategy of imitation and substitution can be very beneficial to universities aiming at going global. Let's have a further discussion by examples.

"Officium et Civitas " is the Latin translation for the motto of City University of Hong Kong "敬业乐群". Officium captures the rich connotations of the word and denotes a high-minded sense of duty, including high office, with a very positive moral connotation. Civitas refers to both town/city and "union of citizens (commonwealth) " which is most appropriate for City University."

The motto of The University of Hong Kong（明德格物）is translated into the

Latin phrase Sapientia et Virtus, meaning "wisdom and virtue" or sometimes cited as "Foresight & Socia."

We can see the implied meanings of the Chinese university mottos are well transferred into the translated mottos, and the translations bear the brief, concise and aesthetic qualities of university mottos.

Accordingly, we can translate Chinese university mottos into English by imitating or substituting, and achieve the better effect.

① Southeast University: Strive for Perfection.

（东南大学：止于至善）

② Xiamen University: Pursue Excellence, Strive for Perfection.

（厦门大学：自强不息，止于至善）

③ Hong Kong Polytechnic University: To Learn and to Apply for the Benefit of Mankind.

（香港理工大学：开物成务，励学利民）

We must always keep in mind that strategies of translation are to serve the purpose of achieving dynamic equivalence in translation, and they are seldom used alone, but in combination with several other strategies. During our translation of a Chinese university motto we ought to do our utmost to retain its full meaning or at least replace it by other appropriate ones in order to deliver the spirit essence of Chinese university education.

To sum up, translating university mottos is a tough and fascinating job. The strategies proposed in this essay cannot be counted as perfect, and they are likely to leave much to be desired. In addition, we must always bear in mind that every successful translation is attained by using an effective combination of several strategies. Therefore, in the process of translating Chinese university mottos into English, it is very important for translators to make the right decision on what should be contained in the combination.

Bibliography

[1] PETER N. A textbook of translation [M].London: Prentice Hall International (UK) Ltd., 1998.

[2] NIDA E A . Toward a science of translating[M]. Leiden: E.J.Brill, 1964.

[3] NIDA E A. Language, culture, and translating [M]. Shanghai: Shanghai Foreign Language Education Press, 1993.

[4] 陈文伯. 英语成语与汉语成语[M]. 北京:外语教学与研究出版社,1982.

[5] 谭载喜. 新编奈达论翻译[M]. 北京:中国对外翻译出版公司,1999.

[6] 李延林,潘利锋,郭勇. Studies of English cultural translation[M]. 长沙:中南大学出版社, 2003.

[7] 包惠南. 文化语境与语言翻译[M]. 北京:中国对外翻译出版公司,2001.

[8] 郭建中. 文化与翻译[M]. 北京:中国对外翻译出版公司,2000.

[9] 刘宓庆. 文化翻译论纲[M]. 武汉:湖北教育出版社,1999.

Functional Equivalence in English-Chinese Idiom Translation

王雨辰

摘　要：如今，习语在日常交流中的应用十分广泛，因此找到一种合适的习语翻译方法也十分必要。多年以来，不同学派的翻译学者们针对习语翻译提出了各种各样的方法。通过学习翻译理论，作者发现奈达的翻译理论，特别是他对于功能对等和文化翻译的观点对于习语翻译是最为实用且理想的翻译方法。基于奈达的翻译理论，本文旨在探究功能对等下的习语翻译策略，证明功能对等理论可以应用于习语翻译，并解决英汉习语翻译中存在的大量问题。

关键词：功能；对等；习语翻译

1 Research Background

An idiom is a word or group of words that cannot be literally translated from the source language into the target language because an idiomatic meaning cannot be understood by literally defining its component parts. English, as the most active and widely used language, enjoys a vast idiomatic basis, which makes its learning very exciting and interesting, with about 4,000 idioms used in the daily communication.

作者简介：王雨辰，北京工商大学助理实验师，外交学院英语翻译专业毕业，研究方向为英语翻译、现代教育技术等。

In view of the difficulty and the significance of idiom learning, as language learners, who are supposed to build a bridge for the Eastern and Western languages, we should become aware of the increasing significance of idiom learning. Due attention and efforts should be given to the study of English idioms and more work needs to be done into this special field. English learners should learn about the meaning and usages of idioms as well as the origins of these idioms for the sake of adequate communication.

2 Introduction of Nida and His Concept of Equivalence

Nida is a famous American translation theorist and linguist. Both in western and eastern countries, translation studies have been greatly influenced by his translation theory which paves the way for the study of modem translation works.

"Functional equivalence" is the core of Nida's translation theory. It was first put forward as "dynamic equivalence" in Toward a Science of Translation (1964) and elaborated in the Theory and Practice of Translation (1969). Nida expounded two fundamental types of equivalence in translation which are formal equivalence and dynamic equivalence. "Formal equivalence" is text-oriented. In such a translation, the translator tries to "reproduce as literally and meaningfully as possible the form and content of the original," and the reader is allowed to "identify himself as fully as possible with a person in the source—language context, and to understand as much as he can of the custom, manner of thought, and means of expression." However, "dynamic equivalence" is reader-oriented. Nida proves the legitimacy of dynamic equivalent translation from the viewpoint of information theory and communication theory.

In 1969 Nida formally defined dynamic equivalence in the book *The Theory and Practice of Translation*: "Dynamic equivalence is therefore to be defined in terms of the degree to which the receptors of the message in the receptor language respond to it in substantially the same manner as the receptors in the source language."

2.1 Functional Equivalence in Idiom Translation

In translation, because of cultural differences, a serious problem may cause amusement and laughter while a harmless statement may cause displeasure and anger. From our daily communication, we can tell that cultural equivalence is more subtle and difficult than linguistically oriented equivalence. A good and exact functional equivalent version may be very effective in eliminating such misunderstandings among peoples from different cultural backgrounds. The problem is how to achieve the highest degree of functional equivalence. The author has worked out some basic principles for the effective use of this equivalence theory in the translation of idioms with cultural messages.

Firstly, understanding the source text is of vital importance. Secondly, dynamic equivalence has the priority over formal equivalence. Thirdly, the translator should be careful to avoid choosing the false equivalent in the target culture. Fourthly, translators must always keep readers in mind.

With these four principles, translators can achieve functional equivalence in idiom translation. And in order to illustrate how to apply the theory of functional equivalence to English idiom translation, three degrees of correspondence between English and Chinese idioms are discussed with examples in the following parts. The three degrees of correspondence are corresponding, semi-corresponding and non-corresponding.

2.2 Corresponding Idioms

Cultural similarities are reflected in many idioms. However, there are also many idioms in similar forms but different meanings and functions in two languages. Therefore, we should use the corresponding idioms with great care because "equivalents" seldom culturally equal. The SL idioms can be replaced by the corresponding TL idioms in the following situations.

2.2.1 Idiom Equivalent Both in Form and Content

In English and Chinese, there are some idioms which are of the same grammatical forms and of the more or less same figurative meaning and function. In this case, such an SL idiom can certainly be replaced by the corresponding TL idiom in translation since they are equivalent both in form and in content. Using the equivalent or corresponding TL idioms to translate SL idioms can transfer the cultural messages from the SL text to the TL text very effectively if the SL idioms and the TL idioms are really equivalent in every aspect of meaning, style, and coloring. For instance,

Out of sight, out of mind.（眼不见，心不烦）

To add fuel to the fire.（火上浇油）

Walls have ears.（隔墙有耳）

Strike while the iron is hot.（趁热打铁）

A bolt from the blue.（晴天霹雳）

To be on the thin ice.（如履薄冰）

To pour oil on the flame.（火上浇油）

To fish in troubled waters.（浑水摸鱼）

In the above group of idioms, the literal translation approach is applied. Take the idiom *walls have ears* for instance, the English idiom uses the rhetorical device of simile, and the corresponding Chinese one contains the same cultural message and the same rhetorical device. We translate them literally for the purpose of reproducing the effect of the closest natural equivalence on the minds of the readers and the original flavor faithfully and vividly. In this instance, the cultural message and the rhetorical device of the original text can be conveyed to us directly and clearly.

2.2.2 Idioms Accepted by the Target Culture

There is another type of equivalent idioms with the similar image and figurative meaning in English and Chinese. These idioms are usually originally transferred into the target culture literally and merged into target culture gradually through a period of time. As a result, people in the target culture are so familiar with such idioms that they use them frequently without knowing where they actually come from. Therefore, the literal translation of these idioms with specific cultural connotations cab also be understood by the TL readers easily. The cultural elements in the SL idioms are accepted consciously by the TL readers.

Here are some English idioms which have already been accepted and extensively used by readers: have the gift of the gab（能说会道）, call a spade a spade（直言不讳）, hole-and-corner（偷偷摸摸）, like a cat on hot bricks（热锅上的蚂蚁）, between the devil and the deep sea（进退两难）, put all one's eggs in one basket（孤注一掷）, escape by the skin of one's teeth（死里逃生）, what's done is done（木已成舟）, no smoke without fire（无风不起浪）.

2.3 Semi-corresponding Idioms

Due to linguistic and cultural diversity, exact equivalence is very hard to achieve. Only a small number of idioms have the same form and idiomatic meaning. Semi-correspondence refers to idioms that are partially equivalent to each other. This can be seen in the following two areas.

2.3.1 Idioms Equivalent Superficially

Some SL idioms may contain the same or similar images and the same or similar literal meaning as the *corresponding* TL idioms, but they may have quite different figurative meanings. If the translator uses such formal corresponding TL idioms in his translation, he will totally change the cultural messages of the SL idioms. Here is the list of different figurative meanings of Chinese and English idioms with similar literal meanings.

（1）pull one's legs: to make fun of someone by trying to make him believe something not real.

（2）wash one's hands of: to refuse to accept any responsibility for something.

（3）a walking skeleton: a living being reduced to skins and bones.

Such kinds of corresponding or equivalent TL idioms should never be used in translation. Unfortunately in the practice of translation such a kind of mistakes are not uncommon. For example, if we use equivalent Chinese idiom 翘尾巴 to translate the English idiom *have one's tail up*, the emotional coloring will be totally distorted because the Chinese idiom is derogative whereas the English idiom is commendatory. Here are some other examples: Diamond cut diamond（棋逢对手）, Murder will out（纸包不住火）, New brooms sweep clean（新官上任三把火）, It never rains but it pours（祸不单行）.

2.3.2 Idioms Equivalent in Content but not in Form

As Chinese and English idioms come into being under different cultural backgrounds, some share the similar figurative meanings and perform the same function but have different figures of speech and different images. These idioms can be replaced by each other in translation. Such replacement keeps much of the original flavor without causing obscurity, or losing the vivid imagery. In English and Chinese, these idioms are not rare to be found: Law of the Medes and Persians（金科玉律）, Great minds think alike（英雄所见略同）, Life up the heel against somebody（暗箭伤人）, Never too late to mend（亡羊补牢，犹为晚也）, Great boasters, little doers（说话的巨人行动的矮人）, Life up the heel against somebody（暗箭伤人）, Ill news comes apace（好事不出门，坏事传千里）, What do you expect from a pig but a grunt（狗嘴里吐不出象牙）.

2.4 Non-corresponding Idioms and Their Translation

Because of cultural differences, most of the SL idioms cannot find their equivalent counterpart in the TL idioms. Non-correspondence means that there are no existing equivalents in the target culture. It doesn't mean that functional equivalence can't be achieved. In translation of such idioms, certain adjustments have to be made in order to achieve highest equivalents. Here the translator's bilingual competence is of help to him only that any equivalence in this case cannot be found but will have to be tactfully created.

2.4.1 Achieving Equivalence by Literal Translation of Idioms with the Addition of Footnotes

Sometimes the limitation of literal rendition of idioms can be removed by the addition of footnotes. Besides. the addition of explanatory phases is an important way to strengthen the advantages of literal translation of idioms. It is also a brief and immediate method to promote cultural exchange.

Usually the implied connotation of an SL idiom is very clear to the SL readers but quite difficult to understand for the TL readers. Sometimes the cultural background and the implied meaning can be conveyed to the TL with the addition of a footnote. Let's look at the following example:

"难道这也是个痴丫头，又像颦儿来葬花不成？因又自笑道：若真也葬花，可谓'东施效颦'了；不但不为新奇，而且更是可厌。"（Cao Xueqin, 1985：425）

"Can this be another absurd maid come to bury flowers like Taiyu?" he wondered in some amusement. "If so, she's Tung Shih imitating Hsi Shih', which isn't original but rather tiresome."

Footnote: Hsi Shih was a famous beauty in the ancient Kingdom of Yueh. Tung Shih was an ugly girl who tried to imitate her ways. (Yang Xianyi, 1994: 602)

In the idiom "东施效颦," it contains some national culture which is not familiar to the TL readers. The cultural message or characteristic can be transferred to the TL text through the addition of a footnote.

This method not only conveys the cultural connotation in the idiom properly but also makes the translated idiom easily understood. The footnotes can solve some problems of untranslatability and increase the target readers' knowledge of foreign culture. However, too many footnotes may interfere with the fluency of the translated text and target readers' appreciation of the target text. What's more, some cultural messages cannot be explained properly with several sentences. Therefore, translators will use free translation of SL idioms in order to achieve functional equivalence.

2.4.2 Achieving Functional Equivalence by Free Translation of SL Idioms

Literal translation of idioms has great advantages in the terms of cultural exchange, but sometimes it may make the readers feel quite puzzled about the meaning of some idioms. The limitation of literal rendition of idioms cannot he removed by the addition of footnotes or explanatory phrases in all eases. In this instance, free translation of SL idioms may have to be applied.

In order to achieve the effect of functional equivalence, sometimes the source idioms will be paraphrased into the target language. The application of free translation can be used in the following situations.

(1) Where incomprehensible for the TL text would otherwise be produced.

A. A truly wise person does not show off his (her) ability.（大智若愚）

B. How stupid of me to forget what I really come for and just to maunder on! (Yang Xianyi: 858)（可是我糊涂了！正经说的都没有，且说些“陈芝麻，烂谷了”的（Cao Xueqin，1985：620））

C. But when thou doest alms, let not thy left hand know what thy right hand doeth.（你施舍的时候，不要大肆宣扬）

(2) Where misunderstanding on the part of the TL reader would otherwise arise:

A. Be born with a silver spoon in her mouth（生长在富贵之家）

B. People who live in glass house should not throw stones.（自己有短处就不要去揭别人的短处）

C. Publication of the draft plan touched off a lively discussion with everybody eager to put in a word.（方案一公布，大家就“七嘴八舌”地议论开了）

Let's take the Chinese idiom “七嘴八舌” for instance. In fact, it doesn't refer to *seven mouths and eight tongues*, but refers to an action. Its implied meaning is that many people are eager to put in a word at the same time. Therefore, it is not sensible to translate it into *seven mouths and eight tongues*.

Frankly speaking, free translation of idioms is the last resort for rendering idioms because it usually greatly reduces vividness of the idioms and the cultural messages transferred to the TL text.

3 Conclusion

In this thesis, the author proposes to apply Nida's functional equivalence as a theoretical guidance to English idiom translation, and adopt functional equivalence translation to achieve "ideal" effect in English idiom translation. The author offers a variety of definitions of English idioms given by authoritative dictionaries and scholars, meanwhile, puts forward the working definition of English idioms in thesis and the features of English idioms. And also, in this thesis, the ways of applying functional equivalence are anglicized in three different categories which are corresponding idioms, semi-corresponding idioms and non-corresponding Idioms. Based on Nida's view of language, culture and translation, and illustrated examples in this thesis, we can see that English idiom can surely be translated into Chinese.

Bibliography

[1] MORGAN B. Teaching and Learning Language and Culture[M]. Philadelphia: Multilingual Matters, 1994.

[2] DAGUT M B. Can metaphor be translated[M]. London: Babel Publishing Company, 1976.

[3] ROSS D. The rhetorical tradition: principles and practice[M]. New York: Hunt Publishing Company, 1978.

[4] NIDA E A. Language culture and translating[M]. Shanghai: Shanghai Foreign Language, 1992.

[5] 包惠南. 文化语境与语言翻译[M]. 北京:中国标准出版社, 2001.

[6] 范家材. 英语修辞赏析[M]. 上海:上海交通大学出版社, 1992.

[7] 金堤. 等效翻译探索[M]. 北京:中国对外翻译出版公司, 1998.

汉英口译中的文化干扰

郝雪琴

摘　要： 本文主要阐述了汉英口译概念种类及特性，口译人员在翻译中应该遵循的三大原则：系统的原则、约定俗成的原则和前后一致的原则；必须经过三大训练：语言训练、语用训练和技术训练。重点举例分析口译中文化背景知识对口译过程的干扰以及回译中应该注意的问题，一定要注意语言中词汇的引申含义或深层次意义，避免造成译文功效上的不对等，形成交流障碍。

关键词： 汉英口译；技巧训练；文化干扰；回译

1 口译的特性

口译常常分为两类：连续翻译（consecutive）和同声传译（simultaneous）。连续翻译可以用在很多场合，如政治会议、商贸洽谈、学术交流以及其他公众事件的交流交际等。同声传译绝大多数用在国际会议之中。

翻译是用另外一种语言解释源语言的意义和思想，是语言交流中的最高环节，在英语学习的五项技能听、说、读、写、译中，翻译的要求是最多的。掌握两种语言以及文化才能充当好交流的桥梁。口译是速度和信度的完美结合。信度有两层意思：理解准确和表达准确。理解准确要求口译人员弄懂说话者的原义，包括言外之意。表达准确包括语言准确和语用准确两个方面。口译的要求更高，不仅要准确忠实于原语言，达到交流的目的，还要追

作者简介： 郝雪琴，山西运城人，英语语言文学硕士，北京工商大学外国语学院讲师。

求快速流畅的在现场短时间内用目标语言表达出说话者的本意。如果不理解说话者的语言，绝对不能装懂，如果找不到适合的词语，可以试着用另外一种方式解释。记得翻译只是双方交流的桥梁，不能夹杂自己的想法和观点。

翻译没有绝对正确的标准。除了极其简单的句子，一般的句子可能会有很多不同的翻译，正确的理解源语言是翻译最基本的先决条件。不同的语言有着不同的语言结构、文化背景和习俗，逐词对应的翻译并不能达到交流的目的。要在英语中找出有对等意义的语言需要作出很大的努力，作为汉英口译人员，不仅要同时掌握好两种语言，还要具备深厚的中国文化底蕴，才能在汉英口译中免受文化干扰，真正流畅完全地交流。

2 口译原则以及训练

口译应遵循下列原则：系统、约定俗成和前后一致。语言有语音、语法和词汇三个要素组成。汉译英除了掌握一般的语言知识外，还要训练某些独特的技巧，遵循系统的原则。

语言具有约定俗成的特点，翻译界的前辈在长期的翻译过程中，对汉语的语汇和说法，逐渐形成了普遍接受的译名和译法。已有固定译法的，我们不可杜撰，例如，中国传统的节日已有固定的译法：元宵节（the Lantern Festival），端午节（the Dragon Boat Festival），春节（the Spring Festival）。有些中国人名也有固定的译法：孔子（Confucius）、孟子（Mencius）、孙中山（Sun Yat-sen）。有些中国特有的词汇也有固定译法：阴阳（Yin-Yang），气功（音译为Qi Gong，意译为Controlled Breathing Exercise），武术（音译为WuShu，意译为Martial Art），太极拳（音译为Taijiquan，意译为Shadow Boxing）。中国地名和名胜也有固定的译法：北京（Peking / Beijing），香港（Hong Kong），澳门（Macao），长城（the Great Wall），颐和园（the Summer Palace），天坛（the Temple of Heaven）。

前后一致的原则，是指句法结构做到前后呼应，包括主谓关系、人称、格、单复数、时态、语态、逻辑关系、用法和搭配方面的呼应或一致。

口译训练包括语言、语用和技术。从语言要素来看，语言训练涉及语音、词汇和语法，是基础。而技术训练涉及听、说、读、写、译五种基本功的综合能力，以及诸多的翻译技巧。当然，汉英口译偏重说和译两种能力的训练。语用训练则是关键的一环，口译作为一种跨文化的交际方式，涉及语用问题。熟悉英语国家风土人情、风俗习惯、历史传统及国情现状，可以大大提高口译质量。

3 口译中的文化干扰

语言是文化的载体，语言所表达的含义与各个国家的文化有千丝万缕的联系。汉英口译人员，对于中国文化和英语国家的文化都应该有全面细致的了解，以免闹出笑话或引起不必要的误会。

汉语中的成语和俗语，谈话中经常会遇到，如何做出准确、流畅、快速的翻译，口译人员必须多加注意。比如“司马昭之心，路人皆知”，缩省法译为：The villain’s design is obvious，译文中不提司马昭也同样表达了说话者的意图，这种省略还是有必要的。同样的还有“说曹操，曹操就到”可译为：Talk of the Devil and he’s sure to appear；或者：Talk of an angel and you’ll hear the fluttering of his wings。只要意思相同，没有必要把曹操翻译出来。

原语词语和译语词语的指称意义相同，但一个有语用意义，另一个没有。英国是一个岛国，捕捞业和航海业在其经济生活中占有重要地位。就像汉语中有大量包含数字的成语一样，英语中也有众多以水产和航海作比喻的成语。这些成语大部分的喻义都难以从字面看出，虽然它们表层所指对中国读者来说并没有什么不清楚，例如：fish in the air（水中捞月）；have other fish to fry（另有要事）；drink like a fish（牛饮）；a fine kettle of fish（乱七八糟）；a cold（queer）fish［一个冷漠的（怪）人］；neither fish，flesh，nor good red herring（不伦不类）；You can’t make a crab walk straight（江山易改，本性难移）；know the rope（懂得诀窍）。

在不同的文化中，相同的词汇给人们的联想意义却是完全不相同。汉语中表示嫉妒情感的“红眼”“眼红”，英语用green-eyed。如果说：He is red-eyed，英美人会认为他因患眼疾、熬夜或挨打而眼睛红肿，以为有生理的变化。

同类的例子还有不少。

"白象"牌电池，"白象"直接翻译成White Elephant销路就不会很好，因为在英语中White elephant的含义是大而无用的东西。最合适的翻译是Baixiang或者Silver Elephant。

"金龙"牌电扇，"金龙"按字义直接翻译为Golden Dragon就不妥，因为在英语中龙是指可怕的、有破坏力的怪物，也可以指脾气暴躁的人。为了避免歧义还是翻译为Jinlong更好些。同样的道理，"亚洲四小龙"就可以翻译为Asian Four Little Tigers。老虎在英语中的含义是"猛士、勇士"，有"朝气蓬勃、充满希望、富有活力"的含义。如果把"亚洲四小龙"翻译为Asian Four Little Dragons，西方人看来就变成了"亚洲四个小魔鬼"。"望子成龙"如果翻译成expect one's children to become dragons，英语国家的人会不理解，还是翻译为expect one's children to have a bright future更能传达本意。

"芳芳"化妆品牌，"芳芳"如果音译为Fang fang，就忽略了fang在英文里的含义是"毒蛇的牙齿"，试问谁还敢抹上这样的唇膏呢?

"金鸡"牌鞋油，"金鸡"起初翻译为Golden Cock。岂不知cock一词在英语中已经赋予了男性生殖器官的含义，改换成Golden Rooster就好了。

这些效果很差的译文，让我们意识到，在翻译中一定要注意语言中词汇的引申含义或深层次意义，避免造成译文功效上的不对等。

4 口译中的回译

中国文化和西方文化的交流有相当长的历史。汉语从西方语言中借进了大量的词语，汉语的许多词语也进入了西方语言。转借的方式不外乎音译（transliteration）、仿译（loan translation）和释义等。在许多时候，译者必须将原语中借自译语的词语回译成它在译语中的原来的形式。

音译词语的回译如：沙丁鱼（sardines）、芝士（cheese）、迷你（mini-）、贴士（tips）、道林纸（calendered paper）、sampan/sanpan（舢板）、typhoon（台风）、yangko（秧歌）、chop-suey（杂碎）。孔子、孟子的英语为：Confucius，Mencius。有的译者居然回译成了孔休斯、孟休斯，不了解这些就会闹出很大的笑话。

仿译词语的回译：Long March（长征）、洗脑（brain wash）、视野（field

of vision）、葱皮纸 / 半透明纸（onionskin）、趁热打铁（strike while the iron is hot）、战争贩子（war-monger）、夹着尾巴（with the tail between the legs）、武装到牙齿（armed to the teeth）、披着羊皮的狼（a wolf in sheep's clothing）、火中取栗（pull the chestnut out of the fire）。

5 结语

汉语的学习难度，在世界语言中应该是首屈一指的。英语是国际上大多数国家讲的语言，而讲汉语的人口是最多的，如果能学好汉英口译，中国传统文化在未来会得到很大程度的弘扬。要学好汉英口译必须从细微处着手，持之以恒，避免文化干扰，做好中西文化交流的桥梁。

参考文献

[1] 刘和平. 口译技巧[M]. 北京：中国对外翻译出版公司，2001.

[2] 朱佩芬. 新编实用英汉口译技巧[M]. 上海：华东理工大学出版社，1997.

[3] 何高大，陈琳. 实用英汉汉英口译技巧[M]. 长沙：中南大学出版社，2002.

[4] 何自然. 语用学与英语学习[M]. 上海：上海外语教学出版社，1997.

[5] 吴冰. 汉译英口译教程[M]. 北京：外语教学与研究出版社，1995.

[6] 蒋磊. 英汉文化差异与广告的语用翻译[J]. 中国翻译，2002(5).

功能语篇分析在英汉口译学习中的应用

佟梦瑶　王琼娅　徐冬妮

摘　要：本研究以英语专业三年级学生在交替传译课堂上的口译语音材料为素材，从语言使用的角度，分析语篇特点及这些特点所反映出的语言学习特别是口译学习问题，并就发现的问题提出建议。

关键词：功能语篇分析；口译学习

1 引言

语篇分析自结构主义者Zellig Harris（1952）提出以来已有了半个多世纪的历史。语篇分析从语言使用的角度分析语篇（口头语篇或书面语篇），为语言学的发展和语言教学的研究都起到了推动作用。

对于英语专业学生而言，作为口译的初学者，在课堂练习中的译文及学习方法都存在一定问题。本研究以北京工商大学英语专业三年级学生为对象，收集口译课堂的语音材料，建立一个小型的语音文本语料库。解释语料的同时，在照应、替代、省略、连接、词汇手段上对语料进行评估，有针对性地选取语篇进行分析解释。

项目/基金：本文为大学生科研与创业行动计划项目（编号：SJ201502058）。

作者简介：佟梦瑶，女，北京人，北京工商大学外国语学院英语专业2012级学生。王琼娅，女，山西长治人，北京工商大学外国语学院英语专业2012级学生。徐冬妮，女，北京人，北京工商大学外国语学院英语专业2012级学生。本文指导教师为田芳。

2 语料分析

2.1 照应

照应指语篇中的指代成分与它在同一语篇中所指的对象之间语义上的相互解释关系，是汉英两种语言共有的衔接方式。按照Halliday的衔接理论，照应可分为人称照应（personal reference）、指示照应（demonstrative reference）和比较照应（comparative reference）。

例1： Now we are at the third floor. This is our company's conference room.

译文： 现在我们在三层。这是我们公司的会议室。

例2： 这是我的朋友彼得。他对中国文化非常感兴趣。

译文： This is my friend，Peter. He is very interested in Chinese culture.

以上两例均出现在课堂模拟参观口译的背景下，原文与译文中出现指示指称this、人称指称he，指代上文中提到的地点、人物。由于学生口语中出现的简单句较多，且与上文连接较为明显，所以在所选取语料中，学生能够在翻译中体现人称照应、指示照应及比较照应，照应上文，使上下文整体篇章连贯。

2.2 替代

替代指用替代形式去替代上下文出现的词语，可分为名词性替代、动词性替代和分句替代。

例1： 但是其它公司的产品质量不如我们。

译文： But other companies' goods are not as good as ours.

例2： OK，let's do it now.

译文： 好的，我们现在就打吧。

通过分析发现，在口译过程中，同学们能够灵活使用one、do等词汇进行名词性替代、动词性替代及分句替代。可以看出，代词（即代词代替名词，如here、that、it……），there be句型，名词性物主代词（ours……）使用居多，替代上下文出现的词语，简单明了。唯一需要注意的就是表意清晰，离所指不要太远，避免出现指代不明。

2.3 省略

省略指省去句子中某一成分。

例1：Did she get there at six?

No，（she got there） earlier （than six）.

例2：您是想喝茶还是咖啡？

译文：Tea or coffee，please?

省略这一特点在使用上非常灵活，我们可以省略主语、谓语、状语等，某结构中未出现的词语可以从语篇的其他分句或句子中找回。对于这一技巧，需要具体语境具体分析，合理使用，才能不造成误解。

2.4 连接

连接是通过逻辑联系词等过渡性词语来体现句子间逻辑关系的衔接手段，可以让人们更好了解句子之间的语义联系以及理解整个语篇。有学者认为，连接表达了增补、转折、因果和时空等四种关系。

（1）增补关系。

增补连接指说话者在说完第一句话后又添加了另一种情况。该类连接词包括and，what's more，in addition to，in other words等。

例：...And if you want to try some food with typical taste，you can go to the second floor. And if you want to try some fast food，you can go to the third floor.

译文：……二层提供风味小吃，三楼是快餐。

（2）转折关系。

转折连接指连接词后语句与之前表达语义相反。该类连接词包括but，however，or，on the other hand等。

例1：...but other company's products are not as good as ours.

译文：……但是其他公司的产品质量不如我们。

例2：It's really hard to say goodbye but we have to say it.

译文：很难说再见，但我们不得不分离。

（3）因果关系。

因果连接指连接词所连接的语句表示原因或结果。该类连接词包括as a result，why，so，because，consequently等。

例：Yes，indeed. So we have enough time to do the boarding tasks.

译文：确实是。所以我们现在有足够的时间登机。

(4) 时空关系。

语篇中经常存在时空关系。该类连接词包括then，later，first，next等。

例：再往前走是我们的体育馆。

译文：And then is our gym.

以上例子皆选自学生课堂口译语料。很明显，在口译中，学生能够很好翻译出增补关系，以及采用连接词连接另一种情况，熟练使用so，because等词汇准确表达语篇的因果关系。相比之下，转折关系及时空关系在学生课堂口译中出现次数较少，时空关系在参观口译中频率较多，其他口译情况下基本没有出现。

在增补关系中，学生连接词的使用过于单一，多数同学普遍采用and，而忽略了其他增补关系词。遇到语篇转折关系时，若源语出现明显转折词如“但是”“可是”等，学生能够准确抓住并有效转译出来，但如果源语有暗在转折逻辑，却没有明显标志词，同学们在口译的时候就不会使用连接词，而是按照字面意思生硬地翻译出来，造成语篇断连，让听众感觉不顺畅。

2.5 词汇

词汇衔接是语篇中出现的一部分词汇相互之间存在的语义上的联系，对语篇连贯起着基础而关键的作用。

词汇连接分为两大类：复现（reiteration）和同现（collocation）。其中复现又包括重复（repetition）、同义词或近义词（synonym or near-synonym）、上义词（superordinate）和泛指词（general word）四种。

(1) 复现。

a. 重复，即具有同样语义、同一形式的词汇在语篇中的反复出现。重复一般多为关键词，词汇的重复使句子相互衔接得以连贯。

例：I just saw there is a Starbucks and we can buy a coffee，let's go to the Starbucks right now.

译文：那里有星巴克，我们可以买杯咖啡，我们现在就去吧。

b. 同义词或近义词，指具有相同意义和相近意义的不同词在语篇中的接应关系，不管这个词是指人、物、过程或性质。

例： It is elegant and has good quality. I think it is very comfortable.

译文： 这件高端大气上档次，而且很舒服。

c. 上下义词。上下义关系体现了词语间的分类关系。上下义的主要意义为内包，即意义概括的词内包意义更为确定的词。

例： I love Chinese food，do you provide Beijing roast duck?

译文： 我喜欢中国菜，你们有北京烤鸭吗？

d. 泛指词。在语篇中遇到出现过的人、事、物时，可用泛指词替代，如：person，thing，place 等。

例： There're so many people study here.

译文： 有很多学生在这里学习。

（2）同现。同现，又称搭配，是词汇衔接重要手段之一。有些词搭配与之对立的词，构成意义互补关系。

例： The winter is really cold，but when we sit around the hot pot，we can always get a very warm and a harmonious atmosphere.

译文： 冬天很冷，但是当我们围着火锅坐下来的时候，就会感到温暖和谐的气氛。

在八组学生课堂口译中，泛指词使用较多，掌握情况很好，同学们能有效用泛指词替代出现过的人事物。此外，同学们也能很好使用上下义词，在口译过程中，能对一个概念词进行更为确切的解释。由于语料出自学生课堂口译，多为日常交际的短对话，所以重复、同现等词汇手段出现频率较低。

3 结语

以上分析表明，学生在口译过程中能够做到有意识地运用多种手段衔接上下文，实现语篇连贯，但对于词汇连接等手段的使用仍然不够主动、熟练。

在口译学习过程中，同学们应积累更多词汇及表达方式。连接词汇积累不够会使口译选用不恰当的词汇，或者用词单一，造成译文枯燥，甚至会打破原文的逻辑关系，不能清楚表达原文意思。同时，通过分析语料发现，由于对经贸、文化等方面的专业词汇积累不足，再加上心理紧张，常常导致口译中断，在一定程度上也影响了语篇的连贯程度。

另外，同学们在口译学习中经常把重点放在将表面意义翻译准确，而忽视语篇逻辑。有些语句没有明显的逻辑关系，但其联系却潜藏在深层含义中。建议在今后的口译学习和练习中，多加思考，找出每个语句间的内在逻辑，并选用合适的连接手段，使译文更加流畅、连贯，完整表达出讲话者的意图。

参考文献

[1] 胡壮麟. 语篇的衔接与连贯[M]. 上海:上海外语教育出版社,1994.

[2] 张金平. 从语篇衔接理论看中国学生的英语写作[J]. 中州大学学报,2011(1).

浅析英文招股书的语言特点与翻译策略

郑昊霞　冀于希　贾钟灵

摘　要：招股说明书是企业在上市过程中必须具备的最重要的法律文件。英文招股书的汉译可考虑在翻译目的论的总体框架下针对其词汇、句子和文本层面的特点采取相应的策略。

关键词：招股说明书；翻译策略

1 招股说明书及其翻译

随着中国经济发展日益全球化，越来越多的国内企业瞄准国际市场，开展资本运作，通过在国际市场上发行股票的方式来获取更多的发展资金。依照相关法律规定，拟公开发行股票的企业，必须以招股说明书（prospectus）的形式向社会公众和投资人提供有关企业募集股份的真实、准确、完备的信息，内容通常包括首页及重要提示、预期时间表、目录、正文和附录五个部分。其中正文是最重要的，通常由十多个部分组成，如概要、释义、风险因素、公司资料、历史及重组、行业概览、业务、董事及高级管理层、股本、财务资料、未来计划及前景，等等。

招股说明书（以下简称为招股书）是企业在上市过程中必备的最重要的法律文件，通常由拟上市的企业聘请中介机构如投资银行、律师事务所、会计师事务所等负责撰写，其中律师事务所负责文件的执笔，企业和中介机构

项目/基金：本论文为2015年北京市级大学生科研与创业行动计划项目的成果，项目编号SJ201502070。

作者简介：郑昊霞，英语语言文学硕士，北京工商大学外国语学院讲师，研究方向英美文学与翻译研究。冀于希、贾钟灵，北京工商大学英语专业2012级本科生。

负责提供相关部分的内容。招股书完成定稿后，须报请监管部门审批，获批后再向社会公开发布。选择在香港或新加坡发行股票的企业，其招股书（香港称之为招股章程）除必须用英文撰写之外，在英文定稿之后还须译成汉语，最终向社会公众和投资人提供英汉双语版本的招股书。汉语版的招股书，内容虽然与英文版完全对应但却不具有英文版的法律地位。一旦投资者对于招股书有任何疑问均以英文版为准。

对于招股书的翻译，国内译界少有探讨。仅李克兴、张颖、王彬等几位学者有过专门的著述。本文作者认为，招股书作为企业的一种重要文本，其翻译实有研究的必要性。

2 英文招股说明书的语言特点

2.1 词汇层面

英文的招股书属于专门用途语言（English for special purpose，ESP），是法律英语与财经英语的混合体，其词汇方面有以下特点：①通常大量使用专业术语，包括法律术语如principal（委托人/当事人）、verdict［（陪审团）裁决］、default［违约（行为）］等；金融证券术语如Offer Price（发行价）、Stock Code（股票代码）、retail investors（散户）、sale charge（认购费）等；商业贸易术语如cushion（存货）、spot delivery（现场交易）、tradable quotation（交易报价）、aggregate investment（投资总额）等。②频繁使用缩略词，如GEM（growth enterprise market，创业板）、OTC（over-the-counter，场外买卖）、IPO（initial public offer，首次公开募股）、S-day（settlement day，交收/结算日）等。③经常出现新词如private key（私人密钥）、electronic signature（电子签名）等，与古词如thereto（此外）、thereat（在那里）等。

2.2 句子层面

首先，作为法律文件的招股书非常讲究语言表述的准确、严谨和规范，通常采用较多的并列结构和同位成分，形成复杂的主语、谓语、宾语以及附加修饰成分，因而句子普遍较长。如： The following is a summary of the audited combined of the Group for the two years ended 31st March，1999 and the ten months ended 31st January，2000（“the relevant periods”），which have been prepared on the basis that the existing Group structure was in place throughout the Relevant Periods and which，save as the information on loss per share，have been extracted from the accountants’ report set out in appendix I to this prospectus. 在这个复杂长句中，除了简洁的主句“the following is a summary”之外，还有两个并列的扩展的介词（for）宾语，两个并列的which引导的定语从句，前一个which从句中包含另一个that引导的定语从句，后一个which从句中包含一个插入语“save as...”，等等。

其次，为了凸显其客观真实性，英文招股书中使用大量的被动语态句型。在上面的例句中，就有两个被动语态句，一个是“which have been prepared on the basis...”，另一个是“which...have been extracted from...”。

最后，英文招股书中还有相当数量的套语。各国的招股书都有基本的格式，而招股书的每个部分都要求程式化、规范化和条理化，所以大量使用固定套句。如香港的招股书（或招股章程）中几乎都有“Important（重要提示）”这一项，其措词如下：If you are in any doubt about this Prospectus，you should consult your stockbroker，bank manager，solicitor，professional accountant or other professional adviser. 对应的中文是：“如阁下对本招股章程存有任何疑问，应咨询阁下之股票经纪人、银行经理、律师、专业会计师或其他专业顾问。”

2.3 文本层面

任何交际行为都有其意图或目的，而书面文本的意向性尤其突出，或表达自我，或试图以特定方式影响读者，或表达祝愿、感谢、道歉等。弄清文本的功能和意图，既是创作语篇、选择恰当的文本类型和表达策略的关键，也是理解语篇、确定其文本类型和相应的翻译策略的前提。

招股说明书是企业为了让广大投资者和社会大众了解其真实的运营状况和股票发行的基本情况，以期募集资金、扩大规模而撰写并公布的法律文本，既有提供真实、客观、准确、完整的信息的功能，也有以特定方式影响读者和（潜在）投资者，使其最终实施认购股票的行为的功能。因此，招股书其实是一种混合型的法律文本，其主要功能既有叙述和描写，也有呼吁和说服，翻译时需要采取一些灵活实用的策略。

3 英文招股说明书的汉译策略

总的来讲，法律文本翻译的主要策略是直译和解释性翻译。英文招股书作为法律文本中的一种特殊类型，其翻译策略需要在对语言特点进行分析的基础上加以细化和变通。

首先，鉴于招股书的词汇特点，翻译时应力求表达上的准确、专业和前后统一，对于不熟悉的专业词汇、缩略语等，务必查阅相关的专业书籍或请教专业人士，切忌主观臆测。如“arm's length transaction”，不能草率地译为“保持距离的交易”，而要译为“公平交易”；“balance sheet”不能想当然地译成“平衡表单”，而应译为“资产负债表”。

其次，针对招股书中大量使用的长句、被动语态句以及套语等，译者应该分别应对，逐一破解。长句结构复杂、修饰成分较多，翻译时应分析并把握其语法结构，理清句中各成分的逻辑关系，再将原句的信息按目的语的表达习惯完整、准确地表达出来。英文原句中的被动语态在翻译时可以适当转化为主动语态以避免生硬不当和有碍于信息的传达。如：Any information or representation not made in this prospectus must not be relied on by prospective investors as having been authorized by the company，the sponsor，the Underwriters，any of their respective directors，or any other person or party involved in the offering. 译文是：准投资者不应依赖并非载于本招股章程的任何资料或陈述，将其视作经本公司、保荐人、包销商、他们各自的董事或参与售股的任何其他人士授权发表。对于套语，在确保样例准确无误的前提下，翻译时可以直接照搬，如前文中的Important（重要提示）这一套语的翻译。这样既保持了规范性和一致性，也节省了时间提高了效率。

从整个文本的层面而言，翻译的目的论对于招股书的翻译有较强的指导意义。德国功能派理论认为，翻译是人类的一种有目的的行为活动。翻译目的论强调翻译方法和翻译策略必须由预期的目的或功能决定，主张以目的语文本和文化为导向，采用适用于目的语境的翻译方法。译者在翻译过程中应从目的语读者的角度出发，根据译文的预期目的来决定自己的翻译策略，以达到译文的预期功能，产生预期的效果。因此，在招股说明书英译汉的过程中，译者应以符合汉语及汉语文化为准则，充分考虑英汉文化差异等诸多因素，采用相应的策略，以求译文符合译文读者的需要，这样才能最大限度的发挥招股说明书的作用。

4 结语

招股说明书是企业上市过程中最重要的法律文件。对于招股书的翻译，国内译界的探讨尚不多见。本文主张英文招股书的汉译可考虑在翻译目的论的总体框架下针对其词汇、句子和文本层面的特点采取相应的策略。

参考文献

[1] CHRISTIANE N. Translation as a purposeful activity: functionalist approaches explained [M]. Manchester, UK: St. Jerome Publishing, 1997.

[2] 李克兴,张新红. 法律文本与法律翻译[M]. 北京:中国对外翻译出版公司,2006.

[3] 王彬. 招股说明书英语文体特点及翻译[J]. 河北理工大学学报:社会科学版,2011(1).

[4] 张颖. 从功能理论角度评招股章程的翻译[D]. 广州:广东外语外贸大学,2006.

浅析英文专利文献中法律术语的翻译方法
——以复合副词为例

马 蓉 董丽卓 刘 凡

摘 要：随着中国与世界各国在经济、科技等各领域的交流日益加强，国外的专利文献越来越多地被中国企业所利用。因此，英文专利文献翻译的准确性也受到了考验。专利文献既是一种技术文件，也是一种具有法律效力的法律文件，是技术与法律的结合物。它有着独特的语言特质和规律，其中包含一套习惯使用的复合副词，比如hereby，herein，thereafter，therein，therefor，thereupon等。在翻译中，译者该如何准确把握这些词汇的含义？如何精确表达明晰的概念？这些都是很值得探讨和分析的。

关键词：专利文献；法律术语；复合副词

全球经济一体化正日益加速，中国企业越来越频繁地引进外国专利技术，从而使得翻译英文专利文献成为目前翻译工作者的主要任务之一。专利文献属于科技文献范畴，几乎涉及全部的技术领域。但是，由于翻译工作者的科技专业知识有限，加上这些文献作者本身的英语水平也参差不齐，给翻译工作增加了很大难度。因此，本文将从分析英文专利文献翻译的原则入手，进而以复合副词为例，深入论述在翻译英文专利的法律术语时的基本要

项目/基金：本论文为北京工商大学2015年"大学生科研与创业行动计划"项目的成果，项目编号为SJ201502074。

作者简介：马蓉，女，北京工商大学外国语学院讲师，研究方向为应用语言学。董丽卓，女，北京工商大学外国语学院2012级本科生。刘凡，男，国家知识产权局专利局工作人员。

求、常见结构等，希望能为翻译工作者和专利工作者以及企业技术人员提供有益的参考。

1 专利文献的语言特点及其翻译的原则

专利文献属于科技文献，是科技文献中最重要的一种类型。专利文献的功能主要在于依据法律（专利法）来公开一项新的技术，有较为统一并固定的格式和书写方法，同时详细记录了新发明、新技术、新材料、新产品、新方法等内容。专利文献一般采用书面文体完成，主要由专利代理人或专利律师撰写。由于专利文献本身同时承载着技术信息和法律效应，使其成为了一种特殊的文献，因此，它的文体是独特的。一方面，它秉承了科技文献用词简练、专业术语较多的特点，另一方面，它又被赋予了法律文件严谨的独特风格。

由于专利文献这些特殊的性质，在撰写的时候代理人或律师会遵循一定的格式，使其具备了比较典型的结构及文法规则，因此会出现篇章布局大同小异的情况，在语言上也常有反复出现的雷同模式，比如句式相对固定，形式或内容大致相同等。因此，这些套语的翻译基本上也是相对固定的。

专利文献中的英语语言使用不仅仅局限于英语本身的规则，在词汇方面也更多地涉及各个领域的专业术语和一些法律文书中特定的习惯用语。所以，在翻译这些英文专利文献时，不光要考虑语言学的因素，更要关注专利英语的语言特点。

在英语翻译中，我们常常要依据信、达、雅这三个基本原则。而在翻译专利文献的时候，“信”和“达”是应该得到更多关注的。在“信”的原则下，要做到译文与原文内容基本相符，在语义上没有任何的出入和缩减。那么“达”则要求译者在翻译的过程中做到译文语句通顺、清晰易懂、无语法错误等。在保证“信”和“达”两个首要原则之后，译者应该努力使译文更加自然、符合正常的目标语言表达习惯。

总之，在翻译专利文献的过程中，译者要做到尽量忠实原文，以准确地道、流畅通顺的语言圆满地传递原文中的各种信息以及意义。

2 复合副词在专利文献中的用途以及翻译技巧分析

专利文献既是一种技术文件，也是一种具有法律效力的法律文件，是技术与法律的结合物。它有着独特的语言特质和规律，其中包含一套习惯使用的复合副词，比如 behoove，forthwith，hereby，herein，hereinabove，thereafter，therein，therefor，thereupon，thereto，therewith 等。这些复合副词即为法律写作中常用的法律术语，在专利文献当中常常起到省略的作用。也就是说，在专利文献当中使用这些复合副词通常是为了避免词语的重复而采用这些词语来表达省略的内容。与此同时，语言的结构也因此更加紧凑，从而充分体现了专利文献的技术性特质。这些词不仅在专利说明书的正文里经常可以见到，在专利说明书的标题中也不时地出现。

以下列举一些专利文献当中涉及复合副词的句子及翻译。

例 1：Thereafter the mixture was heated between 89 and 103 deg C. for 6 hours during which time the system became clear.

参考译文：之后，在89℃至103℃之间加热混合物6小时，在这段时间内，体系变得透明。

例 2：The system of claim 42，wherein each distributed system performs an operation with respect to a search request distributed thereto in accordance with information associated with the search request.

参考译文：根据权利要求42所述的广告信息检索系统，其中所述检索设备为多台，每一检索设备根据预先设定的分组响应部分用户标识的检索请求。

例 3：Method 150 may further comprise flattening the corrugation ridges （on either inner or outer faces，or both） to thin the corresponding film supported thereupon（stage 165）.

参考译文：方法150还可以包括使波纹化凸脊（在内面或外面的任一个上或者在二者上）平坦，以使支撑在其上的相应的膜变薄（阶段165）。

例 4：As a result，the NIR radiation method enables powder coatings to be melted and cured in a single process step without the disadvantages associated with conventional thermal curing and/or UV curing processes as described hereinabove.

参考译文：结果使NIR辐射方法能熔化粉末涂料，并在单一加工步骤中固化，而没有上述常规热固化和/或紫外线固化方法涉及的缺点。

例5： The invention may be broadly characterized as a method of thermally processing a hydrocarbon stream which comprises the steps of heating a feed stream, which comprises a mixture of hydrocarbons having boiling points above 600 F., by indirect heat exchange against a hereinafter characterized first bottoms stream; passing the feed stream through a visbreaking zone, and admixing a resultant visbreaking zone effluent stream with a relatively high temperature quench stream to thereby form a first process stream.

参考译文： 本发明可以概括地称为烃气流热处理方法，这包括用下文所说的和第一底流进行间接热交换来加热沸点600°F（315℃）以上烃混物的原料气流；使原料气流流经减粘裂化区并使减粘裂化区流出气流与温度比较高的骤冷气流合成物相混而形成第一处理气流。

专利文献中类似这样的用法不胜枚举，复合副词的形式也多种多样。可是在实际的专利文献翻译中，这些复合副词要么被错误地翻译，要么是完全被忽略，从而造成了很多不必要的误解和麻烦，进一步会导致专利权人的巨大损失，比如说无法阻止他人仿冒或专利被宣告无效等。因此，复合副词的翻译方法应该得到高度的重视。目前，国内翻译界虽然有人在研究如何翻译专利文献，但涉及复合副词的却很少。而复合副词恰恰在法律写作中出现频率很高，扮演着举足轻重的角色。因此，需要翻译工作者投入更多的时间和精力去细细琢磨、反复推敲，如此才能更加准确、到位地传递专利文献中的信息。

参考文献

[1] 庄一方. 专利文献的翻译[M]. 北京：知识产权出版社，2008.
[2] 程宗璋. 论专利英语的语言特点及汉译[J]. 大庆高等专科学校学报，2001(2).
[3] 谌登峰. 专利申请翻译中应注意的几个问题[J]. 南昌高专学报，2007(5).
[4] 史玉琴. 标准文献的语言特点[M]. 北京：中国对外翻译出版社，1998.
[5] 宋新智. 基于科技问题特征的翻译策略[J]. 中国科技翻译，2008(1).

论四字格在英汉翻译中的语义对等

吕 绵 张 倩 张孟璐

摘　要：四字格是汉语成语的常见形式，也是汉语使用者最喜欢的形式之一。四字格在英汉翻译中的运用得当可使文章增色不少，可以解决英汉文化差异和翻译偏离现象导致的翻译错误。本文重点讨论四字格的正确运用在英汉翻译语义对等中的重要作用。

关键词：四字格；语义对等；翻译

1 四字格的结构和形式

汉语四字格结构是汉语言特有的一种语言现象，如成语“浑水摸鱼”“打草惊蛇”“胸有成竹”等。四字格结构在汉语语言中的使用频率非常高。在英语语言的行文和会话中，几乎没有结构和意义都对等的词语、四字格词语。汉语具有强大的生命力和深刻的影响力，在汉译英的过程中理解汉语言的四字格的结构特点，顺应语境的需求变化，正确运用四字格结构，对翻译有很大帮助。

1.1 汉语四字格的结构概述

四字格，也叫四字结构，是一个较为宽泛的概念。它包括四字成语、四字谚语、四字叠音词和所有临时组合而具有类似四字成语修辞功能的四字词

项目/基金：本文为北京工商大学北京市级大学生科学研究与创业行动计划(SJ201502057)的部分科研成果。

作者简介：吕绵，女，北京工商大学外国语学院讲师。张倩，女，北京工商大学外国语学院2012级学生。张孟璐，女，北京工商大学外国语学院2012级学生。

组，但不包括某些偶然形成的四音节片断。四字词组由四个词素构成，通常分为前后两个部分，按词语的稳定性，可以分为固定词组和自由词组。固定词组是一个整体，不能拆散使用，其中的任何词语都不能随意更换，如“负荆请罪”“捉襟见肘”“东施效颦”等。自由词组是临时组成的，可随意拆散使用，重新组合。按前后两部分的语法关系，可以分为主谓关系词组（如：市场繁荣），动宾关系词组（如：发展经济），偏正关系词组（如：富裕生活），并列关系词组（如：改革开放）。

1.2 英译汉译为四字格的基本要求

在英汉翻译中尽量不要逐字翻译，翻译的精华之点不在于形式上的对等，而是在忠于原文的情况下追求语义上的对等，在保证译文通顺流畅的同时还要兼具修辞之美，这样译出来的文章才更有文学价值，更值得拿来品读。因此，在理解原文的基础上，英语单词、习语、词组甚至整句，都可译为汉语四字格。

2 语义对等及文化因素对四字格翻译的影响

翻译的目的是提供原语与译语之间的语义对等。在整个翻译过程中，翻译都应该在语义对等的基础上进行。也就是说，这是从原语到译语的一种语义转换，是把一种语言表达的内容用另一种语言的恰当形式表达出来。

在英汉两种语言中，一对字面对等的文字往往在语义上却不对等。而英汉语义的不对等源自中英文化间的差异，因为语言和文化密切相关。语言是文化的载体，可以反映文化、表达文化、记载文化、传播文化。因此，在深入了解中英文化的前提下，四字格翻译方可消除或弱化文化差异，以达到语义对等。文化差异包括语言所代表的民族历史传统、思维方式，以及地理等因素。

2.1 四字格翻译错误示例

由于文化因素对四字格翻译造成的语义不对等，产生了许多翻译错误。如：

例1：Skate on thin ice 译为“自讨苦吃”或“引火自焚”，而非“如履薄冰”。“如履薄冰”则译为 To walk on eggs。

例2：Still waters run deep，若译为“止水流深”，看似不错，然而却不便于汉语读者理解和接受，因而可套用汉语中特有的成语“大智若愚”。

例 3：To sing a different tune 很容易受中文思维影响而译成“唱对台戏”，然而其实际意思则是“改弦更张”。

例 4：To pull one's leg 同样也很容易受字面影响而直译为“拖某人后腿”，其实正确意思是“拿某人开涮”。

例 5：“班门弄斧”被直译成 Display your axe at the door of Lu Ban，the carpenter master。这并没有语法错误，但在以英语为母语的人看来则太过生硬，甚至无法理解。

2.2 民族历史传统因素

四字格翻译时，需要考虑英汉两种语言所代表的文化差异，第一条就是民族历史传统因素。英汉两种语言由于所处的民族历史传统不同，翻译的时候要适合国情，结合目标语所在国家的传统进行翻译，才可能有意义。举一个简单的例子，西方人人皆知的滑铁卢，或者人们经常所说的“他真是遭遇了自己人生中的滑铁卢”，其义不言自明，就是失败的意思，但翻译成汉语，最好采用中国人熟知的历史典故。所以，meet one's Waterloo 译为“败走麦城”。

其他类似的翻译如：as poor as Job 译为“家徒四壁”（《圣经》）；a Cleopatra 译为“国色天香”；cross the Rubicon 译为“破釜沉舟”；as rich as Crazes 译为“富可敌国”；carry coals to Newcastle 译为“运石进山，多此一举”。若没有相关的历史传统知识而生硬地套用原文的典故会让人一头雾水。

2.3 思维方式因素

“语言是思维信息的载体，文化则是思维信息流通的规则，它可以促进信息交流，也可以阻遏交流。因此，跨文化理解是翻译的大前提之一。”由于中英思维方式差异造成的文化差异在翻译的时候也必须给予足够的重视。如：land of milk and honey 译为“鱼米之乡”；at the end of one's rope 译为“山穷水尽”；help a lame dog over a stile 译为“雪中送炭”；be full of beans 译为“精力充沛”。

2.4 地理因素

由于英国的岛国地理特点，语言中有海和鱼的因素。如：“天涯何处无芳草”可译为“There are plenty of fish in the sea”；“缘木求鱼”可译为“To fish in the air”；“茫然无措”可译为“To feel at sea”。

3 四字格翻译的原则、方法及实例

关于翻译的标准，中外翻译理论家们提出了不同的主张，如玄类采用“译场”的方式保证译文的准确性和可读性；严复的“信、达、雅”近似赫伯特·罗森斯坦（Herbert Valtier）所提出的“Triness”（三个“ness”，即faithfulness，expressiveness，gracefulness）；鲁迅的“信、顺”，保持原作风格；傅雷的“重神似而不重形似”；钱钟书的“化境”说；刘重德的“信、达、切”。从上面列举的翻译标准中，可以发现，尽管各家观点不尽相同，但翻译标准大致可以概括为三点：一，“信”，即忠实原作。二，“顺”，即译文要流畅自然，确切完整，使读者看了能一目了然。三，“功能对等”，即“指从语义到文体在译语中用最贴近而又是最自然的对等语再现原语的信息”。因此，在汉语四字格的翻译中，我们应当尽量达到这三点翻译标准的统一，即“信”“顺”“功能对等”的统一。为此，本文根据汉语四字格与英语习语的文化差异，在以语义对等为翻译标准的基础上，讨论汉语四字格的不同翻译方法，并举例说明。

3.1 套用法

套用译法是翻译中最普遍且最重要的翻译方法。汉英成语对等率较低，最理想的汉译法就是能找到与之相对应的同义成语来翻译。汉英语言、文化的共通之处，使得在汉译过程中，套用同义英语成语成为可能。含义相同且形象一致的英语成语可以直接采取套用法。例如：

浑水摸鱼：Fish in troubled waters.

趁热打铁：Strike while the iron is hot.

一箭双雕：To kill two birds with one stone.

白纸黑字：To put down in black and white.

在套用成语时作者应根据其真正的内涵意义去套用，这样可以使读者在欣赏外国文学作品时不光了解其中意义，更可以细品其中的思想内容。

3.2 直译法

英语和汉语两种语言中也有形同意合的四字格。英语中的“Hedges have eyes，walls have ears”与汉语的“隔篱有眼，隔墙有耳”形意都极为吻合。这种形意相合的四字格对于译者来说是可喜的。例如：

祸不单行：Misfortunes never come alone.

画蛇添足：To draw a snake and add feet to it.

沧海一粟：A drop in the ocean.

谋事在人，成事在天：Man proposes，God disposes.

言多必失：The tongue cuts the throats.

直译法的好处在于可以给读者带来新鲜感，增加文字的表现力，同时也保留了原文的比喻形象，且明确易懂。采用这种方法可以明确地将原文译出，较好地体现了原文的信息并保持了文章的美感。

3.3 意译法

有些四字格成语既无法保留原来的字面意义和形象意义，又找不到对应的可借用的同义成语，所以只好牺牲原文成语的风格，配合上下文进行意译，以便保持原作思想内容的完整性。例如：

树大招风：Names are debts.

红白喜事：The weddings and funerals.

天网恢恢，疏而不漏：Justice has long arms.

随遇而安：Don't trouble trouble until trouble troubles you.

意译法可以有效避免英汉翻译中的误译，如果全部按照直译法翻译会给读者带来莫名其妙的感觉，对文章的理解也会出现偏差。因此，四字格的翻译要视情况而定翻译的方法，找到最合适的方法与之对应，这样语义对等的四字格才可称之为翻译的最高境界。

4 结语

英汉之间的文化差异以及语言特点导致了其各自不同的语义，源语言的意思可能会在目标语中缺失。在四字格翻译中，文化因素极其重要，忽视各自语言背后的文化会使译文读起来啼笑皆非。除此之外，在传达原文意思的基础上还应生动形象，不生硬死板。概言之，深入了解相关的文化背景以及专业知识是保证译文质量的关键。

参考文献

[1] 陈智勇. 汉语四字格结构与翻译原则探析[J]. 考试周刊:文学语言学研究,2014,92:24-25.

[2] 吕洁. 论英译汉中汉语四字格的使用[J]. 陕西师范大学继续教育学报,2002,19(4):73-76.

[3] 张丽艳. 文化差异和汉语"四字格"成语翻译[J]. 忻州师范学院学报,2013,29(3):63-67.

[4] 刘学华,文珊. 论翻译的"信"[J]. 长沙电力学院学报:社会科学版,2002(5):116.

[5] 唐义均. 汉英翻译技巧示例[M]. 北京:外文出版社,2011.

[6] 龚光明. 翻译思维学[M]. 上海:上海社会科学院出版社,2004.

[7] 包惠南,包昂. 中国文化与汉英翻译[M]. 北京:外文出版社,2003.

翻译研究

语言学与教学研究 ☜

外国文学与文化研究

教育、教学探讨与实验教学研究

CBI教学理念与英美概况课程教学改革

史　云

摘　要：大学英语延续课“英美概况”在实际教学中面临诸多问题。以内容为依托的外语教学（content-based instruction）模式将学科内容学习和语言学习有机地结合起来，激发学习兴趣，激活学习热情，提高语言应用能力，促进个人全面发展，有助于培养应用型、复合型人才。其对该类课程的教学有很好的借鉴作用。

关键词：英美概况教学；CBI教学理念

1 引言

国内许多高校四级后的英语学习基本断线，学生们不是抱怨考完四级学校就不管他们的英语学习了，就是感觉到英语课的教学由于内容重复而引起学习自满、懈怠、学习兴趣的下降，学习的动力不足。另外，许多学生虽然通过了大学英语四、六级的考试，具有一定程度的英语水平，但是由于长期应试教育的影响，英语综合能力还有待提高。因此，在完成基础阶段的EGP（English for general purpose）教育后，多数高校通过设置后续课程体系拓宽大学英语的课程功能，使英语教育向应用型、实用型方向转变。英美概况课程，作为旨在提高大学生人文素养的一门通识课，其重要性正在得到越来越多的认可。与注重语言知识和语言功能学习的大学英语基础阶段的教学不同的是，该课程所涉及的内容非常广泛，目的在于使学生了解英美两国的历

作者简介：史云，北京工商大学外国语学院教师，主要研究方向为外语教育、二语习得。

史、社会、政治、经济、教育、节日、宗教信仰、种族关系及社会问题等方面的情况，拓宽学生的知识面，提高学生对文化差异的敏感性、宽容性和处理文化差异的灵活性，培养学生跨文化交际能力。然而该课程在实际教学中面临诸多问题，如生词量大，词句晦涩难懂，教材内容相对于世界形势的变化具有一定的滞后性，内容庞杂，教师备课负担重，课时紧张，班容量大，课堂以教师讲授为主，学生的主体性和积极性不足。久而久之，学生对英美文化的兴趣和自主学习的热情被消磨，课堂死气沉沉，教师授课热情也受到影响。有鉴于此，国内外语教学专家陆续地提出了一些改善文化课程教授的方法，其中，融合了学科内容与语言学习的以内容为依托的外语教学（content-based instruction，CBI）模式不失为一种很好的借鉴和指导。

2 CBI教学理念

CBI理念在于将语言教学基于某个学科教学或基于某种主题教学来进行，被认为是将外语同内容结合起来学习的一种有效教学途径。CBI教学理念发端于20世纪60年代的加拿大幼儿园浸入式教学法，后来广泛传入美国的中学和大学外语教学中。在欧洲，类似的教学法称为CLIL（content and language integrated learning），许多欧洲国家如爱沙尼亚、芬兰、拉脱维亚、荷兰和西班牙都普遍实行了CLIL教学法。在CBI和CLIL教学模式中，外语是学习各学科的媒介，学科内容是语言学习的源泉，语言能力的获得则是理解这些学科信息的“副产品”。学习内容可以学生感兴趣的体育、流行音乐等内容为主题，但通常以历史、科学等学术内容为主，这些学科内容被认为是学习语言的最自然和真实的材料。

CBI提供了理想的语言学习条件。Grabe和Stoller指出，在以内容为依托的课堂上，学生学习学科知识的同时接触到大量的语言材料，具备可理解性、与过往学习经历相联系、符合学习者需求等特点的语言材料正是成功的语言学习的重要标准。CBI支持语境化学习，学生学到的是与文本内容相关的有意义的语言，而不是孤立的语言片段。处理复杂的信息和参与有挑战性的任务可以提升学习者的兴趣和内在动机。CBI天然地具有辅助合作式学习、体验式学习和以项目为基础的学习等特点。此外，教师根据需要可以在课程中增加额外的主题以满足学习者的兴趣和需求，也使得CBI课堂具有更多灵活性。最后，CBI教学有利于开展以学习者为中心的课堂活动，在选择特定内容和学习任务上学生有选择和表达个人喜好的机会，大大增加了参与性。

CBI课堂成功与否取决于实施细节。Stoller总结了成功的CBI课堂的八个特征：①大量的输入、有意义的输出、对语言和内容掌握的反馈；②信息的收集、处理和报告；③综合听说读写各项技能，如以读促写，听讲座以理解文本内容，采访同伴后撰写数据收集的结果；④合作学习原则下的任务和项目活动；⑤策略训练，不是教授一个一个孤立的学习策略，而是立足于培养学生成为善于使用策略的学习者；⑥直观教具，使用诸如图表、时间线、条形图等图表结构图引入单元主题，帮助学习者理解晦涩的文章内容，指导学习者分析课文架构和语篇组织；⑦语境中的语法教学，语法项目练习直接来源于学习者产出和处理的文本；⑧综合任务，学生将多渠道来源的信息加以综合，以口头、书面形式展示学习成果。

3 英美概况课程中应用CBI

3.1 处理好内容和语言的关系

当学生使用外语学习一门学科知识时，必然需要大量的帮助来理解课程内容，同时还要学习使用与课程内容相关的学术语言来进行交流。英美文化课本中大量关于西方文化的术语是学习者的首要障碍。因此，除了课程内容学习目标之外，教师必须要提前设定好明确的语言学习目标，涵盖词汇、语法和篇章组织等方面。课堂练习的设计应包括语言内容（词汇、句型、组织结构等）和学科内容两方面。语言练习要侧重特定学科语言的使用特点。还应注意的是，教师要避免将大部分精力放在学科信息的收集和扩充上而忽视制定具体而明确的语言学习目标。同时，也要避免把重点仅放在解释生词和长句，将课堂变成枯燥的英语精读课。教师对于学生的英语水平要有深入的了解，在此基础上选择内容真实的教学素材，传递有意义的信息，用真实的目标语言完成现实任务。要根据每届学生的英语水平及时更新教材，调整教材的难易度，以此避免学生因所学内容枯燥或太难而失去兴趣甚至放弃。

3.2 采取适当、灵活的教学手段

CBI只是一种教学理念而不是教学方法，也没有单一的模式。

英美概况课通常采取主题模式，教师可以事先征求学生意见，选择几个重要、趣味性强的主题重点学习。教师要设法将大量有趣、相关的教学材料带入课堂，同时也要尽量使学生接触不同来源、观点迥异、体裁各异的学习资料。以美国20世纪60年代的民权运动为例，可以利用的丰富历史资料包括录音、视频、图片、实物、历史文献以及互联网上海量的资料。

掌握学科内容和词汇学习一样都需要相关知识的反复重现。一些有效的课堂复习活动包括：要求学生进行拼图式阅读（jigsaw reading）然后各自报告学习成果；针对同一篇文章或同一视频，复习活动可以设计不同的阅读和视听目的；使用不同模式复习内容，比如听写；要求学生创建个性化的图表式组织图（graphic organizer）重组学习要点；为测验和口头汇报做准备的常规单元复习。

3.3 提高语言综合技能的手段

合作听写（dictogloss），教师将听写材料读两至三遍，学生听第一遍时不记录，整体感受语篇信息；听第二遍时记笔记，但不要求逐词记录。听后学生小组讨论、整理笔记，并重写文本，要求符合原文信息，语法正确，语意连贯，合乎逻辑。教师对各小组的语段进行反馈，鼓励学生比较、讨论以提高运用语言的能力。最后通过对照、分析听力原文，学生进一步了解原文的语篇及语法特征。

对话式日记（dialogue journals），要求学生每周课上或课下进行笔头记录，可以规定具体的写作重点如本周学习过程和心得，也可以是学生希望表达的任何内容。教师作为对话的另一方，写出相应的反馈，但不需要改正任何语法错误。

4 结束语

CBI教学是语言学习的一大创新，应用于国外各种不同的教学环境，已经有了很多成功的范例。英美概况课堂采用CBI教学理念，将外语学习与学

科内容有机地结合起来，可以使学习变得更有意义，增强学习者的动机和主动性，提高他们的语言综合能力和探索学科知识的积极性。目前国内相关的实证研究还比较薄弱，外语教师在如何更好地认识、理解和实施这种教学理念，以及提高自身学科知识、技能传授方面，还有很多工作要做。

参考文献

[1] GENESEE F. Learning thorough two languages: studies of immersion and bilingual education [M]. Cambridge, MA: Newbury House, 1987.

[2] GRABE W, STOLLER F.Content-based instruction: research foundations[M]//SNOW M A, BRINTON D.The content-based classroom: perspectives on integrating language and content. New York: Longman, 1997.

[3] STOLLER F. Promoting the acquisition of knowledge in a content based course[M]//CRANDALL J, KAUFMAN D. Content-based instruction in higher education settings.Alexandria, VA: TESOL, 2002.

[4] STRYKER S B, LEAVER B L.Content-based instruction in foreign language education[M]. Washington: Georgetown University Press, 1997.

[5] 戴庆宁，吕晔. CBI教学理念及其教学模式[J].国外外语教学，2004(4): 16-20.

[6] 戴炜栋. 建构具有中国特色的英语教学"一条龙"体系[J]. 外语教学与研究，2001(5): 322-327.

[7] 王蒙. CBI与大学英语四级后教学[J]. 山东外语教学，2006(2): 29-32.

[8] 谢琳琳. 大学英语选修课程"英美文化"教学初探[J]. 高教研究，2010(10).

浅议英语学习者如何通过看美剧学英语

许兰贞

摘　要：随着互联网的普及，以美剧为代表的英语影视剧迅速在国内传播开来，一些制作精良、情节有趣的美剧受到了人们的追捧，尤其是广大英语学习者的热捧。许多英语学习者甚至认为看美剧是真正的快乐学习，是学习英语语言和文化的最佳途径。本文旨在讨论英语学习者该如何有效地看美剧才能使自己真正地从中受益。

关键词：美剧；英语学习者；学习方法和步骤；学习态度

1 前言

随着互联网的普及，以美剧为代表的英语影视剧迅速在国内传播开来，中国观众对于美剧的喜爱不分年龄、性别、职业，几乎男女老少、学生教师都有几部自己钟爱的美剧。早至20世纪90年代开始的《老友记》《欲望都市》，以及后来的《迷失》《越狱》《反恐24小时》《别对我说谎》《豪斯医生》《绯闻女孩》，还有近些年备受好评的《纸牌屋》《国土安全》《疑犯追踪》等都受到了人们的追捧，尤其是广大英语学习者的热捧。究其原因，这些美剧制作精良，其生动有趣的情节、富有异域特色的文化很容易激发人们的观赏热情，继而激发人们对英语语言和文化的兴趣。甚至许多英语学习者认为看美剧是真正的快乐学习，是学习英语语言和文化的最佳途径。然而根

作者简介：许兰贞，北京工商大学外国语学院讲师。

据笔者的观察和经验，很多人美其名曰看美剧、学英语，其实更多关注的只是故事内容、剧情发展，英语学习效果却并不明显。本文旨在讨论英语学习者该不该看美剧、如何有效地看美剧才能使自己真正地从中受益？

2 看美剧学英语的可行性

不可否认，看美剧学英语是无数英语学习者梦寐以求的学习方式，一边观看美剧享受精彩剧情，一边放松身心、娱乐自己，同时又能提高英语、了解国外的文化生活，何乐而不为呢？所以，答案是肯定的，英语学习者应该看美剧，应该多看美剧。

首先，美剧等英语影视剧是英语学习者绝好的学习资源，我们没有任何理由浪费互联网时代带给我们的免费资源。此外，美剧通过声音和图像的共同作用，将视觉和听觉刺激有效结合，这是其他学习手段所不能达到的，因而也比阅读英语书籍和听英语广播等音频材料等方法能更充分地调动学习者的学习兴趣。这是学习者所推崇的寓学于乐、快乐学习的第一步。

其次，美剧中包含的丰富的文化信息以及地道的生活化口语对于学习者建立英语思维方式、改进英语语感、理解美国社会文化，发挥着积极有效的作用。从某种意义上来讲，看一部美剧相当于在美国社会体验和生活了一段时间，而这样的体验对于中国学生来讲是非常必要的。因为我们的日常生活没有英语听说的语言环境，作为美国人日常生活的缩影和提升，美剧则人为地给英语学习者创造了一种原汁原味的英语语言环境，还展现出多姿多彩的美国文化以及真实丰富的语言场景，让我们身临其境般地听到纯正地道的英语、亲眼目睹美国式的生活和文化。

3 看美剧学英语的具体操作方法

基于对美剧积极作用的理解，笔者提倡英语学习者应该观看美剧，而且看美剧学英语不失为一种快乐的学习方法。那么英语学习者到底应该怎样看美剧才算是真正有效的，并能从中获益良多呢？笔者推荐具体方法步骤如下。

第一，选择一部合适的美剧，适合自己的兴趣爱好和英语水平。兴趣是最好的老师，有了兴趣就会有源源不断的动力坚持边看边学。当然，看美剧不能仅凭一腔热血追求剧情的精彩和刺激，否则就是纯粹的娱乐方式。以学英语为目的来看美剧，应该尽量选择贴近日常生活、故事情节平淡却不失趣味的影视作品。像《反恐24小时》《越狱》《疑犯追踪》这类动作片，虽然情节紧张、场面恢弘，但感官刺激过后能留给你的东西少之又少，所以此类美剧暂时先不要涉足。有些美剧太过专业，如《实习医生格雷》《豪斯医生》《律师本色》《波士顿法律》等，适合相关专业的、有学专业英语需要的学生。所以，在数百部流行美剧中，大家选择的基本原则是生活化和口语化，尤其是情节交代比较详细，剧情发展比较缓慢却不失趣味的电视剧，如《绝望主妇》《摩登家庭》《查理成长日记》。这三部美剧的共同特点是以家庭生活为拍摄重点，故事贴近日常生活，语言比较简单、规范、地道，没有《老友记》《生活大爆炸》等情景剧中那么多的流行语和俚语，特别有助于英语学习者的学习。

第二，采用正确有效的观影和学习方法。看美剧、学英语绝非在于所观看的美剧的数量，其关键在于观看的质量和效果。笔者认为每一集美剧至少需要反复看三遍、听两遍才能达到学英语的目的。第一遍应该照顾个人的观影热情和兴趣，所以不要有任何学习的压力，只需要完全投入地享受剧情，基本理清人物关系和故事情节。至于字幕的去留、中文或英文，则因人而异。如果基础比较薄弱，词汇量不足以驾驭和理解情节大意，建议保留中英文字幕，以便随时获取帮助、跟上故事情节。对于有一定英语基础的学习者，第一遍就隐去字幕、努力去听，不必在意能听懂多少，主要以了解剧情为目的，看看自己是否能了解故事脉络。我们从实际交际理解的经验得知，口头语言（oral language）只占交流信息的35%，而非语言因素（body language，指除了听说之外的眼神交流、肢体动作等）则占65%。所以有一定英语基础的学习者完全可以不要字幕就看懂故事情节。这种根据肢体语言猜测、推断对方所表达的意思的能力不论是在考试中还是和外国人的日常交流中都是非常重要的，而且可以通过这种锻炼出来的猜测能力逐步培养学习者的英语语感和思维能力。通过第一遍观看对人物关系和剧情的大概了解，第二遍建议附上英文字幕进行逐字逐句的精听，更理想的方法是把该剧的电子版剧本打印出来，放在电脑旁边随时备用。这一遍需要仔细听，拿起笔认真记，有疑难的地方就果断暂停播放，对照打印好的剧本认真研读语句，把重点、难点一一标注下来，以便加深印象。有了第二遍的精听训练，第三遍建议关掉字幕，看看自己是否能听懂第二遍没能听出来的语句，甚至对于第二遍中遇到的特别好的对话或者旁白、独白，可以选一个小片段进行听写训练。这一步至关重要，应该反复地做，直到能把一集完全看懂、听懂为止。看完三遍之后，相信对故事的情节已经了然于心，对于影片中的人物特征也了如指掌，但是离成功还有两步之遥：泛听和精听各一遍。最后两遍都是只听不看，把看美剧演变为听美国“相声”，一边听，一边想象故事画面，加强自己对故事的理解和融入。泛听是真正享受美国相声的正确办法，虽然你仍然会漏掉和忘记许多细节，但是不必在意，只需好好放松心情去享受美国“相声”带来的快感和惬意。最后一遍是精听，需要一手拿着打印的剧本，一手随时单击暂停键，对于没有听懂的语句需要反复听，直到完全听懂为止。

第三，循序渐进、坚持不懈的学习态度是不可或缺的。一集美剧看三遍、听两遍，这会不会太浪费时间了？这个过程确实很耗时，但是功夫不负有心人，坚持不懈一定会有很好的回报。可以记录一下自己完成以上五个步骤各需多少时间。可能第一集需要2个星期，第二集还需要10天，到了第三集可能只需要一个星期。慢慢地你会越来越有成就感，最终实现和美国观众同步享受美剧视觉、听觉的美好愿望。何况，学英语从来都是不容易的，大家之所以打着看美剧、学英语的旗号，不就是因为美剧吸引人，可以为你提供源源不断的动力和坚持不懈的毅力吗？

4 结语

互联网时代的英语学习者是幸运的，因为他们有了美剧这一取之不竭、用之不尽的宝贵资源。美剧将美国人的现实生活场景搬到了我们眼前，尽管有些内容不无夸张，甚至是虚构的，但是足以让我们这些外国人得以管中窥豹，更好地了解美国社会和文化。观看美剧的过程使得英语学习者有机会完全浸泡在生动有趣的故事情节中，跟上美国人的英语思维习惯去理解他们的逻辑和情感，超越时空去体验美国人原汁原味的生活细节，最后得以逐步了解美国社会和文化。

参考文献

[1] 王红. 美剧与英语学习[J]. 电影评价,2008(11).

[2] 吴晓敏. 看经典美剧,学地道美语[J]. 安徽文学(下半月),2011(1).

[3] 饶素玉,魏庆平. 英美影视作品在大学英语教学中的应用研究[J]. 科技风,2010(2).

[4] 王利伟. 美剧的中国发展历程及流行背后的思考[J]. 才智,2010(1).

基于Blackboard教学管理平台的任务型教学
——以创建多模态Wiki百科之商务英语课程为例

石洪宇　李子嘉

摘　要：本文基于多模态理论，采用了任务型教学法，研究了学生利用Blackboard教学管理平台工具Wiki建立商务英语小百科的过程。笔者发现，多模态互动给学生的语言学习创造了有利的环境，但是Wiki工具的某些性能尚需完善。在小组任务中，学生的协作是一种优势，然而如何让学生都均衡地参与到任务中去有所收获是教师要考虑的问题。

关键词：BB平台；任务型教学；多模态；Wiki工具；商务英语

21世纪以来，科技的进步和教学资源的短缺给大学英语教学带来了前所未有的机遇与挑战。各高校开始引进网络学习和教学管理平台，与之相关的语言学与语言教学理论也蓬勃发展，为新的教学方法提供了理论基础，其中，任务型教学法和多模态理论占有非常重要的位置。

北京工商大学从2013年引入Blackboard教学管理平台（以下简称BB平台），为广大师生的教与学提供了一个强大的平台和有效的工具。至今，BB平台已经在发布通知、教学大纲和教学日历的上传、测试的实施与成绩的管理、教学资源的分享等方面发挥了极为重要的作用，但是交流互动功能以及平台工具尚未得到充分地开发与使用。为了进一步发挥现代技术教育手段的

项目/基金：本论文为2015年北京市级大学生科研与创业行动计划项目的成果，项目编号SJ201501035。

作者简介：石洪宇，女，天津人，北京工商大学讲师，主要研究方向为英语教学法、语言学。李子嘉，女，山西人，北京工商大学商学院学生。

作用，充分利用BB平台，增强学生之间的互动，帮助学生更好地自主学习并提升语言学习效果，本文基于多模态理论，采用了任务教学法，研究了学生利用BB平台工具Wiki建立商务英语小百科的过程。

1 任务型教学法

任务型教学法（task-based language teaching approach）兴起于20世纪80年代，它以系统功能语言学、社会建构主义学习论等为理论依据，是一种以“任务”为核心单位，计划、组织语言教学的途径。任务教学法与传统教学法不同，它把交际中的意义放在首位，强调语境的作用，学习者利用真实的语料，在学中做、做中学，在用目的语完成任务的过程中，与其他学习者进行合作和协商，在掌握语言形式的同时，能够意识到语言的功能意义。任务型教学法有效地解决了传统教学法中只关注语言形式和结构，忽视语言内容及意义的弊端，是将语言的输入和产出相结合的一种教学方法。

2 多模态理论

从20世纪90年代起，“多模态”（multimodality）越来越受到语言学界的关注。多模态话语是指运用视觉、听觉和触觉通过话语、声音、图像及动作多种手段和符号资源进行交际。过去在交际中人们往往强调文字的作用，随着科技的进步、各种媒体的发展，人们逐渐认识到图像、动作也都传达了一定的信息，为文字提供了一定的语境，因此，多模态话语所传达出的信息要比单一模态传达出的信息更为准确、充分。因而，多模态话语给学生的学习也带来重要的影响。顾曰国以行为主义心理学和认知心理学为基础，构建了多模态外语学习的模型，并指出通过视觉及视频流进行互动，具有直观性和体验性。与其他模态相比，学习效果可以说事半功倍。张德禄基于系统功能语言学，分析了多模态话语综合理论框架，并把框架分为文化层面、情景层面、内容层面以及表达层面。他认为，多媒体技术的发展为提供尽可能真实的语境创造了便利条件。

3 研究对象及研究方法

本研究的研究对象是北京工商大学2013级A班130名学生，他们来自于全校各个专业，又分为A1、A2、A3三个班。A班属于快班，学生英语基础较好。在实施本研究初期，有部分学生已经通过全国大学英语四级考试，并取得不错的成绩。根据学校的教学计划，这些学生在第一、二学期进行基础英语的学习，第三、四学期学习商务英语，教材是《BEC剑桥商务英语》中级。由于学生来自各个专业，文理皆有，学生之间的差异较大。经济类和商科的同学在学习商务英语时已经具备了一定的背景知识，对学习材料理解起来相对容易一些。而理工专业的同学对某些话题往往会显得比较生疏，也缺乏兴趣。为了尽可能弥补这种差异，帮助学生熟悉商务英语的背景知识及语言知识，增加学生对商务英语的学习兴趣，促进学生学习的积极性和自主性，我们在第四学期对学生采用了基于BB平台的任务型教学，具体实施方法如下。

根据本学期商务英语各单元的话题及所要掌握的商务技能，要求学生利用BB平台上的Wiki工具，建立自己的商务英语小百科，内容可以包括商务英语词汇及名词解释，介绍商务英语背景的文章、图片、图表、视频等，具体形式可以参考互联网上的维基百科。学生分成3~5人的小组，每个小组的同学可以根据单元数量及内容自行分工，可以每人负责一个单元，也可以大家共同建立一个单元。此项任务贯穿整个学期，在任务进行的过程中可以随时进行师生、生生之间的探讨和咨询，无论是技术层面还是语言文化层面上的，包括学生的使用心得，在不同时期还进行了阶段性的检查，了解学生的任务进行状况。学期末进行教师评估和学生之间的互评，评分按照百分制，最终计入平时成绩。另外，针对使用情况对学生进行了访谈。

4 研究结果及分析

经过一个学期的学习和协作，期末的时候大约80%的学生基本完成了这项任务。这里的完成是指每个单元都建立了相关的内容。内容以每个单元的商务英语词汇为主，配一些跟单元主题相关的介绍背景的文章，也有技能型介绍，比如如何写电子邮件。从模态上来看，主要使用的仍然是文字性材料，有少部分学生配了图片和图表，没有学生使用音频和视频。从材料的组织来看，大部分学生都是简单地罗列了材料，材料之间没有呈现紧密的联系。仅有一组同学把所掌握的材料按照一定的逻辑组织在一起，并按照材料的安排给出目录。

利用BB平台提供的Wiki工具建立商务英语小百科这一任务符合建构主义及任务型教学的相关理论。在这一任务中，学生变成了学习的中心，由外部刺激的被动接受者和知识的灌输对象转变为信息加工的主体、知识意义的主动构建者。老师不再是知识的传授者和灌输者，而变成了帮助学生构建意义的促进者和帮助者，利用情景、协作、会话等学习环境要素充分发挥学生的积极性、主动性和创造性，最终帮助学生实现意义的构建。完成这一任务的过程包括对所学单元主题及内容的理解与回顾，对接触到的知识和信息的消化和掌握，对文化背景知识的拓展和语境的感知，对商务技能的获得，对所掌握的材料之间的逻辑关系的分析及组织，必要的word和excel等计算机办公软件的使用，以及个人独立学习和小组协作学习的能力。由于学生搜集到的资料有可能是文本、图片、图表、音频、视频，所以学生、教师、多媒体课件与资源创造出了一个多模态互动的语言学习环境，每种模态都构成了符号资源，都对学生的意义建构起了一定的作用。因此，按照要求完成这项任务有助于学生对课堂知识的吸收和课外知识的延续，丰富语言知识和背景知识，提高学生发现问题、分析问题、解决问题的能力。总之，无论是吸收性知识还是产出性知识，完成这一任务的过程将会对学生语言知识、语言能力、科研能力及协作能力有一个全面的促进。做得最好的一组学生的反馈也证明了这一点。他们认为，这一任务不仅锻炼了他们的语言能力，也锻炼了思维能力。

但是，应该看到，研究结果还存在不尽如人意的地方。无论是使用人数、创建的内容、模态的使用，与最初的设想出入很大。总结对学生的访谈内容，技术原因占了很大的比例。首先，学生在进行这项任务时要熟悉Wiki工具的使用。总体来说，Wiki工具使用是便捷的，也能支持文本、图片、音频、视频等多种格式的文件，同一小组的学生可以单独也可以共同编辑一个条目，而且每一位学生的编辑都会有详细的记录，比如编辑人及编辑时间。编辑人还可以自行设置字号大小、格式等。但是由于某些文本的编辑或文件的上传需要预先规划好，这种预设性从某种程度上影响了其使用的便利性。加之受到网速的影响，视频上传需要较长时间，进而影响了学生尝试多种格式文件上传的积极性。要解决这个问题，一方面生产厂家应不断改进产品，从技术上做到用户友好，另一方面应加强对学生的技术指导，在任务开始之前对学生进行培训。其次，小组协作方面还需要更多的规范。分小组完成一项任务的优势在于进入小组协作的模式后，同一组的学习者可以对某一问题提出自己的见解，也可以请求同组其他人帮助自己学习中存在的问题，因而可以提高学生共同解决问题的能力。但是如果这种求助最终成为对于其他人的依赖，那么这种小组任务又会成为某些学生懒惰的屏障，会让积极完成任务的学生感到不公平，从而影响完成任务的动力和兴趣。再次，评价小组任务的方式也有待商榷，评分标准有待细化。学生以小组为单位完成任务，评价往往也是以小组为单位的。以本次利用Wiki工具创建商务小百科为例，评分主要是看是否每个单元都有内容，然后靠主观感受来评定任务完成的质量，这样的标准在研究结束时再看显得过于笼统和模糊。事实上，材料的数量、组织以及使用模态的种类都可以作为评分的标准。最后，虽然BB平台的Wiki模块能够体现每个小组成员贡献，但是评价方式没能根据小组成员个体所做的贡献打分，这也是此次研究的一个缺陷。这也给今后的分小组完成任务的教学方式提供了一个借鉴，评价小组任务完成情况时如何兼顾集体成果和个人贡献是教师需要考虑的问题。此外，作为评价的一部分，最后加入面试环节也会促进学生对自己所学材料的理解和吸收。

5 结语

总之，任务教学法已经被证明是帮助学生建构意义的行之有效的方法，但是如何让协作不变成依赖，加强监控，让小组每个成员完成相当量的任务，还是任务教学法面临的一个问题。随着计算机网络的发展，学习者接触到的信息是多模态、多渠道的，得到的帮助也会是多模态、多渠道的，这为学生的语言学习提供了一个有利的环境。教师如何利用好这一网络时代的优势，加强自身的学习，迎头赶上，帮助学生利用好各种资源，有的放矢地为教学服务，是教师自身发展要解决的一个课题。

参考文献

[1] 方文礼.外语任务型教学法纵横谈[J]. 外语与外语教学,2003(9):17-20.

[2] 顾曰国.多媒体、多模态学习剖析[J]. 外语电化教学,2007(4):3-12.

[3] 黄立鹤.基于多模态理论的大学英语拓展学习体系研究[J]. 语言教育,2014(8):11-16.

[4] 黄若妤.建构主义与外语多媒体教学模式[J]. 外语电化教学,2000 (6):16-19.

[5] 覃修桂,齐振海.任务及任务教学法的再认识[J]. 外语教学,2004 (5):69-74.

[6] 谢蓉蓉.多模态虚拟课程——基于多模态话语分析理论的未来网络课程新模式[J]. 中国电化教育,2012(4):74-79.

[7] 王炤.多媒体英语写作中的多模态互动模式[J]. 外语电化教学,2010(11):14-19.

[8] 岳守国.任务语言教学法:概要、理据及运用[J]. 外语教学与研究,2002(9):364-367.

[9] 张德禄.多模态话语理论与媒体技术在外语教学中的应用[J]. 外语教学,2009(7):15-20.

[10] 张德禄.多模态话语分析综合理论框架探索[J]. 中国外语,2009(1):24-30.

[11] 朱永生.多模态话语分析的理论基础和研究方法[J]. 外语学刊,2007(5):82-86.

浅谈大学英语写作课程中的问题与改善

赵 聃

摘 要：外语学习中写作的重要性不言而喻，是最终也是最重要的输出。但写作的教学效果并不尽如人意，这与写作课程的内容与安排有很大关系。因此本文首先回顾了国内学者对于大学英语写作课程存在问题的研究，其次探讨了大学英语写作课程应当从主观意识和实际操作上做出怎样的改善。

关键词：大学英语写作教学；课程安排；观念改善

语言学习的目的最终在于能够实现交际功能。简单来说，练习“听”以能明白别人在表述什么；练习“读”为了看得明白同时积累语言素材；练习“说”为了能够表达需求与思想；练习“写”是更为标准和正式的输出，同时承载着传承。在大学英语教学的听、说、读、写中，写是最终也是最重要的输出，但同时也成为了大学英语教学和学生学习中感到最头疼的环节。从学生而言，经长达数年的练习，但是仍感觉收效甚微，仍旧不会写、写不好。从老师而言，写作教什么、怎么教、课堂如何安排、布置了写作如何修改、修改后如何保证学生的提高，也成为困扰老师的问题。大学英语写作教学，一直以来都为国内英语学界学者关心。

本文将回顾近些年来学界所探讨的国内大学英语写作现状和问题，并且给出一些在意识观念、教学手段、训练方法等方面可能的解决方案。

作者简介：赵聃，女，2006年毕业于北京大学，现为北京工商大学讲师，主要研究方向为英美文学、国际关系等。

1 对大学英语写作课程存在问题的研究

在大学英语逐渐成为大学必修课，但同时也一直在被质疑的这几十年中，一些学者对于大学英语写作课程存在问题和革新的研究一直没有停止过。较早用数据进行分析的研究是在1995年。有学者根据该校200名学生的写作测试成绩统计分析，得出结论，认为大学生英语写作中最大的问题是写作内容的贫乏，主要表现在主要思想和细节技巧的运用不理想。2003年李至雪、李绍山，2004年王文宇、王立非，2005年姚兰、程骊妮等学者都分别通过检索，深入探讨了国内大学英语写作研究状况。尤其是姚兰从英语写作中存在的问题、影响写作的因素、导致英语写作教学相对滞后的原因等几个角度对历年文献归类分析。英语专家李赋宁也曾指出，目前我国知识界的英语听说能力已经有了很大的提高，但是英文写作水平仍不能令人满意。

就这一长期以来的问题，总结各位专家学者的研究，主要有以下几方面原因。

客观因素来说，首先，写作在整体英语课程中缺乏比较系统的框架结构。一直以来，非英语专业的大学英语课程主要以阅读为主，测试时，阅读也是占了很大比例。因此，大学英语教学的内容在于强调阅读理解技能和词汇学习；课堂上没有专门的写作时间，就连批阅和讲评都很难找出时间。其次，很多时候写作成为了考试通过的手段，而非目标。于晓红在2007年也指出这一问题，由于过级考试的需要，应试教学获得了空前的发展。再次，在教学方法上，老师一般都是讲授写作技巧、模仿练习，更有甚者，为了应试而背诵范文例句然后直接套用。所以可能四、六级能通过，雅思托福也会有好成绩，但是真实生活中的邮件、论文摘要、信函等却难以胜任。这就是课程内容的安排问题。除了以上原因，还有学者提出中西方思维的文化差异也导致了中国学生写作质量比较低，比如选词、结构和修辞等方面。

主观因素而言，首先，对写作的不够重视其实源自于整体英语教学大环境，比如大纲里对写作的要求和比例分配。其次，学生整体的语言基础不扎实，同时又对写作缺乏热情。另外，大部分学校的公共英语课中一般都是大班授课，班级学生人数多，而每位教师需要在有限时间内完成课时任务，没有办法进行细致的修改和给出评语，更不用说对着学生进行一对一的修改。

学生看不到不足之处，就会慢慢失去兴趣。这也是一个恶性循环，教师也因此越发丧失对写作教学的信心和积极性。

2 对大学英语写作课程提高和改善的方法探究

写作是一个复杂的过程，它是建立在大量输入后的一项输出，需要学生已经有了一定的语言基础，同时也需要教师采取合理的教学方式和安排。除此以外，还应了解写作能力的提高是一个渐进的过程，不可能一蹴而就。在这个过程中，不仅仅要意识到写作教学的问题所在，同时也要尽最大可能改善教学方法、优化写作课程、提高教学质量。

（1）要从大局上进行观念的转变。国内现存的四、六级考试，要逐渐但是坚定地进行考试改革，不能让考试束缚了学生的思维模式和写作定式。比如，写作的命题类型可以从议论文转向对未来工作更实际的应用文写作、图表分析等。在教学大纲和教材编写上，要给写作更多的空间和地位，使写作教学更加系统和连贯。

（2）要在主观层面上重视写作。教师和学生都要充分意识到“写”这个最终的输出和最重要的语言传承途径。就算不能够把写放在最重要地位，也一定要在实际教学中增加写作时间，包括理论讲解时间、批阅时间、课堂分析时间等。

（3）在课堂教学模式上，要注重写作过程的指导。从传统的“学生单独写作，教师单独评阅”的单向交流模式转向不仅仅重视写作结果，更要注重写作过程，即采用过程写作法。从学生的写前准备、初稿、反馈、修改、讨论、重写几个阶段展开。在初稿阶段，鼓励学生尽可能地把自己的想法写下来，不必过多地担心语言形式的正确与否。在反馈阶段，教师在内容和结构方面指出学生初稿中的优点和存在的不足，学生之间可根据教师提供的标准进行互评，为彼此的文章提供建设性的意见。在修改阶段，学生应根据教师和同学提出的意见和建议对初稿进行修改，不断完善文章内容，寻求最佳表达方式。必要时，学生再作修改和重写，如此反复，直至形成较好的成品。这一过程会促进学生的反思，同时也会减轻学生压力。

（4）在学生语言能力提高方面，需要保证大量语言输入，即阅读。大量的阅读是学生获得语言输入的最重要的途径，所以要通过读来促进写，同时也要在写的点评中使用阅读中出现的语言点来鼓励学生继续读。阅读的内容可以广泛涉猎名家名作、各类文体文章。阅读方法上，需要鼓励学生做读书笔记，多写勤读，同时摘抄、临摹和仿写，将他人的真正转化为自己的。这可以帮助学生意识到东西思维模式的差异，发现英汉语言差别，并且有目的地进行思维模式的模仿。这种模仿才能潜移默化地帮助他们写出地道的英语来。

（5）在网络时代，要充分使用网络教学平台所提供的各种便利。教师可以根据学生特点和要求进行课程的设计，可以改变比较枯燥的写作局面。老师能监控全过程，并能直接发现问题、解决问题。同时网络平台也是一个极好的能够增强学生自主学习意识、提高写作积极性的方式。

3 结语

本文不仅仅就大学英语教学写作部分存在的问题做出了一个整体的回顾，同时也做出了一些可提高改善的方案。尽管在实际教学中，确实还要教师和学生共同努力，但对于学生和老师来说都是一样的，随着写作教学研究的不断深入，相信英语写作的教学水平一定会有提高，学生也能获得事半功倍的效果。

参考文献

[1] 蔡慧萍. 我国高校英语写作教材的现状调查分析与思考[J]. 外语与外语教学，2005(6)：29-31.

[2] 杜金榜. 从学生英语写作错误看英语教学[J]. 外语教学，2001(2)：43-47.

[3] 秦朝霞. 国内大学英语写作研究现状及发展趋势分析[J]. 现代外语，2009(5)：195-204.

[4] 王立非，孙晓坤. 汉语写作能力对英语写作质量的影响[J]. 外语与外语教学2005(4)：24-27.

[5] 王丽敏. 对大学英语写作教学的思考[J]. 外语研究，2006(4)：167-169.

[6] 王文宇，王立非. 二语写作研究：十年回顾与展望[J]. 外语界，2004(3)：51-58.

[7] 姚兰,程骊妮. 我国20世纪80年代以来英语写作研究状况之研究[J]. 外语界,2005(5):2-16.

[8] 张在新,吴红云,王晓露,等. 我国英语写作教学中的主要问题[J]. 外语教学与研究,1995(4):43-49.

[9] 张艳红,程东元. 网络环境下大学英语写作能力培养模式的设计与实践[J]. 外语电化教学,2007(8):26-31.

大学英语四、六级汉译英中语篇意识的培养

陶 爽

摘　要：在大学英语四、六级考试中，汉译英段落翻译的出现增加了对学生语言综合运用能力的考核。对学生汉译英中语篇意识的培养对于提高学生的翻译能力，改善译文质量有着重要的意义。

关键词：四、六级考试；汉译英；语篇意识

1 引言

随着大学英语教学改革的不断推进，大学英语四、六级考试也在不断地进行改革。2013年，大学英语四、六级考试中的句子翻译改成了汉译英段落翻译。汉译英段落翻译是对学生学以致用能力的考查，是对学生语言应用能力的又一个综合性考核，这也对日常的语言教学提出了更进一步的要求。

在日常的大学英语四、六级汉译英段落翻译练习中，我们发现学生在翻译时普遍存在字对字、句对句的死译、硬译现象，缺少整体的语篇意识，往往只见树木，不见森林，译文呆板、生硬，甚至不准确。《大学英语》主要授课、学习对象和大学英语四、六级考核的主要对象是在校非英语专业的大

项目/基金：本文为2015年北京市级大学生科学研究与创业行动计划项目，项目题为“大学英语四、六级翻译中的语篇意识”，项目编号为SJ201502075。

作者简介：陶爽，女，北京工商大学讲师，主要研究方向为外国语言学及应用语言学、语篇分析及功能语法。

学本科生，学生对诸如语篇等语言学的概念及相应的训练少，这就要求我们在日常教学中，适当引入语篇等概念，从而帮助学生有意识或者下意识地从整体上对原文和译文进行把握和审视，使其在语言综合运用时更加灵活，准确。

2 语篇及翻译中的语篇意识

对于语篇（discourse）这一概念，不同的语言学家及学者有不同的表述。韩礼德和哈桑（Halliday and Hasan）认为，语篇是语义单位，不是形式单位，语篇不是由句子构成的，而是由句子实现的。具体来说，语篇可以是篇章、段落，也可以是一个或几个词，但是不受语法约束的在一定语境下表达完整语义的自然语言。胡壮麟认为，语篇指任何不完全受句子语法约束的在一定语境下表示完整语义的自然语言……目的是通过语言这一媒介实现具体交际任务或完成一定任务的行为。语篇可以是口头的，也可以是书面的，是语言使用中的一个单位。黄国文认为语篇可以从形式和功能两个角度来看，从形式的角度看，语篇是大于句子的语言单位；从功能的角度看，语篇是使用中的语言。总之，语篇是在交际功能上相对完整和独立的一个语言片段；可以是一段或者几段有意义的，表达一个完整信息、逻辑连贯、语言衔接、具有一定交际目的和功能的语言单位或交际事件。它是一组使用中的语言，既不是小句或句子之类的语法单位，也不受长短的限制。由此，我们可以看出，大学英语四、六级中的汉译英翻译段落可以称之为一个独立、完整的语篇。把语篇意识引入到大学英语四、六级汉译英翻译教学中是可行的。

把语篇意识引入到翻译中就是要把语篇当作一个有机的整体来对待，而不是孤立地一字、一词、一句的简单对等翻译。译者要从整体上了解原文的语言使用、文体风格及表达特点等，从而使译文读者在语言使用、文体风格及表达方面的整体感受同原文读者欣赏原文时的感受尽量相同或者接近，这对于非英语专业的大学本科生来说无疑是个高要求！要使学生，尤其是非英语专业的本科生具有语篇意识并能在实践中进行运用并不容易，这就要求英语教师将语篇意识贯穿到整个语言教学过程的始终。

3 如何培养学生汉译英中的语篇意识

要培养学生在汉译英中具有一定的语篇意识，教师要有较完善的语篇知识和翻译技巧，并在平时的汉译英练习中采取一定的教学策略。

首先，在汉译英翻译练习时，要在翻译的各个步骤上对学生进行一定的引导，使其具有一定的语篇意识。翻译前，要引导学生养成通读原文的习惯，把原文当作一个有机的整体来对待，了解原文的语言使用、文体特征及表达特点等，从而对原文有较好的掌握，并为翻译后提高译文质量奠定基础。翻译过程中，在做字、词、词组及句子的翻译时，引导学生在头脑中时刻保持对原文的整体感，选词、造句时顾全原文语义的同时，要注意译文的整体语篇。翻译结束后，除了做基础的如语法、词汇方面的检查，还要对译文从整体上进行完善，包括对照原文的语言使用、文体特征及表达特点等进行改进，使译文对读者产生的感受尽量接近原文读者对原文的感受。

其次，在平时授课时，用一定的语篇知识对学生进行引导，使学生在翻译时有据可依。语篇作为一种交际活动（communicative occurrence），有其自身的标准。Beaugrande 和 Dressler 认为，语篇应该具有七项标准，即：衔接性（cohesion）、连贯性（coherence）、意向性（intention）、可接受性（acceptability）、语境性（situationality）、信息性（informatility）和语篇参照性/互文性（intertextuality）。在这七项标准中，衔接和连贯是最基本的标准，直接影响着译文质量的高低，这两个概念也是最容易被学生理解和接受的。衔接是语篇的有形网络，主要有词汇和语法手段。语法层面的照应、替代、省略和连接现象，词汇层面的重复、同义、反义、下义、搭配等现象容易被学生识别、理解和掌握，这将在很大程度上改善学生的译文质量。连贯是语篇的无形网络，需要借助有形的语法和词汇手段来实现语篇中的语义关联，从而达到语义上的连贯。

最后，在汉译英教学和练习中，要引导学生观察、体会汉、英的语篇差异，从而采取相应的翻译策略，帮助学生提高译文质量。如英语语篇多注重“形合”，语篇的生成多依赖语法、词汇等衔接手段，而汉语语篇属于“意合”，语篇的生成更多地靠意义间的逻辑衔接来实现；在句式上，英语句子多长句，汉语多短句；在词语使用方面，英语多避免词语的简单重复，在不影响语义的情况下常使用同义词来替换，而汉语常用词语重复来达到一定的语言效果。汉语语言博大精深，富有成语、典故、俗语、谚语及诗、词句等，英语虽然也有自己的成语、典故等，但不如汉语丰富。这些在汉译英时将给学生带来一定的难度。大学英语四、六级汉译英的语篇虽然相对比较简单，但在2013~2015年的汉译英试题语篇中，成语和四字格的使用频繁出现，如果学生对英语、汉语语篇特点没有一定的了解，将给他的翻译带来很大的困难。相反，如果学生在做汉译英时能意识到英语、汉语语篇的差异，在面临四字格等翻译时，便会相对容易地采取相应的翻译策略对原文进行翻译。对英语、汉语篇差异的认识对于译文的修改和完善也是十分重要的，便于学生在整体上对译文进行修改、完善，从而使其符合译入语篇的特点，提高译文质量。

4 总结

大学英语四、六级汉译英语篇篇幅虽然相对比较短，但内容丰富，对于非英语专业本科生来说，想要翻译出高质量的译文并不容易。在日常教学中，培养学生的语篇意识，从整体上对原文汉语语篇和译文英语语篇进行把握，对于帮助学生提高译文质量有重大的意义。

参考文献

[1] DE BEAUGRANDE R W, DRESSLER W.Introduction to text linguistics[M]. London: Longman, 1981.

[2] HALLIDAY M A K, HASAN R.Cohesion in English[M]. London: Longman Group, U.K.Ltd., 1976.

[3] 黄国文.语篇分析的理论与实践:广告语篇研究[M]. 上海:上海外语教育出版社,2001.

[4] 胡壮麟.语篇的衔接与连贯[M]. 上海:上海外语教育出版社,1994.

浅析BTBU2014级研究生的学习类型对学习方法的影响

陈秀珍

摘　要：本文采取问卷的方法考察部分在读研究生的学习类型。受试对象是北京工商大学2014级学术型硕士研究生一年级的96名研究生。问卷包括18个问题，是英国英格兰地区在中小学校普遍使用的测试学习类型的问卷。本文中的学习类型分为三种：视觉型、听觉型和动觉型。本研究的目的一是使学生对自己的学习类型有所了解，在今后的学习和研究中更有效率地学习；目的二是使教师本人对学生的学习类型有所了解，在今后的教学中更有针对性地使用不同的教学手段从而使授课效果更佳。

关键词：学习类型；学习方法

1 学习类型和不同类型学习者偏好的学习方法简介

1.1 学习类型简介

根据O'Brien的学习风格（learning styles，也译作学习类型）理论，我们往往把学习者分为视觉型学习者、听觉型学习者和动觉型（也译作触觉型）学习者。他们有各自不同的学习方式。

视觉型的学习者处理世界的事情倾向于先用眼睛去看，而眼睛的学习能

作者简介：陈秀珍，女，山东烟台人，北京工商大学教师，主要研究方向为应用语言学。

力快，可以在同一时间内接收到很多信息，日子久了，发挥视觉能力熟练后，他们的行为模式会有以下特征：

① 通常喜欢颜色鲜明、线条活泼、外形美丽的人、事或物。

② 能够在同一时间中兼顾数项内容，并引以为荣。

③ 喜欢事物多变化、多线条、节奏快。

④ 要求环境清洁，摆设整齐。

⑤ 坐不定，有小动作。

⑥ 衣着得体，颜色搭配很好。

⑦ 说话简短轻快、声调平板、不耐烦冗长说话。

⑧ 说话喜欢开门见山，直接切入主题，两三句便说完。

⑨ 在乎事情的重点，不太在意细节。

听觉型的学习者惯用听觉，日子久了，发挥听觉能力熟练了，他们的行为模式会有以下特征：

① 说话内容详尽，或许会有内容重复的情况出现。

② 重视事物的细节。

③ 说话多，而且往往不能停下。

④ 重视环境的安静，难以忍受噪声，注重文字的优美，发音正确等。对用字很注重，不能忍受错别字。

⑤ 喜欢事物有节奏感，做事喜欢按部就班，注重程序和步骤。

⑥ 说话中常有描述性或象征性的声音，并常用连词。

⑦ 说话声音悦耳，有高低快慢，往往善于歌唱，喜欢找聆听者，本人也是良好的聆听者。

⑧ 坐着时眼球多转动（内心在自言自语），常常有具备节奏感的身体语言。

动觉型的学习者处理世界的事情多考虑内心的感受，他们的行为模式常会有以下特征：

① 注重人与人之间的关系。

② 喜欢别人的关怀，注重感受、情感、心境。

③ 不在乎好看或好听，而重视意义和感觉。

④ 不善多言，可长时间静坐。

⑤ 说话多提及感受、经验；但是往往不能说一句完整的句子，需要分多次说完。说话低沉而慢，给人以深思熟虑的感觉，多用含价值观的字。

1.2 不同类型学习者偏好的学习方法简介

视觉型的学习者比较倾向于通过眼睛看的方式来学习。比如他们通过看示意图、视频、电影、海报、概念图、图表、宣传画册、教科书、图画、拼贴画和用彩色荧光笔画重点等的方式学习，且通过这样的方式学习效率较高。

听觉型的学习者比较倾向于通过耳朵听的方式来学习。他们会比较喜欢通过下列方式进行有效地学习：讨论、团组互动活动、两人互动活动、辩论、采访、详细阐述、看展示、听演讲、写下帮助记忆的词句、记笔记、写诗歌、写散文、写故事以及阅读等。

动觉型的学习者比较倾向于通过亲自动手操作和感受的方式来学习。他们会喜欢角色扮演活动、舞蹈、制作模型、制作卡片和即兴创作等学习方式。他们常常会把观点和动作联系起来，喜欢在实地考察活动中学习，喜欢运动和竞赛等。

2 研究对象

笔者于2015年3月对所教授的北京工商大学（以下简称BTBU）2014级在读一年级硕士研究生进行了问卷调查，受试者共计96名。其中男生26名，女生70名。受试者年龄介于22岁至28岁，来自全国各地（城镇和农村均有）。受试者就读于北京工商大学的六个学院，专业涉及数量经济学、统计学、管理科学与工程、环境科学与工程、机械制造及其自动化、机械设计及理论、会计学和财务管理。含理科专业学生38人，文科专业学生58人。

3 研究工具

调查问卷取自英国英格兰地区中小学普遍使用的学习类型测试问卷，共18个问题，将学习类型分为视觉型（visual）、听觉型（auditory）和动觉型（kinaesthetic）。问卷是全英文书写，为避免理解失误，笔者在对受试者进行问卷调查时用汉语给予了适当的解释说明。

4 研究结果与讨论

受试者中，学习类型基本属于视觉型的学习者有30人，约占所有受试者的31%；基本属于听觉型的学习者1人，约占所有受试者的1%；基本属于动觉型的学习者有10人，约占所有受试者的10%；三种学习类型基本均匀分布的学习者有28人，约占所有受试者的29%；基本属于视觉和听觉两种类型兼有的学习者11人，约占所有受试者的11%；基本属于视觉和动觉两种类型兼有的学习者14人，约占所有受试者的15%；基本属于视觉和动觉两种类型兼有的学习者2人，约占所有受试者的2%（见表1）。

表1　学习类型分布

学习类型	V	A	K	V&A&K	V&A	V&K	A&K
人数	30	1	10	28	11	14	2
占总人数百分比	31%	1%	10%	29%	11%	15%	2%

注：V=visual learners（视觉型学习者），A=auditory learners（听觉型学习者），K=kinaesthetic learners（动觉型学习者）。

调查数据显示：约1/3的受试者属于视觉型学习者（31%），该部分受试者专注力强，能够比较充分利用课堂授课和图书馆资源进行有效学习，比较易于完成自己的学习任务。另有约1/3的受试者同时兼有三种学习类型（29%），这一结果表明该部分受试者可以通过多种方式进行有效地学习，在广泛涉猎多种知识方面具有优势，并且成绩优异。极少数的受试者属于听觉型学习者（1%）或听觉和动觉型兼有的学习者（2%），这也说明在BTBU2014级的研究生当中单一通过听觉学习的人属于特例。值得关注的是近2/3的受试者并非单一类型的学习者，作为研究生，在校就读期间需要完成繁重的学习任务和科学研究项目，他们不通过单一的方式学习，更能够高效地完成学习目标，也意味着大多数的BTBU2014级研究生在各自的研究领域均可以通过不同的方式进行学习和研究。

在96份有效问卷中，有一名受试者在18个听觉型问题中选择为零。经过采访，该受试者表示自己无法通过听的方式进行有效的学习，必须通过认真看教师的演示、课后阅读以及动手操作等的方式学习。另有一名受试者在18个动觉型问题中选择为14个，经过采访，该受试者表明自己在课堂授课中常常无法集中精力认真看教师的演示或者听教师的解说，需要自己另外花时间去理解和领悟。值得一提的是，该受试者所学专业是机械设计及理论，根据动觉型学习者所具有的特征来看，这一专业也许非常适合该受试者。

5 结语

综上所述，北京工商大学2014级在读一年级学术型硕士研究生中有约31%的学习者倾向于通过视觉的方式进行高效率的学习，有约29%的学习者学习的方法比较多样，他们通过看、听或者动手操作的方式均能进行有效的学习。有近60%的学习者基本属于两种或两种以上学习类型，他们能够通过多种方式进行有效的学习，毫无疑问，这一特点对于学习任务多，科学研究项目繁重的研究生来说是非常有利的。极少数的学习者学习类型单一，学习方法相对单一，需要课后花更多时间去理解和领悟教师在课堂上讲授的内容。

从调查结果来看，为适应不同类型学习者的学习方式，帮助大多数甚至所有学习者在课堂上进行高效学习，教师在授课过程中可以尽可能多地选择使用多种教学媒体和方法进行讲解。在安排课堂活动时，尽可能安排不同学习类型的学习者用自己所擅长的方式参与活动，从而达到更佳的教学效果。

参考文献

[1] http://www.360doc.com/content/13/0817/11/_307780273.shtml.

话语分析的认知视角

王红莉

摘　要：话语分析研究从萌芽到兴盛历经60年，在不同的理论框架下用不同的方法论展开研究，形成了突出的跨学科综合性特点。本文在回顾话语分析发展历程的基础上对话语分析的认知视角做简要评述。

关键词：话语分析；认知语言学；认知视角

1 引言

“话语分析”（discourse analysis）从第一次作为专门术语出现，到现在已经走过了60年，经历了从萌芽到发展兴盛的各个阶段，涌现出众多有造诣的研究学者，分别在不同的理论框架下采用独特的方法从不同的视角对话语进行分析讨论并撰文著说，硕果累累。本文在简要回顾话语分析发展历程的基础上对话语分析的认知视角做简要评述，进一步展现话语分析的跨学科特点，拓宽话语分析的研究空间。

2 “话语”与“话语分析”

关于“话语”（discourse），一般认为其覆盖的范围较广，包括词、短语、句子、片语、篇章甚至完整的著作。在整个话语分析历史过程中，不同的学者在不同的理论背景下从不同视角做出不同的定义解释。有的认为是具

作者简介：王红莉，女，北京工商大学副教授，研究方向为理论语言学和认知语言学。

体的会话或篇章，而有的则看作社会文化语境中的一种语言使用形式，还有人把话语看成是一种言语交际活动。如Widdowson认为话语是句子的组合运用；Brown和Yule认为交际过程本身就是话语，话语的具体表现形式是语篇；Van Dijk认为话语包括语言使用、思想传递和社会情景中的交际三个方面。Caire Kransch认为话语是讲话、阅读和写作的方式，也是话语所在地域的人的行为、交际、思维方式和价值观念。

对"话语"的界定，众说纷纭，各有各的道理和根据。由此看来，要对其诸多方面进行综合讨论和研究，注定是一项跨学科的综合性研究。

关于"话语分析"，一些学者如Stubbs、Sinclair和Coulthard等主要是对自然发生的连贯的口头语或书面语进行研究，关注语篇衔接和话语连贯等方面的问题；另一些学者如Widowson、Brown和Yule除了关注话语的语言形式特征更重视对话语交际功能的研究；还有一些语言学家如Labov、Haliday和Van Dijk采用社会分析法分析人类是如何理解彼此话语的。话语分析方法林林总总，归纳起来主要有结构分析法、社会文化分析法、批评分析法、认知分析法和综合分析法五大类。其中认知分析法关注话语的生成与理解，强调认知在思维过程和思维呈现中的作用。认知法还认为除了个人的认知之外，话语还涉及社会文化认知，话语分析应该重视交际双方构建和理解话语的动态过程。

3 话语分析发展概述

追溯话语分析的发展历史，一般都认为从1952年开始，因为在这一年美国结构主义语言学家Z. Harris在《Language》杂志上发表了题为《Discourse Analysis》的论文。语言学历史上第一次出现了"话语分析"这个术语。但也有学者认为话语分析其实远在古希腊和古罗马时代就存在了，只不过那个时候以修辞学形式存在，主要研究政治、法律演说的结构和机制，研究劝说的有效性。所以我们不妨把古希腊罗马时期的修辞学看作现代话语分析的前身，两者之间有着一定的传承关系。

现代话语分析的启蒙阶段普遍认为是从Harris第一次提出"话语分析"概念到20世纪60年代末。主要代表人物有从成分分布角度研究话语结构的

Z. Harris，结合语境研究买卖对话特点的T. F. Mitchel，探索言语交际形式的D. Hymes，从功能角度研究话语的M. A.K. Halliday，和关注言语行为的语言哲学家J. L. Austin和J. Searle。在这个阶段，话语分析初露头角，没有系统、成型的理论和方法论，研究者们各自为政，提出零星个人观点而已。

之后的10年，随着理论语言学和社会语言学的快速发展以及计算机语言学和语用学的出现，受到H. P. Grice、Levinson、G. Leech等的言语行为、会话含义、合作原则、礼貌原则等理论成果的影响，现代话语分析得以起步发展，取得了丰硕的研究成果：Lehister、Van Dijk、W. Labov、M. A. K. Halliday等出版了话语分析方面的专著，除此之外，还有很多论文集出版。这一切都标志着话语分析已经朝着独立学科的方向起步。

从20世纪80年代至今，现代话语分析蓬勃发展，步入欣欣向荣的兴盛阶段。这个阶段话语分析有了突破性的发展，标志性事件是1981年话语分析的第一本学术刊物《TEXT》创刊，Van Dijk任主编。从此，话语分析有了自己的学术园地。1978年创刊的杂志《Discourse Process》编委中也有多名话语分析研究领域的知名学者，如J. B. Carroll、Hymes、R. Lakoff等。这两本杂志常被看作是话语分析成为一门独立学科的重要标志。在这一阶段，从事话语分析的学者人数迅速增长，分布范围日渐扩大，由欧美扩大到了亚澳地区，中国也涌现出一批学者，如胡壮麟、沈家煊、顾曰国、申丹、陈平、黄国文、张德禄、朱永生等。话语分析蓬勃发展还表现在学术成果如专著和论文集的出版方面，国外有M. Bakhtin、G. Brown和G. Yule、M. Coulthard、M. A. K. Halliday和R. Hassan、D. Tannen、Georgakopoulou和D. Goutsos等的专著以及Van Dijk主编的四卷论文集；国内如王佐良和丁往道、秦秀白、黄国文、程雨民、胡壮麟、张德禄等也纷纷著书立说。总之，这个阶段基本廓清了话语分析的研究对象与任务，除语言学外还积极吸收相关学科如社会学、人类学、心理学、计算机科学和认知科学等的精华，成为一门跨学科的综合性研究。

4 话语分析的认知视角

近30年，认知语言学不断发展兴盛，其中G. Jackoff和M. Johnson的隐喻理论，D. Sperber和D. Wilson的关联理论，以及G. Fauconnier的心理空间映射理论，对话语分析的发展起到了非常积极的指导和推动作用。有学者认为，认知语言学有可能成为未来话语分析方法论的基础。

认知语言学认为，语言不是一个自足系统，语言的结构与人类的概念知识、身体体验以及话语的功能有关，并以此为理据。现代认知心理学认为，人的一切行为都受其认知过程的制约，所以，话语行为必然也是一种认知活动。说到底，话语行为牵涉从情景到话语和从话语到情景两个方向上的推理过程，交际双方只有通过推理才能获得、理解并传递、交流信息。推理是个典型的认知过程，其概念系统结构源自身体体验，在这个认知过程中除了经验概念外还必然要结合隐喻和心理意象等所形成的概念。所以，从话语行为发生的过程到产生的结果，认知都是话语行为不可否认的基础。下面谨以Gee的话语分析认知观为例做简单说明。

Gee认为，人类的话语交际本质是利用“社会语言”（语言与行动、非语言符号系统、物体、工具、技术、思维方式、价值观、感情、信念等的集合体）构建一个由符合系统、现实世界、活动、交际者的社会身份及联系、政治（权利地位善恶美丑等)、相互关联组成的“世界”。他提出了“文化模式”概念，认为人体与客观世界的相互作用在语言上表现为“模式”，人脑对客观世界里任何一种体验都可能会有无限量的“模式”，人们善于利用脑中原有的旧经验来处理新模式，这些旧经验就是话语行为发生的“情景意义”以及交际者所处社会群体所具有的“文化模式”，这些“情景意义”和“文化模式”一起构成人的“社会语言”。情景意义、文化模式和社会语言是Gee提出的三种基本的话语分析工具，是话语分析的认知视角和社会视角的融合。

当然，Gee还从认知视角提出了很多切实可行、易于操作的话语分析框架和具体方法，篇幅所限，本文不做赘述。

5 结语

纵观话语分析发展历史，虽尚存不足，如还没形成作为独立学科的一套完整理论体系和方法论，但国内外研究成绩不容置疑，专著和论文数量可观，研究者队伍日益壮大，与各相关学科间的渗透和交融特点越来越突出。话语分析与认知语言学的结合是其跨学科表现之一，为全面深刻地分析真实自然的话语提供了比较科学的研究视角。

参考文献

[1] GEE P J. An introduction to discourse analysis: theory and method[M]. London: Routledge, 2005.

[2] 朱永生.话语分析五十年:回顾与展望[J]. 外国语,2003(3).

[3] 陈莉萍.建立认知语言学为基础的话语分析方法[J]. 扬州大学学报:人文社会科学版,2008(9).

[4] 陆恩.国外话语分析研究综述[J]. 牡丹江大学学报,2008(7).

思维导图与大学英语写作教学

吕 绵

摘　要：思维导图广泛应用于生活、工作的方方面面，其快速准确整理、归纳、筛选所需要的观点的功效在大学英语写作中尤其有效。本文借助批改网，通过对同一题目要求的两篇作文进行对比，试图发现思维导图在帮助大学生提高写作质量方面的作用。

关键词：大学英语；写作；思维导图；批改网

1 引言

思维导图（mind-mapping）可以对某一个主题或观点及其和主题、观点相关的复杂信息以一种直观的、视觉图像的方式呈现出来，从而达到帮助学生理解概念，创造新的信息、想法，并发现、建立信息、想法之间的相互联系。这一原理应用于大学英语写作教学，可以极大地帮助学生整理、归纳写作时的观点，把握文章整理思路和脉络，达到事半功倍的效果。

2 思维导图应用于大学英语写作教学实例研究

为了检验思维导图在大学英语写作过程中的作用，我们以一篇雅思常见作文为例，进行了实验。题目要求如下：

Present a written argument or case to an educated reader with no specialist knowledge of the following topic.

项目/基金：本论文为2015年北京市级大学生科研与创业行动计划项目的成果，项目编号为SJ201502057。

作者简介：吕绵，女，北京工商大学外国语学院讲师。

In most parts of the world, the volume of traffic is growing at an alarming rate. Discuss the traffic problems in your countries, their causes and possible solutions.

You should write at least 250 words.

You should use your own ideas, knowledge and experience and support your arguments with examples and relative evidence.

2.1 操作步骤

2.1.1 第一次布置作文

2014年9月16日在批改网上布置作文358297号，没有特别的提示，只公布了题目和要求（如上），截止日期2014年10月8日。截止日期后共有37名学生提交了作文。来自批改网的主要统计数据如表1所示。

表1 358297号作文(修改前)数据概述

文章篇数	37篇
最短句	1个单词
最长句	77个单词
总句数	634句
总词数	12120个单词
平均句长	19.12个单词
成绩均值	73.56

2.1.2 课堂思维导图训练

2014年11月下旬，在课堂上对学生进行了思维导图的讲解和训练，并有意识地对同一题目进行了思维导图写作提纲的提示。具体步骤如下。

（1）在黑板上画下面一个图形（见图1）。

图1 提示引导图

（2）让所有学生进行头脑风暴，构建自己的思维导图。随后让学生随意到黑板前，把自己想到的观点都写在图形上。

（3）在学生进行思维导图构建的过程中特别提示学生，尽量记下所有想到的观点，先不要急于评价或评估这些观点是否有用。

（4）思维导图构建结束后，提示学生找出所列信息或观点之间的相互联系或关系。① 找出造成交通拥堵的原因。相似的造成交通拥堵的原因，用同一种颜色标注。② 进行归纳整理，总结出3~4条最主要的原因。③ 找出解决交通拥堵的办法。同样，类似的解决办法，用同一种颜色标注。接着，进行归纳整理，总结出3~4条主要的解决办法。④ 针对主要的原因，找到相应的解决办法。原因和解决办法必须是一一对应、相互呼应的。如果学生不进行思维导图的训练，写作时往往会出现原因和解决办法脱节的问题。⑤ 要求学生以小组为单位，列出自己的写作提纲。要求写出第一段引言中的主题句、文章主体中的一一对应的交通拥堵的原因及解决办法、最后结尾段落的主题句。

2.1.3 第二次布置作文

2014年12月1日第二次在批改网布置同一篇作文（391369号），题目要求同前，但参考课堂上所列的写作提纲。截止日期后有34名同学提交了作文。来自批改网的主要统计数据如表2所示。

表2 391369号作文（修改后）数据概述

文章篇数	34篇
最短句	1个单词
最长句	66个单词
总句数	578句
总词数	10996个单词
平均句长	19.02个单词
成绩均值	86.72

2.1.4 实验结果统计

实验结束后，我们对相同题目和要求的作文358297号（修改前）和作文391369号（修改后）的数据在批改网进行了统计和对比，主要包括数据概述、词性分布、搭配分布、句长分布、维度概述、薄弱点分析、错误分布、词频、分级词汇、数据比对等方面，发现在作文成绩和错误分布两方面数据变化明显。

修改前的358297号作文学生的成绩均值为73.56，修改后的391369号作文成绩均值为86.72，而且提交了两次作业的34名学生成绩都有了明显提高。表3是来自批改网导出的学生两次作文薄弱点统计对比表。可以看出34名学生的成绩均有了显著提高，最高提高17.5分，最低的也有6.5分，平均提高12.9分。表4是批改网导出的两篇作文学生出现错误的分布图。可以看出修改后的作文错误率大幅降低，除了搭配错误（11项）比修改前（8项）稍多外，其他包括名词错误（15项对6项）、句子不规范（30项对23项）、动词错误（14项对9项）、用词错误（4项对2项）、低频警示（241项对0项）均明显降低。

表3 作文358297号(修改前)和作文391369号(修改后)薄弱点统计

学号	成绩		维度分析/%							
			词汇		句子		篇章结构		内容相关	
	修改前	修改后	修改前	修改后	修改前	修改后	修改前	修改后	修改前	修改后
1	75.0	85.5	89.14	88.09	92.67	85.52	83.42	85.57	94	68.33
2	71.0	85.0	87.34	85.11	79.64	83.64	88.79	90.96	88	73.33
3	77.5	88.0	88.38	92.23	95.87	86.39	89.74	90.56	85	60.00
4	76.5	91.5	85.07	95.62	92.82	92.43	86.03	90.56	87	65.00
5	73.0	88.0	89.59	94.98	73.38	77.87	90.40	90.56	97	65.00
6	78.0	90.5	88.16	90.72	94.96	94.08	87.91	90.56	100	75.00
7	74.5	89.5	87.64	91.81	87.02	87.91	91.52	90.56	97	71.67
8	70.5	87.5	85.47	87.28	85.28	84.8	90.94	90.56	100	80.00
9	74.0	86.5	84.94	89.05	87.04	86.69	88.35	90.56	86	52.50
10	70.5	84.5	84.17	84.76	86.17	85.44	84.69	90.56	93	84.00
11	73.0	86.5	87.53	88.52	93.34	90.11	81.38	90.56	83	61.67

续表

学号	成绩		维度分析/%							
			词汇		句子		篇章结构		内容相关	
	修改前	修改后	修改前	修改后	修改前	修改后	修改前	修改后	修改前	修改后
12	76.5	83.0	86.58	87.9	91.85	86.18	86.28	90.56	86	30.00
13	74.0	86.5	84.28	88.07	84.95	86.67	88.66	90.56	97	61.67
14	75.0	86.5	85.16	86.96	87.38	93.42	89.09	90.56	100	66.67
15	71.0	83.5	89.37	86.13	81.38	77.47	83.65	90.56	88	78.33
16	70.5	85.5	88.79	88.25	87.06	88.19	91.02	90.56	100	65.00
17	71.5	87.5	81.74	85.77	90.28	92.36	87.19	90.56	92	73.33
18	73.0	88.0	79.39	89.14	87.27	91.14	82.96	90.56	95	68.33
19	70.0	87.0	89.19	88.3	91.27	89.53	89.08	90.56	100	60.00
20	74.5	88.0	90.92	86.61	91.74	90.72	88.58	90.56	100	76.67
21	73.0	83.5	82.17	83.14	80.06	88.26	89.83	90.56	96	52.50
22	77.0	86.5	89.98	89.14	92.69	91.18	90.53	90.56	90	45.00
23	75.5	87.0	87.34	91.22	96.85	86.89	83.89	90.56	84	52.50
24	69.5	87.0	86.17	88.18	95.31	88.66	89.48	90.56	100	65.00
25	76.0	87.5	84.36	90.69	84.36	84.43	81.05	90.56	99	65.00
26	71.5	86.0	85.33	88.17	93.68	86.67	90.63	90.56	100	52.50
27	73.0	88.0	88.48	89.22	83.3	87.47	91.02	90.56	99	68.33
28	73.0	86.5	82.93	87.97	95.78	91.83	77.23	90.56	95	65.00
29	74.5	82.0	82.08	85.89	86.98	75.46	82.31	90.56	96	80.00
30	78.0	90.0	87.42	91.86	89.79	86.88	91.22	90.56	100	81.00
31	76.5	88.0	87.32	91.01	85.7	84.78	82.38	90.56	100	80.00
32	67.5	78.5	81.57	76.92	87.45	80.95	86.64	90.56	90	60.00
33	77.5	89.0	87.93	93.42	96.77	89.42	91.98	90.56	100	52.50
34	76.5	88.5	84.08	90.67	96.86	89.37	88.52	90.56	95	63.33

表4 批改网导出两次作文中的错误分布

全部	修改前	312
	修改后	51
名词错误	修改前	15
	修改后	6
句子不规范	修改前	30
	修改后	23
搭配错误	修改前	8
	修改后	11
动词错误	修改前	14
	修改后	9
用词错误	修改前	4
	修改后	2
低频警示	修改前	241
	修改后	0

3 结语

从批改网导出的数据可以清楚地看出，修改前后的两篇作文在总体及个体成绩表现及文法到句法的正确率方面都有了显著的提高。这清楚地说明思维导图在大学生英语写作方面的积极效果。如果学生在写作过程中思路清晰、观点明确、论据充分，则有助于他们清楚地表达，提高写作质量，同时降低错误。思路清晰能帮助减少语法错误是偶然的发现，但也充分说明思维导图在写作中的重要积极作用。

参考文献

[1] 陈敏. 思维导图及其在英语教学中的应用[J]. 外语电化教学，2005(1).
[2] 东尼·博赞. 思维导图大脑使用说明书[M]. 北京：外语教学与研究出版社，2005.
[3] 东尼·博赞. 思维导图[M]. 北京：中信出版社，2009.
[4] 吕绵，侯霞. 思维导图在大学英语写作教学中的运用[J]. 学园，2014(32).

BTBU商务英语阅读教学之我见

陆 敏

摘 要：随着世界各国全球化步伐的加快和我国改革开放的深入，特别是中国加入WTO以后，越来越多的跨国企业来到中国寻求发展，国内企业的对外交流与合作也不断扩大。商务英语在经济全球化的今天无疑成了越来越重要的介质。顺应企业对商务英语专业人才的需求以及培养"既有出众的语言能力，又熟悉商务知识的复合型、应用型人才"的社会发展要求，国内高校纷纷开设了商务英语专业或增设了商务英语课程。本文就北京工商大学（BTBU）外国语学院商务英语阅读课程的教学现状进行了分析，并根据教学实践对课程的发展提供了一些建议，以期对学院专业的发展尽绵薄之力。

关键词：商务英语阅读；教学现状；发展建议

1 引言

随着世界各国全球化步伐的加快和我国改革开放的深入，特别是中国加入WTO以后，越来越多的跨国企业来到中国寻求发展，国内企业的对外交流与合作也不断扩大。商务英语在经济全球化的今天无疑成了越来越重要的介质。顺应企业对商务英语专业人才的需求以及培养"既有出众的语言能力，又熟悉商务知识的复合型、应用型人才"的社会发展要求，国内高校纷

作者简介：陆敏，女，内蒙古鄂尔多斯人，北京工商大学外国语学院讲师。

纷开设了商务英语专业或增设了商务英语课程。

商务英语阅读是商务英语专业的一门必修课程。作为商务英语教学的重要组成部分，商务英语阅读在培养应用型、复合型的商务英语人才中起了重要的作用。我们都知道，阅读是汲取有效信息的最佳途径。通过商务类报刊、文章的阅读，学生不仅可以进一步培养良好的阅读习惯，提高阅读技巧，扩大商务词汇量，而且可以获取大量的商务背景知识，培养学生的商务英语交际能力及国际商务从业能力，为进一步提高商务英语专业综合技能奠定坚实的基础。近年来，笔者一直在高校从事商务英语阅读等商务英语专业课程的教学。如何高效的教与学，使得学生既提高了阅读理解能力，同时又能最大限度地汲取商务知识，是每一位专业教师需要不断摸索和总结经验的一个重要课题。

2 商务英语阅读教与学的现状和发展

如上所述，商务英语阅读的教学不仅应重视语言能力的培养，更应该重视通过大量商务背景知识的输入和模拟情境的训练来培养学生在商务环境中的实际操作能力。

由于商务英语专业设置的特殊性，本校商务英语专业的学生都是在一年级进行英语听、说、读、写的学习以培养学生的基本英语技能，二年级开始逐渐增加如商务英语读写、综合商务英语、高级商务英语等商务类课程。可想而知，学生相关的背景知识严重不足。从目前教学的情况来看，作为一个相对新生的事物，商务英语阅读的教与学两方面都多多少少存在着一些问题。

2.1 学生的商务背景知识匮乏

笔者认为，学生在商务英语阅读中遇到的最大难点不是语法、句式等，而是商务的背景知识。首先，学生从高中到大一的学习以英语基础技能为主，几乎不接触任何跟商务有关的信息。其次，目前国内商务英语阅读的教材大多取自国内外知名的杂志、报刊，内容涉及国际经济合作、人力资源管理、市场营销、金融、货币政策、财务管理等各个领域。从专业的角度来看，每一个话题的学习都需要很长的时间完成，而本专业的学生根本就没有这个过程。如果没有一个商务理论的框架构建，仅仅通过一篇文章的学习，学完也不知所云，完全达不到预期目的。以笔者所授的“政府与贸易”一课为例，从学生上课的反馈来看，没有输入背景信息之前，学生只是简单的完成阅读任务，对于老师所提到的贸易壁垒、贸易保护政策、政府与贸易之间的关系等一无所知，而且由于缺乏相关的商务专业知识作铺垫，学生对该篇文章的理解存在很大的偏差。

2.2 商务英语阅读教材的质量参差不齐

近几年来，各高校出版社有关商务英语阅读的课本种类和数量逐日增多，然而其质量却不尽如人意。笔者在选用教材时就发现，很难看到既具备了英语水平高，同时商务知识丰富的教材。有些教材商务知识丰富，但语言水平过浅；有些教材提供了不少语言技能训练的练习，可惜商务知识欠缺，对所选内容只是蜻蜓点水，不够系统，不能构建很好的知识框架；还有些教材来自国外，难度过大，学生理解起来比较费劲。

2.3 商务英语阅读的教学方法亟待改进

目前，国内大部分高校商务英语阅读的课堂教学仍以教师为主，某种程度上忽视了对学生积极主动思维的培养。从客观上来讲，学生自有的信息量不够，商务词汇量小，学习中阻力不小，如何激发学生学习的主动性也是一个值得探索的问题。

3 对BTBU商务英语阅读教学的若干建议

针对上述问题，结合教学经验，笔者认为目前可以从以下几个方面来改进商务英语阅读的教学。

3.1 构建商务背景的知识框架

对商务基础薄弱的学生来说，建构相应的背景知识对提高商务英语阅读理解能力尤为重要。仍以“政府与贸易”一课为例，为了让学生对两者之间的关系有更为形象、立体的理解，笔者认为背景知识的构建可以分三步走。首先，是商务信息的输入。教师可以在正式阅读课文材料之前，输入诸如自由贸易、比较优势与绝对优势、贸易收支平衡、贸易保护政策、关税壁垒与非关税壁垒等相关内容。这部分内容通常具有信息量大、词汇多的特征，需要学生投入很大的精力去消化。其次，结合输入的信息，学习课文内容：政府与贸易是什么关系。根据笔者的经验，在前期大量背景的输入之后，这一部分内容的理解要容易很多。既然是阅读课程，教学的重点应该在大意的理解与把握上，而且主题句与段落的匹配也是BEC的考点，满足学习知识与应试的双重要求。最后，通常来讲，学习情境与外部世界环境越接近，学习者越有可能将他们的能力转化到解决实际问题的情境中去。为了体现商务英语的实际操作性，在完成课文的教学后，可以选用商务新闻材料，第一手的真实的教学语料，来检测学生对这一部分知识的掌握情况。如笔者在这一课后就选用了如下的材料：美国对华为、中兴展开的“337调查”、欧盟对俄罗斯实施的经济制裁等。通过这样的一个框架构建，丰富了教学内容。同时也弥补了国内教材的种种缺陷。

3.2 改进商务英语阅读的教学方法

首先是教学模式上的转变，从传统的以教师为中心转向以学生为中心。运用典型的任务教学法、情景教学法、案例教学法等，调动学生的学习积极性，突出学生在课堂上的主体作用。在课外，积极发挥学生的主导作用，通过library research、PPT preparation等形式督促学生进行课外学习，并将学生的表现打分计入平时成绩，从而更好地促使学生自主学习和合作学习。这不仅弥补了课内阅读量不足的缺陷，也可以拓宽学生的视野，激起了学生的学习兴趣。这样课内课外双管齐下，调动学生的主观能动性，提高教与学的效率。

3.3 借助现代化的教学手段，提高教学效果

目前我们的商务英语专业已经有了自己的商务英语在线学习平台，同时我们还与北京外国语大学合作，搭建了国际法商英语在线学习平台，两个平台相融合，实现了本硕学科在线学习平台的一体化建设。平台涵盖学习、研究、反馈、管理的完整过程，真正实现课上课下教学研究不断线。这也给学生提供了一个不错的接触商务知识的平台。

4 结语

综上所述，为了改进商务英语阅读课程的教学效果，提高学生的商务英语阅读能力，教师要在教学实践中不断研究探索，发现并分析商务英语阅读课程教与学中存在的问题，进行教学改革，最大限度地提高教学效率，从而在商务英语阅读的教学中将商务语言知识和商务专业知识完美地结合起来。只有这样，才能力争培养出合格的复合型涉外商务英语专业人才，满足社会的需求。

参考文献

[1] 姚维鹏. 建构主义理论在商务英语阅读教学中的运用[J]. 现代商贸工业,2015(3):163-164.

[2] 刘静静,张常亮. 商务英语阅读教学探究[J]. 外语教学与研究,2007(26):82-83.

[3] 刘亚珍. 利用报刊资源促进商务英语阅读教学的研究[J]. 长春师范学院学报:人文社会科学版,2013(5):169-172.

[4] 徐晶,秦拓. 多媒体课件在商务英语阅读教学中的应用[J]. 山东教育学院学报,2010(3):61-63.

[5] 王兴孙. 对国际商务英语学科发展的探讨[J]. 国际商务研究,1997(1):24-28.

[6] 林妮斯. 浅析商务英语阅读教学[J]. 科教文汇:下旬刊,2008(10):147.

[7] 张亚智. 案例教学法在商务英语教学中的运用研究[J]. 开封教育学院学报,2014(1):179-180.

语篇语言学应用于礼仪致辞开场白口译教学

田　芳

摘　要： 口译是通过口头表达的方式把所理解和感知的信息准确、完整、即时地由一种语言转换为另一种语言。口译教学中应用语篇语言学的理论是有建设性的。本文通过使用语篇语言学的理论框架分析中文礼仪致辞开场白口译教学中的三个实例，说明语篇语言学的理论应用于口译教学中的实际意义和作用。

关键词： 口译；口译教学；语篇语言学

口译是把所理解和感知的信息通过口头表达方式由一种语言转换为另一种语言，而达到准确、完整而即时地传递与交流信息之目的的交际行为。口译的评价标准是准确及流利。这里的准确指的是意义和风格准确；流利则反映了口译的速度。在口译教学中，要帮助学生达到这两个标准，不仅需要教授语言知识，介绍口译技巧，还需要帮助学生了解所译篇章的特点，就需要应用到语篇语言学的理论。

"语篇语言学"又被称为"语篇分析"（discourse analysis）"或"篇章分析"（text analysis），是开始于20世纪60年代的一门学科。语篇语言学吸收了语言学、心理学、社会学、符号学、文学等多个学科的研究成果，形成一个涉及多个学科的研究交际中语言使用的科学。

语篇分析和语用意义是翻译研究的语篇语言学方法所重视的两个问题。因此，翻译研究的语篇语言学方法的研究对象不仅是源语和目标语的语言体

项目/基金： 本论文为北京工商大学青年教师科研启动基金的成果，项目编号为QNJJ2014-03。

作者简介： 田芳，女，北京工商大学外国语学院讲师。

系，还包括语言体系外的其他因素，如“情景语境”和“文化语境”。

根据Neubert & Shreve的观点，受传统语言学影响的翻译是从下而上的（bottom-up），也就是说，翻译是从句及互不相连的语言单位开始的，形式上会贴近源语，但对目标语读者来说译文会不通顺甚至难以理解。而语篇语言学的翻译方法是从上而下的（top-down），也就是说，先决定译文在目标语中的属性、类型和交际功能，再通过不同的语言结构来翻译源语语篇。

礼仪致辞时开场白受其所处情景的影响，也是深受源语的文化习惯影响的。在中文的礼仪致辞开场白中，经常会先对时间、地点或参与人员进行赞美，然后才进入主题。例如习近平总书记2013年在博鳌论坛上的致辞。

例1 椰风暖人，海阔天高。在这美好的季节里，同大家相聚在美丽的海南岛，参加博鳌亚洲论坛2013年年会，我感到十分高兴。首先，我谨代表中国政府和人民，并以我个人的名义，向各位朋友的到来，表示诚挚的欢迎！对年会的召开，表示热烈的祝贺！

语篇中“椰风暖人，海阔天高”这样的表述若不分析其语篇意义，会使学生非常困惑，不知该如何下手。若按传统语言学模式操作，翻译是自下而上的（bottom-up），而很多学生也是这样操作的，即从句及互不相连的语言单位开始，则例1会被翻译为：

The coconut breeze warms people，the ocean is wide and the sky is high. In this balmy season，I meet you all in beautiful Hainan to attend the Annual Conference 2013 of the Boao Forum for Asia. I am so glad. Let me begin by extending，on behalf of the Chinese government and people and also in my own name，a heartfelt welcome to you and warm congratulations on the opening of the Annual Conference of the Boao Forum.

这样翻译在语义上并没有错，基本做到形近于源语，但有两个问题。

（1）在中文中“椰风暖人，海阔天高”这种写意的铺垫在英文译文中没有意义，且不符合英文重心在前的结构，很难被目标语使用者认同。因此，有必要分析“椰风暖人，海阔天高”的功能意义。这句是对下一句中“在这美好的季节里”时间状语的细节描写，是时间状语的一部分，因此在译文中把中文中单独成句的“椰风暖人，海阔天高”译为官方参考译文中的时间状语更为恰当。

(2) 译文中表达原文“在这美好的季节里，同大家相聚在美丽的海南岛，参加博鳌亚洲论坛2013年年会，我感到十分高兴”时，重心有误。有必要使学生认识到“在这美好的季节里”及“在美丽的海南岛”是整句的时间状语和地点状语，并相应将重心调整为重心前置。

官方参考译文如下：

In this balmy season with clear sky and warm, coconut-scented breeze, I am so glad to meet all of you at the Annual Conference 2013 of the Boao Forum for Asia here in Hainan, a picturesque island embraced by the vast ocean. Let me begin by extending, on behalf of the Chinese government and people and also in my own name, a heartfelt welcome to you and warm congratulations on the opening of the Annual Conference of the Boao Forum.

例2 在这个美丽无比、繁星满天的夜晚，我谨代表总经理以及公司的全体同仁，感谢各位拨冗光临我们的新春联欢晚会。

本句中“美丽无比、繁星满天”是直接作为“夜晚”这个时间状语的修饰语的，因此无需进行功能的转换。但对于初学口译的同学来说，这个短语仍会是翻译的难点，甚至有的学生口译时会把时间状语的重心从“夜晚”放在词长更为突出的“美丽无比、繁星满天”上，出现误译。但如果在教学中对中文礼仪致辞开场白进行分析，帮助学生了解这种类型语篇的语言结构，学生就可以在口译中避免上文所提到的误译。因此此句的恰当译文可为：

On this most beautiful evening with numerous shining stars in the sky, on behalf of the General Manager and all my colleagues of the company, I wish to thank all the people for taking time to come to our Chinese New Year's party.

例3 我谨代表我们一行的全体成员，感谢董事长先生的盛情邀请，使我们来到装饰得如此华丽的大厅，参加如此欢快的圣诞晚会。

例3中“装饰得如此华丽”是对地点状语“大厅”的修饰，学生在口译此句时如果明白这一点，即这是对地点状语的修饰，就不会因为词汇量不够，翻译不了“装饰得如此华丽”而不知所措。他们只需把地点状语口译出来，就基本完成了任务。这并不是说鼓励学生随意篡改源语表述，而是在能够基本准确的前提下、在保证达到交际目的时的一种应急策略，而这个策略没有语篇语言学的理论框架是无法完成的。因此此句的恰当译文可为：

On behalf of all the members of my group, I'd like to thank you, Mr. Chairman, for your gracious invitation for us to attend such an enjoyable Christmas party in such a magnificently decorated hall.

通过以上口译实例的分析，我们可以看到有必要使用语篇语言学的理论框架来指导口译教学。具有单纯的语言知识并不意味着能够熟练地使用这种语言，同样单纯的知识学习也不意味着具有使用这种语言的能力和技能，单纯具有语言知识并不能产生具有语篇意义和交际意义的语言。帮助学生了解对所译语篇的属性、类型及交际功能，使学生具有语篇能力，能使学生更容易地达到准确和流利的口译标准。

参考文献

[1] 梅德明. 中级口译教程[M]. 上海:上海外语教育出版社,2014.

[2] 张美芳,黄国文. 语篇语言学与翻译研究[J]. 中国翻译,2002(3): 3-7.

四、六级翻译中语篇意识的体现与培养方法

孙龙飞　陶　爽　熊靥諹

摘　要：自2013年12月起，大学英语四、六级的翻译题由句子翻译改为段落翻译，同时增加了分值的比重。新题型的考查重点不仅包括固定搭配、词汇运用、重点语法，还包括句子结构，以及语篇衔接、连贯，是对以句子为中心到以语篇为中心的翻译测试。学者李运兴甚至说"翻译课正在经历一次从以句子为中心到以语篇为中心的改革"。可见，树立和培养语篇意识在大学英语翻译教学中是顺应时代和现实的大势所趋。

关键词：四、六级翻译；语篇意识；培养方法

1 语篇意识在四、六级段落翻译中的体现

黄国文将语篇定义为：语篇通常指一系列连续的话段或句子构成的语言整体，语篇无论是口头表达还是书面表达，都必须衔接合理，符合逻辑，语义连贯。语篇意识，指译者对原文和译文语篇的文体特点、衔接连贯的构成、语篇和语境的关系等，需要有正确的认识和清晰的概念。在目前对语篇意识的研究中，不乏对语篇与翻译教学关系的探讨。但是大都是从教师的角

基金/项目：本文为2015年北京市级大学生科学研究与创业行动计划项目，项目题为"大学英语四、六级翻译中的语篇意识"，项目编号为SJ201502075。

作者简介：孙龙飞，男，汉族，北京人，北京工商大学商学院2013级注册会计师专业学生。陶爽，女，北京工商大学讲师，主要研究方向为外国语言学及应用语言学、语篇分析及功能语法。熊靥諹，女，江西南昌人，北京工商大学注册会讲师专业学生。

度进行研究，并且理论研究占大多数，缺少简明易懂的例子和适合学生操作的具体方法。本文通过总结分析语篇意识这一新要求对四、六级翻译的影响，探寻考生建立语篇意识、提高翻译能力的有效途径，从而帮助考生更好地把握这一题型。

本文以2015年6月的六级考试段落翻译题和两篇译文为例，对比总结语篇意识在四、六级段落翻译题中的体现。

原文：汉朝是中国历史上最重要的朝代之一。汉朝统治期间有很多显著的成就。它最先向其他文化敞开大门，对外贸易兴旺。汉朝开拓的丝绸之路通向了中西亚乃至罗马。各类艺术流派繁荣，涌现了很多文学、历史、哲学巨著。公元100年中国第一部字典编撰完成，9000个字，提供释义并列举不同的写法。其间，科技方面也取得了很大进步，发明了纸张、水钟、日晷（sundials）以及测量地震的仪器。汉朝历经400年，但统治者的腐朽最终导致了它的灭亡。

译文1（无语篇意识）：The Han dynasty is one of the most important dynasty in Chinese history. There are a lot of great achievements during the reign of Han dynasty. It was the first dynasty to open the door to other cultures, and it had prosperous foreign trade. The Han dynasty developed the Silk Road and reached the West Asia and Rome. At that time, there were many kinds of art. There existed many great works on literature, history and philosophy. The first dictionary in China was completed in 100 BC which including 9000 words. It provided meanings and displays different ways of characters. In the meanwhile, technology made great impact. Paper, sundials, clock in water and instruments used to detect earthquake were invented. The Han Dynasty lasted 400 years. However, its rulers' corruption led to its dying out.

译文2（有语篇意识）：Han Dynasty was one of the most important dynasties in Chinese history. There were many significant achievements during the Han Dynasty. It was the first dynasty to open its door to other cultures. Foreign trade flourished during this period. The Silk Road initiated by Han Dynasty led all the way to the West Asia and even to Rome. Various forms of art prospered, with the emergence of a lot of literature, history and philosophy masterpieces. 100 A.D. witnessed the completion of the first Chinese dictionary which included 9000 words, providing interpretation and various styles of writing. Meanwhile, technology had also achieved great progress. Paper, water clocks, sundials and earthquake detectors were invented. The reign has lasted for 400 years. However, the corruption of the rulers eventually led to its downfall.

译文1由于只是机械地将原文一一对照直译，而没有从宏观上把握语篇的特点，所以无法准确体现语篇内部的逻辑关系和句法等细节。同时因为忽视了句子间的前后呼应，造成了句式的零散混乱，使译文的准确性大大降低，没有将原文的主题解释清楚。

与译文2相比，译文1的不当主要体现在以下三处。

（1）没有体现逻辑关系。译文1在翻译“各类艺术流派繁荣，涌现了很多文学、历史、哲学巨著”时，将其拆分成两个独立的句子，没有体现出“各类艺术流派繁荣”和“涌现了很多文学、历史、哲学巨著”之间的因果关系或包含关系。译文2使用“with the emergence of a lot of literature”准确清楚地表达了前后句之间逻辑关系。

（2）没有体现强调的内容。译文1在翻译“汉朝开拓的丝绸之路通向了中西亚乃至罗马”时，采用了and连接“West Asia”和“Roma”，没有翻译出“乃至”表达的强调语气。译文2使用“even to”体现了强调语气。

（3）打破了长句的连贯性。译文1在翻译“公元100年中国第一部字典编撰完成，9000个字，提供释义并列举不同的写法”时，将其拆成两个单句。而译文2将“9000个字”作为定语从句，从而使得多层意思能够在一个句子中表达，使译文更加连贯流畅。

2 学生缺乏语篇意识的原因

通过与学生交流在翻译过程中的想法和思维，我们发现了以下造成学生缺乏语篇意识的原因。① 不清楚语篇意识在翻译中的重要性。学生对语篇意识的作用缺乏基本的概念和重视。多数学生没有在翻译前通读全段，而是马上字对字地进行翻译，从而缺乏对整个语篇内容的宏观把握，忽略了语句之间的逻辑关系。② 词意辨析不明确。学生在选择词汇时，缺乏对前后语境的理解和对词义的精准辨析。例如把“各类艺术流派繁荣”，直接译为“There are many kinds of art”。然而many不能表达“繁荣”的意思。③ 句子结构安排不当。学生在翻译复杂句，以及处理句子间的衔接关系时，句子结构安排比较混乱。如在翻译“公元100年中国第一部字典编撰完成，9000个字，提供释义并列举不同的写法”时，将包含多层意思的长句分拆译为两个并列句，肢解了原句的连贯性。④ 句子间的衔接与连贯不当。句子的衔接和连贯指的是各部分的排列、连接及内容都要符合逻辑，贯通且有完整的语义关系。为了达到这一目的，可采用添加连接词，用替代成分避免重复，以及适当的省略等方法。然而考生对连接词的使用普遍不熟练，同时对可以相互替代的近义词也积累不足。

3 建立语篇意识、提高翻译能力的方法

3.1 建立语篇意识

语篇意识要求学生在不拘泥于个别词句的基础上对语篇进行分析，自上而下地把握语篇的特点。学生在阅读语段时，可以通过提出问题帮助自己对语篇进行全面的思考和分析，如该段落的主题是什么及主题是如何通过事件或者事物展开的；翻译时如何体现事物之间的关系；原文中出现的一些词是否可以直译等。在解决这些问题的过程中，学生可以通过逐步的思考来弄清语篇的主题、句子之间的关系及词语的特殊含义，从宏观上把握段落。运用语篇分析方法，把握好主题，可以使语气连贯，各个句子之间有机地联系起来。

3.2 结合语篇进行选词

词汇的选择合适与否是由语篇决定的，而不仅仅要求意思相对。汉语中有些词语在英语中找不到对应词，或者勉强找到，其所指也不完全相同。比如汉语中的“房子”，在汉语中，各种形式的屋子均可统称为“房子”，然而“房子”在英语中的对应词可以是house、apartment等。但是house在英语中专指是“独门独户的房子”，apartment则是指“公寓”。所以，只求字面意义对应，不顾词语的具体指称含义必定会导致误译。结合语篇选择词语，同时

注意积累英语近义词的细微差别可以尽可能避免这类误译。

3.3 注重语篇中的词汇及结构衔接

词汇衔接指语篇中前后词语之间的语义联系。在语篇中，词语之间有时会产生同义关系、重复关系、反义关系等。译者要仔细研读原文，捕捉这些起衔接作用的词语，从而对原文做出正确解读。结构衔接是语篇中某一部分与上文另一部分存在着承启关系或其他逻辑关系。学生可以多训练连接词的使用，如so that、because、for等，用替代成分避免重复，以及适当的省略等方法。

3.4 学习翻译理论及技巧

多数学生由于没有系统地学过专业翻译知识，翻译时往往只追求词句的对等，而出现“中式英语”，因此学生加强翻译理论及技巧内容的学习极有必要。学生可选择一些典型的句子或者段落进行练习，学习一些翻译理论和技巧，如常用的几种翻译技巧，即重译、增译、减译、词类转换、词序调整、分译、正说反译与反说正译、语态变换等。此外，还可以请老师进行必要的翻译讲评，对翻译中出现的问题有针对性地进行分析，再进行练习。如此通过理论学习强化实践，并在实践中体会理论和掌握运用技巧，从而提高翻译能力。

3.5 培养学生注重译文应与文化语境相结合的意识

在翻译的过程中，有时需要将情景语境与文化语境结合起来去加深理解，并针对原文的文化背景对译文做出必要的信息补充和诠释，使译文更加准确。如果学生的文化意识和文化感应能力较差，则只能完成汉语中单词和汉字对应成相应的英语表达，却无法实现符合西方阅读者思维习惯的英语转译。四、六级考试改革后的翻译题型涉及的内容包括历史、文化、经济、社会发展等。然而学生往往把重点放在语言知识的学习上，而忽略相关的文化背景知识。这造成很多学生不了解英语国家的语言文化背景，而习惯于用汉语思维方式表达，在翻译时往往纠结于字词表面的意思对等，不考虑社会文化背景因素，生搬硬套，造成词不达意，出现误译、中式英语等。长期来看，这不但会使学生失去学习英语的兴趣和积极性，更妨碍翻译能力的培养。因此，学生可以在平时充分利用各种资源来增加古今中外的历史、政治、宗教、文学艺术等知识，这样能够在进行翻译练习的同时又进行文化的对比和交流，帮助学生更加准确的理解原文。

3.6 夯实汉语学习的基础

四、六级翻译题型的改革，采用了段落汉译英的方式考查了学生的汉英转换能力。汉语是一种注重意合的语言，各部分的逻辑关系隐藏在句子中，需要译者充分理解，才可做到明确含义，否则就有可能张冠李戴。但是，很多学生往往只重视专业课和英语文化的学习，忽视了汉语文化的学习。这造成汉语阅读能力下降，同时影响了翻译中对原文的理解，造成原文理解出现偏差，直接导致译文表达错误。只有拥有深厚的汉语基础和广博的汉语知识，才能准确地理解汉语原文。否则，必将给汉译英带来很大的困难。建议学生坚持汉语文学阅读，保持自己的汉语阅读理解能力。

4 总结

语篇意识的培养是一个长期过程。只有培养良好的语篇意识，才能尽可能避免汉英语篇翻译中存在的误译或错译现象。这需要学生通过积累扎实的基础知识、扩展文化背景知识，准确理解文本材料，并且注重在翻译实践过程中对语篇的分析。同时，在此基础上多做多练，勤于动笔，就一定能译出结构衔接、语义连贯的译文，在学习和考试中取得满意的效果。

参考文献

[1] 孔孜. 语篇分析与英语翻译教学[J]. 考试周刊,2008(6):74—76.

[2] 刘莉. 四六级考试改革后的大学英语翻译教学[J]. 牡丹江教育学院学报,2014(7):82-90.

[3] 王艺. 大学英语四、六级新题型“段落翻译”策略研究[J]. 文教资料,2014(13):189-191.

[4] 周翔. 四、六级改革与大学英语翻译教学[J]. 渭南师范学院学报,2015(4):75-77.

大学英语教学中融入英美文学的价值及可行性

邱国红

摘　要：新形势下的大学英语教学在训练学生基本语言技能的同时，还应注重对学生人文素质的培养。在大学英语教学中融入英美文学和文化知识，不仅可以使学生拥有更加丰富的精神生活和对完美人性的追求，同时也会极大地促进他们各项语言技能的提高，从而使他们成为现代社会所需的既具备过硬技能又拥有良好人文素养的全方位的人才。

关键词：英美文学；人文素养；提高语言技能；全方位人才

近年来，大学英语改革方兴未艾。但在这场改革中，人们依然关注的是如何提高大学生在听、说、读、写等诸方面的应用能力，而鲜有人提及加强大学生在文学和文化上的素养。笔者认为，究其原因，更主要的是人们对于英美文学在大学英语教学中的价值的忽视。很多人以为英美文学是英语专业的主业，而与大学英语教学没什么瓜葛。然而，在笔者看来，高等教育中的英语教学，应该是摆脱了那种纯粹学习语言规则，记忆词汇的老套初级的教育教学方式，而应该步入到其学习的高级阶段，即，将大学生培养成知识结构较为完整，具有较高的文化素养的全方位人才。在大学阶段，大学生的身心日渐成熟，他们对各方面知识的涉猎有着浓厚的兴趣。在此形势下，大学英语的教学应该当仁不让，让学生注意到文学对人的巨大影响力，引导他们

作者简介：邱国红，女，文学硕士，北京工商大学外国语学院副教授，主要研究方向为英美文学。

了解和欣赏文学中人性的光彩，并同时逐渐增加学生的英美文化的底蕴的积累。此外，作为一个培养人各方面素质的高等教育体系，无论从哪个角度都不应该忽略英美文学在大学英语教学中的影响。因此，笔者认为，在当下大学英语改革的形势下，应该将英美文学知识融入到大学英语的教学改革体系中去，不仅要重视语言知识的讲授，训练学生各方面的语言基础技能，为学生步入职场和社会做准备，而且还要重视对于英美文化知识的传授，使学生拥有更加丰富的的精神文化生活和对于完美人性的精神追求。

1 英美文学在大学英语教学中的重要性

教育部的《大学英语教学大纲》中，明确谈及了大学英语教学中几个应该注意的问题。

问题之一就是提出在大学英语教学将打好语言基础作为教学重点，提高学生综合运用语言的能力之外，“还应有助于学生开阔视野，扩大知识面，加深对世界的了解，借鉴和吸收外国文化精华，提高文化素养。文化和语言有着密切的联系，一定的文化背景知识有助于促进语言综合应用能力的提高”。深刻理解这句话，我们所得到的启示如下。

1.1 英美文学文化知识有助于全面提高大学生的人文素质

众所周知，语言是文化的载体。在人类漫长的社会历史发展中，文学主要承担的是传承文化的功能，它展现的是人类的情感、智慧和社会文化的发展。为了全面地了解不同国家的文化和民族发展的历程，汲取不同民族的文化精华和文明成果，仅仅注重对其语言的学习是远远不够的。脱离了对文学文化的了解和学习，而仅仅谈语言，唯语言为独尊，显然是舍本逐末的做法，是一种文化上的“短视”。因此，笔者认为，真正值得推荐的方法是在大学英语的学习过程当中，教师积极引导学生通过语言的媒介，了解异域文化的传统思想和思维特征，借鉴和吸收其精华，从中受到文化和人性上的陶冶，从而开阔视野，培养出健康的人格与个性，全面提高自身的综合素质，成为具有较强交际能力的高层次人才，最终在国际交往中发挥出更大的作用。

1.2 英美文学文化知识有助于提高大学生英语综合能力的运用

重视学生英语综合能力的提高始终是大学英语教学和改革的重中之重，但在实际教学过程中，教师却发现英语语言的教学往往出现普遍的“瓶颈”现象。即，学生虽然花了大量的时间，背了几本词汇书，但真正在运用这些知识时却经常出现让人啼笑皆非的笑话。究其原因，除了学生对于词汇的有效学习和其用法的透彻研究有很大欠缺，并常常有急功近利的思想作祟之外，就是学生对于英美国家的传统思想文化、习俗、宗教等缺乏必要的认识，致使自己在阅读和交谈过程中，即便没有遭遇语言障碍，却依然无法正确理解文本和交流对象所传递的信息，造成文本误读和交流的无效传达。语言是文化的载体，而文学是语言艺术的精华展现。为了有效地改变这种被动局面，教师亟待通过将英美文化和文学知识纳入大学英语的语言教学中，全面提高学生对于英美文化的知识的了解，使其深刻认识中西文化的差异。教师应该帮助学生通过语言，关注到语言表面含义之外的深层次的意义，提高他们的理解和反应能力，并帮助学生找到正确理解文本和舒适传达的正途，使两种文化的沟通和交际变得顺畅，并最终达到大学英语教学要求的最终目的。

2 英美文学在大学英语教学中融入的可行性

2.1 学生有浓厚的兴趣，在文学素养上有了一定的积累

随着大众文化的广泛传播和中学教学要求的逐步提高，很多学生在中学阶段就通过阅读名著或观看影视作品的形式，对英美的经典文学作品有了一部分的了解。例如，对狄更斯作品的了解可以使学生了解到英国19世纪的黑暗社会现实、下层劳动人民的悲惨生活，从而使学生在大学阶段对于英国早期工业革命对人性的压迫和摧残有了更为深刻的理解和认识。再比如美国20世纪小说家海明威的作品在中国流传很广。海明威以他丰富的个人经历在作品中创造出一个又一个的“硬汉”形象，完美地诠释了人类在重压、死亡等挑战面前应该保持的人类自尊和“重压下的优雅”。如果对这些多加引导和介绍，相信学生在学习《A Day's Wait》等课文中就会对文章有更加深刻

的认识。另外，海明威作品中也对“迷惘一代”和“垮掉一代”的形成和表现有了完整的诠释。如果学生能够在老师的指导下，进一步了解这些文学元素和文化流派的形成背景，以及他们对于后世的影响，学生也就能更好地理解美国60年代出现的众多文化现象和社会现象，理解那个时代的年轻人在旧的价值观被破坏，新的价值观尚未建立起来的空档期所出现的迷惘以及各种荒淫放荡和偏激怪异的行为。在此强大的文化背景的基础上，学生会很顺利地理解诸如《新标准大学英语》第二册第一单元的课文《College Just Isn't Special Any More》中以美国加州大学伯克利分校为代表的大学生所展现出的非同寻常的社会责任感、叛逆和改变世界的精神追求。与此同时，教师如果能及时将《阿甘正传》这部经典好莱坞巨作作为教学辅助，通过让学生了解影片中所涉及的大量纪实材料，诸如水门事件，尼克松访华，中美乒乓外交，肯尼迪被刺，越战，吸毒，性解放，朋克，男女杂居等，必定会使学生对60年代的美国社会和文化产生非同一般的认识和了解，于是在此背景下阅读和理解相关的大量资料自然就不在话下了。因此，大学英语的教学一定要充分利用学生之前在文学上的积累和认识，因势利导，在教学中进一步促进学生对英美文学和文化中所展示的各个现象的认识，最终全面提高学生的理解能力和思辨能力。

2.2 教师素质不断提高，在英美文学方面的知识储备使得这种教学成为可能

目前在高校大学英语部门任教的教师队伍中，硕士研究生学历的占据了相当大的比例，其中很多是研究英美文学方向出身的。他们丰厚的知识储备使得在大学英语教学中纳入英美文学文化的教学成为了可能。大学英语教学和英美文学文化的融合，能极大地积累和夯实学生的文学和文化底蕴，发挥教师的专业特长，并同时促进他们的学术专业研究，使得教学和研究相互补充，相得益彰。

在大学英语的教学过程中，把学生的英语基本技能和综合文学素养有效地结合，一定会极大地促进学生对于各项英语语言技能的学习。他们在文学和文化的海洋中汲取的丰富养分，一定会帮助他们更好观察和了解英美文化和社会现实，从而实现更有效的阅读体验和语言的交际功能，成为现代社会

所需的具备过硬的技能和良好人文素养的人才。

参考文献

[1] 曾琛. 学习英美文学的价值和现实意义[J]. 科技风,2013(1):228.

[2] 黄春英. 大学英语教学中开设英美文学课程的必要性和可行性[J]. 考试周刊(外语教学与研究),2007(35):67-68.

[3] 邢小梅. 在大学英语中开展英美文学教学[J]. 英语教学研究,2009(4):20-26.

北京市高校商务英语学习状况调查与分析

卢丹军

摘　要：商务英语是获得适应商务活动的语言的能力为目的的一种学习，内容涉及日常商务活动的方方面面。近年来，随着商事活动国际化程度的增加，各高校也纷纷开设商务英语课程和专业。本文通过对北京市高校商务英语课程的开展现状进行调查和数据分析，粗略分析了北京市高校在校生对于商务英语学习的看法和用人单位对商务英语技能的要求，尝试探讨高校设置商务英语课程对毕业生就业的帮助。

关键词：商务英语；BEC；就业市场；人力资源；课堂学习

商务英语是以教导学习课程的学员适应在职场中的语言要求为目的，内容涉及商务活动的方方面面的一门课程。是在夯实英语基础知识之后，再进一步地增强、提升学生的商务知识与意识，然后自然地促进其沟通能力——当今的商务活动强调实际的商务沟通能力。

商务英语教学正在全国各个高校全面铺开，特别是BEC商务英语的教学。BEC商务英语证书被全球许多知名企业认可，已经成为进入诸如西门子、普华永道、强生等500强企业的敲门砖。很多企业的招聘考试都采用了BEC考试的题目。近几年来，中国BEC考试报名率以每年300%的速度疯狂飙升。但是从官方数据来看，BEC在中国的通过率是远低于其他国家的，中级在30%左右，高级在25%左右。不论是初级、中级还是高级。所以我们必

项目/基金：本论文为2015年北京市级大学生科研与创业行动计划项目的成果，项目编号为SJ201502040。
作者简介：卢丹军，浙江宁波人，北京工商大学外国语学院讲师。

须加强对于商务英语的关注以及提升。

1 北京市高校开展商务英语现状

我们在北京市的多所高校中抽取了12所进行了实地调研，运用了结构性访谈法，大部分高校都开设商务英语课程或专业。其中，部分调查结果如下。

1.1 商务英语课程参与情况

从图1中我们能直观地看出，在受访者中，大部分同学都参与过商务英语课程的学习。而这些学校均属于综合性大学，其中有偏经济类的也有偏理工类的。我们所调查的语言类大学如北京语言大学、北京外国语大学和北京第二外国语大学中均有此专业的开设，可见商务英语在北京市很多高校的进展都十分顺畅。

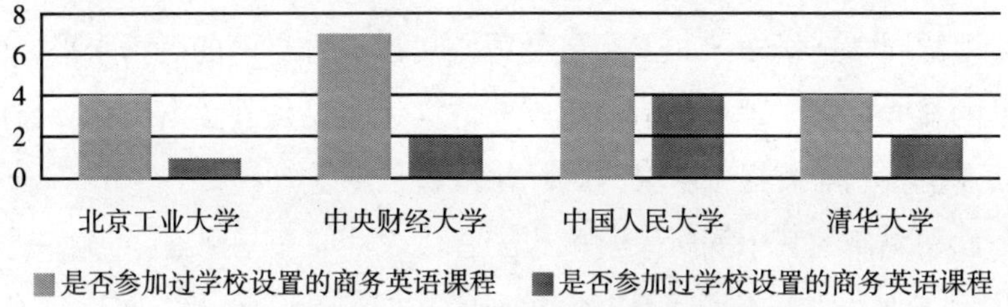

图1 是否参加过学校的商务英语课程统计表

1.2 参与课程学生所处的BEC等级

如图2所示，在我们所调查的高校中没有学习初级商务英语的在校生，一般的起点都是商务英语中级。我们在采访中了解到，出现这一现象的原因是一般高校在课程设置时都会以中级教材为起点，原因有两个。

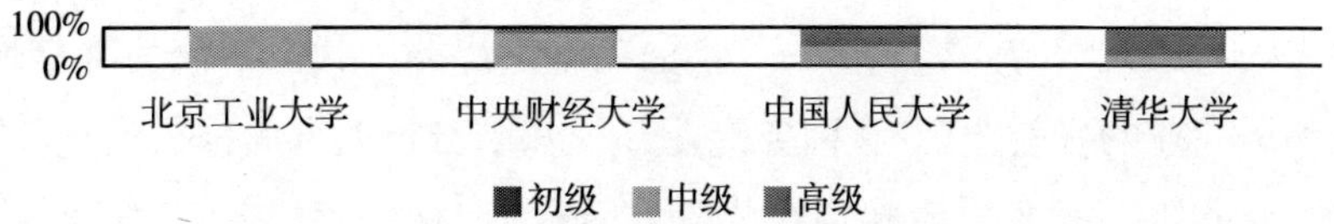

图2 各校学生所处商务英语不同等级所占比例

（1）初级的难度对于大学生来说过于简单，没有教授的必要，高级过难不是一个合适的起点。

（2）每一级的考试报名费都不算低，要尽量让学生的报名费花得值。

从图2中可以看出趋势，高考录取线越高的学校的学生参与学习商务英语高级的人数所占比例越高。但即使在清华大学中，还是有一定比例的在校生选择进行中级商务英语的学习。在北京工业大学中，全部受访者都进行的是中级商务英语的学习，可见商务英语的整体难度有多高。而商务英语就是因为其难度值的保障（换句话说是其证书的含金量）才使得越来越多的人开始进行商务英语的学习。

2 北京市高校在校生对于商务英语的态度

此次调查过程中，我们以问卷的形式了解了来自12所高校的123名在校大学生对于商务英语的态度。其中大部分的同学参加过学校开展的商务英语课程，也对商务英语有着自己的理解。

大多数同学选择学习BEC还是觉得它可以提升自己的英语水平，同时增强自己的就业技能。现在的应届生就业方向大多是是外企、银行。在商务领域的就业也就意味着提升自身的国际化接轨程度。

下面是调研的其中四所大学里比较有代表性的一些回答。

北京工业大学的同学们认为商务英语“在英语运用方面比较有优势”“证书在竞聘外企时还是比较有优势的”“主要是专业技能（听、说、读、写）方面的帮助吧”“挺有帮助的，我找了家实习单位有对商务英语的要求”。

中央财经大学的同学们认为商务英语“对就业挺有用的”“考个证书挺管用的”“学了之后在就业方面更有竞争力了”“除了对英语学习有用之外，对就业好像没多大帮助”“如果要进外企的话，这可能会是敲门砖，学了总比没学强”。

中国人民大学的同学们认为“学商英的没出路，我们学校其他专业貌似都比英语专业的好就业”“在商务专业知识和语言技能方面都很受益”“之前英语不是很好，学了之后感觉在英语方面有很大进步”“去面试的时候，当时就问了一个和以前学的内容相关的问题，很顺利地回答了，所以挺有帮助的”“在银行做翻译，工作基本上和当初学的吻合”。

清华大学的同学们认为“学的足够好的话，去外企，银行等都挺适合的”“学的是国际商务管理方向，一般要就业的话都得考商务英语”“对商务谈判很有用，学到手的东西都是资本”“对搞研究挺有用，能看懂并理解一些相关的文献资料”。

中国农业大学的同学们认为商务英语“对工作是一项很有用的技能”“顺应贸易全球化趋势”“能锻炼口语”“可以接触到一些国外商务案例”。

由此可见，实用性是商务英语为大学生所认可的特点。

3 北京市高校商务英语就业前景分析

在校生对于一个专业的选择或者对于一门课程的学习的根本目的之一在于促进自己未来的职业发展。而商务英语对于职业选择的推动作用应该主要在于商业活动方面。在我们的调查中也显示出这一明确的就业选择导向。大多数在校生倾向于进入外企工作，或从事国际贸易，或从事银行方面。

通过对八家大型企业的访问调查，这些企业进行招聘的岗位涉及客服经理、城市/省区的经理人、总监、经理等职位。对于英语一般来说有着较高要求，但对于是否为BEC持证人的要求是否定的。像特斯拉的客服岗位，他的招聘已经要求到留学回来的硕士，能够自如地进行中英双语转换。我们经过分析，要求并未涉及商务英语的原因如下。

首先，无论是何种形式的资格证书都有一定的获取技巧性，可能企业对于其信任度仍有待提升。其次，企业如果将BEC资格证列为必须项可能会损失优质的求职者，因为商务英语的考证费用相对于很多国内的考试高很多，所以一些英语很好的人也不会去进行这个资格证考试。最后，商务英语在我国的发展还属于起步阶段，仍需要和企业进行大量的磨合。

4 总结

通过对上述群体和市场的分析，可以说商务英语是一门“终身受用”的培训，除了可以提升商务情商、提高商务语言的组织能力、树立正确的商务理念，还能培养国际化的表述，照顾中文中商务语言的表达。无论对于白领，还是希望步入外企的大学生来说，都是一个重要的提升。

我们对于高校商务英语课程的未来规划提出了几点建议。

（1）不将课程重点完全放置于对商务英语证书的取得，而要对于学生的商务素质和英语能力进行综合性提升，这样在大多数企业还未将商务英语列入考量项的时间里，能在求职时占取更大优势。

（2）将商务英语的教材系统化，分类到商务知识系统讲解、商务礼仪、商务用词、商务谈判等不同科目来进行讲解，使得讲解更有针对性。

（3）明确商务英语学习的目的。在国外，大多数进行商务英语学习的主要是从事商务工作的白领。他们有一定的工作经验，所以培训更有针对性、更有效。但是在国内的情况却截然不同，应试的大多是学生，是将商务英语的证书作为了求职的敲门砖。

参考文献

[1] 胡萍萍. 关于大学英语分级教学的几点思考——以浙江师范大学大学英语教学改革为例[J]. 浙江师范大学学报:社会科学版,2008(5):108-112.

利用“意识提升”活动促使学生在英语写作中增强词汇的丰富性

王秀珍

摘　要：本文介绍了“意识提升”活动在词汇学习和写作中的作用。结合学习者在词汇学习和写作中存在的问题，笔者设计了一系列“意识提升”活动，旨在提高学习者的词汇学习效果，进而改善写作水平。

关键词：意识提升；词汇写作

1 引言

词汇在英语作文中的重要性毋庸置疑。没有丰富的词汇，就无法确切生动地表达想要表达的思想内容。研究发现，即使学习者的词汇量很大，他们在作文中能够应用的新词仍然很少。出现这种现象可能是由于以下几个原因：① 教师和学生只强调词汇量的增长，不十分关注掌握词汇知识的应用；② 输入有限，缺乏产出机会；③ 在国内很少有针对把产出性词汇应用到写作中的课程。因此，有必要改善学习者的词汇学习状况、敦促他们把新学到的词汇有意识地应用到写作中去，一方面可以提高词汇学习效果，另一方面可以改善写作水平。

项目/基金：本文是北京工商大学青年基金项目（QNJJ2014-01）“意识提升活动对学习者产出性词汇应用能力产生影响的行动研究”的部分研究成果。

作者简介：王秀珍，北京工商大学外国语学院讲师，主要从事第二语言习得、英语教学法和英语语言学等方面的研究。

2 意识提升与词汇学习和应用

早在1981年，Sharwood Smith就提出了“意识提升”（consciousness-raising）这个术语。“意识提升”指的是教师或研究者为了提升学习者对目标语言形式特征的意识所做的专门尝试。意识包括三个层次：知觉、注意、理解。Schmidt提出了“注意假设”。他指出，外显（explicit）学习，也就是有意识地解决问题，为第二语言学习者提供了形成和检验假设的机会，有意识的活动会促使学习者在记忆中寻找相关的知识，从而确定是否理解了新学知识当中的内容。“意识提升”强调教师要明确解释，把学习者自我发现规律放在首位，呈现目标语形式时要能够吸引学习者的注意力。Ellis认为意识提升活动可以增强学习者对目标语形式的意识，逐渐引导学习者进行正确的产出。Hunston等提出三种增强学习者对词汇模式意识的方法：第一种是让学习者找出课文中给出的模式；第二种是给学习者分享同样模式的词语；第三种是要求学习者识别意群，然后让学习者在课后寻找应用特定结构的词语。

词汇研究权威人士Laufer指出，外显（explicit）词汇学习，也就是有意识地解决问题（conscious problem-solving），是多数第二语言词汇学习的依据。Lee研究了第二语言学习者在写作中的词汇应用以及外显词汇指导（explicit vocabulary instruction）的作用。在阅读指导和理解练习之后，按照要求完成的写作结果表明，研究对象对于认识的目标语词汇有13.19%能够进行产出性应用。在接受目标语词汇外显指导之后，产出性词汇的应用比例增长到63.62%，这是新学词汇产出性应用的显著增长。Jiang和Shu在教授预制动词语块和动词模式（prefabricated verbs chunks and verb patterns）时采用了一系列的意识提升活动。结果表明意识提升活动可以促使学习者注意到词语意义之间的差距、增强学习者学习英语的信心、引导学习者进行词汇学习。

研究者发现，词汇缺乏导致第二语言学习者写作困难，而且词汇是决定写作水平的至关重要因素之一。Duin证实，通过外显词汇指导，学习者可以更多地在恰当的上下文中应用词汇，这是由于“词汇意识”产生了效应，影响学习者在随后的写作中更加注意词汇的选择，从而增强了作文内容的丰富性以及句子结构的多样性。

因此，在教学实践中让学生有意识地应用所学的新词，增强对词汇深度知识的掌握，进而把新词应用到写作当中，学以致用非常必要。

3 “意识提升”活动在教学中的实践

笔者在教学当中，设计了一系列“意识提升”活动，旨在提高学习者的词汇学习效果，把新学词汇应用到写作中，进而丰富作文中的词汇，提高写作水平。以下是意识提升活动的介绍。

首先，在每个单元的词汇教学时，笔者列出学生需要学习应用的词汇，每一组通常为8到10个，称之为目标词汇。通过颜色标记、搭配罗列、句子举例以及翻译练习等活动，笔者引导学生在课上注意并了解掌握目标词汇的应用。然后，笔者给学生留出10分钟左右的时间，要求学生根据自己的兴趣和掌握情况，用其中尽可能多的词语写几句话，最好是一个段落，多用复合句。在这个过程中，教师查看完成较快的学生的情况。待全班基本完成任务以后，分享几个应用较好的例子。此项练习的目的是通过有效输入，引导学生注意并学习目标词汇。产出性练习旨在激发学生的学习兴趣，并且吸引学生的注意力，由此提高词汇教学和学习效果。

其次，在课堂讲解练习完目标词汇以后，课下给学生布置一些笔者自行设计的词汇练习，包括词汇替换、填空、汉译英等。此项练习的目的是强化学生对目标词汇的理解和应用。与此同时，笔者要求学生预习与目标词汇相关的课文，标出目标词汇在课文中的意思，以此引起学生对目标词汇在课文中用法的注意。

再次，教师在课堂上讲解目标词汇所在的课文，通过分析、提问、总结等方式检查学生对目标词汇的理解掌握情况。

然后，学习完目标词汇所在的课文之后，布置一篇命题作文，话题与所学内容相关，列出本单元所学过的目标词汇，要求学生尽量多用列出的目标词汇进行写作。作文的分数与是否能够正确应用目标词汇的多少紧密相关。

最后，在布置下一组目标词汇任务之前，笔者完成批改作文。课上对范文进行分析点评，尤其是指出应用目标词汇较好的句子，加强学生的词汇应用意识，激励学生下次更多地去应用所学的目标词汇。

4 结语

总的来说，在教学当中，通过一系列的意识提升活动，让学生注意并掌握目标词汇的用法，然后有目的地应用到写作中去，不但可以提高学生的词汇学习效果，还可以促使学生增强词汇知识应用的意识，在今后的学习中尽量把所学的新词汇应用到写作中去，一方面能够学以致用，另一方面还可以提高写作水平，从而达到一箭双雕的目的。

参考文献

[1] DUIN A L. Effects of intensive writing instruction on a specific writing task[M]. Minneapolis:University of Minnesota,1983.

[2] ELLIS R. Task-based language learning and teaching[M]. Oxford: Oxford University Linguistics,2003.

[3] HUNSTON S,FRANCIS G,MANNING E. Grammar and vocabulary: showing the connections[J]. ELT Journal,1997,3: 208-216.

[4] LAUFER B. Reading,word-focused activities and incidental vocabulary acquisition in a second language[J]. Prospect,2001,16:44-54.

[5] LEE S H. ESL learners' vocabulary use in writing and the effects of explicit vocabulary instruction[J]. System,2003,31: 537-561.

[6] JIANG J L,SHU B M. An application of consciousness-raising activities when teaching vocabulary to English majors[J]. Chinese Journal of Applied Linguistics (Quarterly),2011, 2: 94-106.

[7] SCHMIDT R. Awareness and second language acquisition[J]. Annual Review of Applied Linguistics,1993,13:206-226.

[8] SMITH S M. Consciousness-raising and the second language learner[J].Applied Linguistics, 1981,2: 159-69.

[9] 邓联健. 二语产出性词汇能力发展研究综述[J]. 外语与外语教学,2006(2):25-27.

浅谈剑桥商务英语课堂的个性化设计

侯 霞

摘 要：剑桥英语证书考试（Business English Certificate，BEC）是英国剑桥大学考试委员设计的一项语言水平考试，旨在培养并测试非英语母语国家人士用英语进行国际商务活动的能力。该项系列测试对考生在普通工作环境下和商务活动中使用英语的能力从听、说、读、写四个方面进行考察，其实用性自不必赘言。近年来，随着大学英语教学改革的深入，英语课的设置更加注重培养学生的语言使用能力，BEC剑桥商务英语因其课程中所提供的案例和情景设置而成了很多大专院校的首选。本文将以作者的实际教学经验为例，对BEC商务英语课堂的个性化设计进行探讨。

关键词：BEC商务英语；课堂设计

1 BEC商务英语对大学英语教学改革的促进作用

最近几年，我校（北京工商大学）提出了大学英语教学改革的口号，教改的目的是培养在校大学生英语实际运用能力。传统的大学英语课堂主要以教师为主导，教学方式多以课堂讲授为主，学生则出于被动学习的地位，长期以来形成一种“满堂灌”的模式。其结果不仅破坏学生学习英语的兴趣，对教师的工作方式和工作热情也造成一定的不良影响。我校英语教改首先引入了BEC商务课程，使用的教材是经济科学出版社出版的《新

项目/基金：本论文为2015年北京市级大学生科研与创业行动计划项目的成果，项目编号为SJ201502071。
作者简介：侯霞，女，北京人，北京工商大学外国语学院讲师。

编剑桥商务英语》，为的是将学生的听、说、读、写能力的培养有机结合起来，为社会输送面向世界、面向未来的合格的人才。BEC商务英语课程是以适应职场生活的语言要求为目的，内容涉及商务活动和职场生活的方方面面。商务英语课程的内容和形式多种多样，既包括案例研究、情景模拟和角色扮演，又提供语言训练的语法词汇练习和跨文化交际的知识。其目的不是简单地提高学生的英文水平和能力，更希望学生能学习到西方的企业管理理念、工作方式和工作心理，了解西方人的生活习惯以及与他们合作的方法，学会如何与他们打交道。BEC商务英语课程的引进符合我校大学英语教学改革的要求。

2 BEC商务英语课本的特点

《新编剑桥商务英语》教材是英国剑桥大学考试委员会推荐的，专为剑桥商务英语证书考试而编写的教材，它以现代商务活动为素材，辅以大量的自测练习。每个单元大致围绕着一个商务专题而展开，其中包括三个部分——商务话题、商务技能和考点分析。相关资料和学习内容以阅读、听力、口语、写作以及BEC考试模拟题等各种不同形式呈现，为教师提供了丰富的案例、商务背景知识、实用范例、情景模拟等通过不同教学手段促进学生参与的课堂活动模式。教师可以利用课本提供的各种素材组织丰富多样的课堂活动，使学生真正参与到教学活动中来，学生作为主导，教师作为辅导，辅助教学活动的进行。下面笔者将以《新编剑桥商务英语》（中级）第十单元为例，对商务英语课堂的个性化设计进行探讨。

3 BEC商务英语课堂的设计

《新编剑桥商务英语》（中级）第十单元的商务主题为管理（Management），根据内容可划分为三个相关的专题，即企业管理简介（包括一篇阅读文章和一篇听力对话）、解决问题的技能（包括两篇听力和一个案例研究）以及项目管理简介（包括两篇电子邮件和一张甘特图），全部内容将在三个时段，即六个课时内完成。

3.1 第一时段——企业管理简介

根据课本提供的材料，这个部分可以以下列线索来贯穿，即什么是管理——优秀管理者的经验——如何成为一个管理者。课本中的阅读文章以美国流行摇滚天后麦当娜的音乐生涯为线索，总结出麦当娜事业的成功模式在企业管理学中的意义和价值，以及管理者从中能够学到的有益的经验。麦当娜虽然被全世界的歌迷奉为流行教母，但对于现在的学生来说已经是奶奶级的人物了，对于她的背景介绍是必不可少的，这部分分配给学生作为课前预习作业，课堂进行汇报展示；此外，关于企业管理知识的材料也将提前给学生作为课前的阅读材料。经过这两方面的准备，上课时就可以组织学生以麦当娜的成功经历为例，对课文内容进行讨论，让学生了解什么是企业管理，管理者应具备的能力以及好的管理经验。这样的讨论有课前的准备、课上的展示和课文阅读作为基础，学生有足够的内容可谈，教师指导学生如何借鉴课文和阅读材料中的词汇、表达等语言知识，使课堂活动可以顺利展开。

第一时段中的听力部分的内容涉及初任管理者时可能遇到的问题以及有意成为管理者的员工应该做好的各方面准备。在经过前面的各项课堂活动之后，学生对管理有了初步的了解，在听的时候有一定的心理准备，有助于他们了解听力材料的内容并对材料进行总结。

3.2 第二时段——解决问题的技能

这部分的主要内容是案例研究，以讨论为主，听力和阅读作为讨论的准备。需要给学生提供的准备包括三个方面：① 了解解决问题的流程，即确定当务之急、提出解决方案、比较各个解决方案、确定最佳方案；② 语法知识，即使用条件句提供解决方案；③ 讨论问题的解决方案时常用的句子或表述。做好以上准备之后，学生先进行听力练习，了解以上内容在实际的商务活动中是如何体现的。经过这两个步骤，教师可以引导学生开始案例分析，带领学生阅读课本中的三份材料——报纸上对一个乐队的乐评、统计乐队周边产品销售情况的柱状图和统计乐队专辑销售情况的表格，从而对文中提到的乐队当前面临的问题进行分析总结。课本中的任务的设置是帮助乐队出谋划策，准备下一张专辑和巡演。学生被分为三人一组的小组，每个人的任务不同，分别为市场调研人员、品牌经理和产品植入专家，三个人要进行角色扮演，根据各自的专业方向为乐队提供建议。在此阶段的讨论中，教师要指导学生使用前面准备阶段练习的语法知识和常用表达。

3.3 第三阶段——项目管理简介

此部分的主题是项目管理，课本内容为两篇讨论乐队巡演安排的电子邮件。教师要先介绍一下项目管理的基本知识和常用词汇，要求学生在阅读两篇电子邮件时将这些知识和词汇“对号入座”，学习这些专业词汇是如何使用的。接下来师生一起讨论甘特图的使用，让学生根据电子邮件的内容，对照甘特图，描述整个巡演项目的安排。根据第二篇电子邮件谈到的安排上的变化画出更新后的甘特图，并用语言进行描述。这样的活动不仅能让学生对专业词汇有一定的了解，同时能让他们练习使用这些词汇来描述实际工作中的安排。

4 结语

剑桥商务英语教材每一课的设置虽然相同，但内容的呈现方式却是多种多样的，课堂活动的方式不能一成不变，因此要求教师要根据每一课的主题和内容、课本提供的教学材料和学生的具体需求对课堂进行个性化设计，充分利用教材的优势，调动学生的积极性，达到从商务知识到语言知识再到语言使用能力共同进步的目的。

参考文献

[1] 剑桥商务英语证书考试大纲(第1-2级)[M]. 北京：机械工业出版社，2004.
[2] 杜慧芳. 讨论式教学法在商务英语课堂中的应用[J]. 太原大学教育学院学报，2009(6)：43-45.
[3] 林菁. 运用案例促进商务英语口语教学[J]. 湖北广播电视大学学报，2006(5)：123-124.
[4] 宫辉. 商务英语课堂中的情境教学法[J]. 科技创新导报，2010(36)：154.

立场词研究综述

刘红艳　尹　喻

摘　要：立场标志着说话者的感情、态度、愿望和价值判断等，立场表达语可以传递这些情感和评价意义。近年来越来越多的学者开始对立场词进行研究和探讨。对立场词的研究主要体现为对比研究，例如不同文化背景之间的立场表达对比，本族语语者与非本族语语者之间的立场词表达对比等。本文将从立场词的定义和立场词的分类两方面对立场词研究进行综述。

关键词：立场词；定义；立场词类

1 立场词的定义

立场标志着说话者的感情、态度、愿望和价值判断等，立场表达语可以传递这些情感和评价意义。近年来越来越多的学者开始对立场词进行研究和探讨。学者们对立场词给出了不同的定义。

Ochs提出，立场词是联系语言与文化的元素之一。可以将立场词定义为“a socially recognized dispositions”。立场词可以分为两类：表达认知的立场词和表达情感的立场词，其中表达认知的立场词是社会公认的认知主题的方式，例如直接认识、间接认识、确定程度和特异性，表达情感的立场词是社

项目/基金：本论文是北京工商大学国有资产管理协同创新中心项目“基于语料库的国有企业组织话语研究”(批准号：GZ20131301)的部分成果。

作者简介：刘红艳，女，汉族，山西太原人，北京工商大学外国语学院教授，硕士生导师。尹喻，女，汉族，贵州遵义人，北京工商大学外国语学院2013级研究生。

会公认的感觉、态度、情绪或者情感强度。

Fairclough将立场词定义为对客观世界的主观评价，立场词不是话语发出者用于直接表达确定性、怀疑和态度的装置。Fairclough还认为话语发出者应该选恰当的词汇或语法来表达他们真正的意图。

Hyland认为立场词是专业学者用于评论准确性、确定性或用于评论主题的工具，立场词还能表现出专业学者想要在多大程度上通过话语表达自己的想法。Hyland提出作者在文章中把话语立场词当作表达他们意见、情感、判断和评价的有效且重要的方法。Hyland研究了学术写作中的立场词。根据Hyland对写作中立场词的研究，立场词是对文本的解释，也是对一些断言的评价。

Biber和Finegan将立场词定义为对态度、情感、判断和承诺的表达，其中包括说话者或作者对“信任”不同程度的表达。Biber和Finegan后来还对表达情感的立场词和表达态度的立场词进行了研究，那意味着他们拓宽了他们的研究范围。根据Biber等的研究，可以将立场词划分为三大类，即表达情感的立场词、表达态度的立场词和表达方式的立场词。

依据Huston和Thompson的研究，立场词是说话者或者作者用来表达他们观点、态度或是对于他们所谈及的话题的感觉的一般词汇。

徐宏亮指出，语法立场标记语是表明作者对于主题或读者立场的语法装置。根据李荣娟的研究，作者用来标记结构位置的语法装置是不同的，这些语法装置属于不同的结构层次，包括词、短语和句子，它们归属于不同的词汇种类，包括动词、情态动词、名词、形容词和副词。立场词成分与合格结构主题之间关系是各种各样的。

2 立场词的分类

目前已有不少学者对不同种类的立场词，诸如动词、副词、形容词、名词和情态动词等进行了研究。例如Biber和Finegan对立场副词进行了研究，Biber和Finegan、Biber等，Hyland对立场动词、立场形容词、立场副词、立场名词和立场情态动词进行了研究。Chafe对立场动词和立场副词进行了研究。

2.1 立场动词

Precht将5种实义动词区分为关系动词、模糊动词、报告动词、精神过程动词和影响动词。关系动词描述文本信息之间的关系；模糊动词限制作者或说话者承诺或提议的强烈程度；报告动词显示了信息的来源，精神过程动词显示出作者或说话者的精神状态或思想状态；影响动词表明作者或说话者的情感和态度。

在学术写作中，报告动词又被称为认知动词。Williams研究了诸如find、show、suggest、seem and appear等报告动词。Hyland对observe、notice、show、argue、believe等实义动词进行了分析。

现在有学者开始把这些动词分为两类：即“to 从句”和“that-从句”。

2.2 立场副词

各类副词被统称为adverbial，包括单一副词、副词短语、名词短语、介词短语、限定性从句等。根据Hoye的研究，adverb属于词汇范畴而adverbial属于语法范畴。根据Biber等的研究，Adverbial可以分为circumstance adverbials，stance adverbials和linking adverbials。在Biber对adverbial的分类中，stance adverbials用于表达作者的立场和态度，同时能被读者识别出来。

Biber等发现立场副词能用于表达各种含义，例如评价、价值判断、预期评估等，同时立场副词还能表达各种认知含义，例如怀疑、现状、局限和观点等。基于Biber的研究，立场副词主要表达以下几方面的含义：怀疑与确定、现状、信息来源、限定与不精确、观点。

根据Biber等的研究，怀疑副词与确定副词包括对主题和可能性的绝对判断；现状副词与现实副词评价该陈述是否是真实；信息来源副词表明信息的来源；限定性副词能表明主题的局限；观点或视角副词能显示从哪个观点出发该主题是正确的。除此之外，不严密副词用于显示主题的不精确。

2.3 立场形容词

形容词常用于描述物体的特征。说话者和作者使用的形容词总会表现出他们的立场。

Biber和Finegan列举出了很多用作立场词的形容词，例如表示确定性的词：clear，definite，evident和certain。Hyland也对用作立场词的形容词进行了研究，包括essential possible、important、probable等。Biber等对诸如sure、certain、possible等认知立场形容词，诸如amazing、angry、essential等态度立场形容词进行了研究。Holmes认为，用形容词表示怀疑和确定性，这种情况在会话中出现得较多，在书面语中出现得较少。形容词补语从句通常表现为adjective+to clause和adjective+that clause。

2.4 立场名词

和前三类立场词一样，说话者和作者也会通过名词表现其态度。Dry分析了态度名词，例如fact、problems、truth等。Holmes研究了认知名词，例如probability、view、opinion等。Hyland分析了doubt、assumption、possibility、implication、prediction等词的特点。除了单独的名词作立场标记词，noun+complement clause的结构也常作为标记立场。

2.5 立场情态动词

情态动词可以分为认知情态动词和义务情态动词。Halliday将认知情态动词定义为"说话者对可能性的估计和预测"。Chafe、Hoye、Hyland、Plamer、Biber等和Quirk等对不同语义类别的情态动词进行了研究。Biber等发现会话中使用的情态动词比书面表达中使用的情态动词更多，书面语中小说类使用的情态动词比其他领域的更多。情态动词是最常使用的立场标记语。

3 立场词研究局限及展望

立场标志着说话者的感情、态度、愿望和价值判断等，立场词是传递这些情感和评价意义的标志和工具。近年来很多学者都在对立场词进行研究和探讨。到目前为止，对立场词的研究在深度和广度上都得到了很大的推进，但目前的研究大部分都是基于Biber、Finegan、Hyland等语言学家的研究成果，对不同文化背景之间的立场表达进行对比研究以及对本族语语者与非本族语语者之间的立场词表达进行对比研究，其中对本族语语者和非本族语语者的立场表达进行对比研究的情况更为常见。同一话语者或作者对不同语言接收者所使用的语言中的立场词有何特征以及有何差异？此类研究甚少，因此，除了以不同文化背景之间的立场表达和本族语语者与非本族语语者之间的立场词为研究对象外，我们还可以研究当话语接收者不同时，同一话语者或作者所使用的语言中的立场词的特征及差异。

参考文献

[1] OCHS E. Cultural universals in the acquisition of language: keynote address[J]. Papers and Reports on Child Language Development, 1990(29): 1–19.

[2] BIBER D, FINEGAN E. Adverbial stance types in English [J]. Discourse Process, 1988 (11): 1-34.

[3] BIBER D, CONRAD S. Adverbial marking of stance in speech and writing[M]. Oxford: Oxford University Press, 2000.

[4] BIBER D, JOHANSSON S, LEECH G, et al. The Longman grammar of spoken and written English[M]. Harlow: Longman, 1999.

[5] BIBER D, JOHANSSON S, LEECH G, et al. Longman grammar of spoken and written English [M]. Beijing: Foreign Language and Research Press, 2000.

[6] WALLACE L C, NICHOLS J. Evidentiality: the linguistic coding of epistemology[M]. New Jersey: Able, 1986.

[7] FAIRCLOUGH N. Discourse and social change[M]. Cambridge: Polity Press, 1992.

[8] HOYE L. Adverbs and modality in English[M]. New York: Longman, 1997.

[9] HYLAND K. Hedging in scientific discourse[M]. amsterdam and philadelphia: John Benjamins Publishing Company, 1998.

[10] HYLAND K. Metadiscourse[M]. London: Continuum, 2005.

[11] PRECHT K. Patterns of stance in English [D]. Flagstaff: Northern Arizona University, 2000.

[12] 曹蕾. 基于语料库的政治语篇立场状语研究[D]. 上海:上海交通大学,2008.

[13] 徐宏亮. 学术语篇中的作者立场标记语研究[M]. 合肥:合肥工业大学出版社,2007.

[14] 李荣娟. 政治专栏语篇中态度意义的评价理论视角[D]. 济南:山东大学,2004.

儿童及青少年的行为问题：诊断标准以及学校心理专家的作用

董 虹

摘 要：本文将探究儿童及青少年时期出现的行为问题，还将把行为障碍的诊断与对立违抗性障碍（oppositional defiant disorder，ODD）和行为障碍与注意力缺陷多动障碍（attention deficit hyperactivity disorder，ADHD）之关联性进行比对。为使人们对这些儿童和青少年身上存在的行为障碍（conduct disorder，CD）和影响予以足够的重视，本文还将给出这些行为障碍的标准医学定义，以及有关这一领域中研究文献。

关键词：行为障碍（CD）；对立违抗性障碍（ODD）；注意力缺陷多动障碍（ADHD）

1 引言

在儿童心理学中，要精准研判儿童是否为行为障碍是极其困难的，因为必须首先清楚地区分开是否是正常儿童行为或是真正的行为障碍的初始或已经到了延伸阶段。但是，当孩子到了入学的年龄，识别和研判该孩子的身上是否存在有行为障碍则显得尤为迫切。

作者简介：董虹，北京工商大学外国语学院讲师，主要研究方向为英美文学、特殊教育。

2 行为障碍

美国儿童与青少年心理学协会（AACAP）针对行为障碍给出的定义是：行为障碍是发生在年轻人身上的一组复杂的行为和情绪问题。患有此障碍的儿童和青少年通常难以遵循规章制度，表现出社会不能接受的行为。这些孩子通常被看成是坏孩子、问题少年，没有人认为他们是患有精神疾病的人。为了能准确识别出这一行为障碍，美国儿童与青少年心理学协会罗列出了患有行为障碍儿童在日常活动中常常表现出的一些行为迹象。这些行为包括：

① 有攻击人和动物的行为；

② 有破坏财物的行为；

③ 有欺骗、说谎、或偷窃的行为；

④ 有严重违反规章制度的行为。

美国儿童与青少年心理学协会除了描述并为行为障碍明确下了定义以外，还指出：患有行为障碍本身并不可怕，可怕的是常常伴随行为障碍而出现的附加障碍。美国儿童与青少年心理学协会指出：

许多患有行为障碍的儿童或许会同时患有情绪障碍、焦虑症、创伤后应激障碍、吸毒、注意力缺陷多动障碍、学习困难，或者思维障碍，然而这些问题是可以治愈的。研究表明患有行为障碍的年轻人如果没有接受早期全面的治疗，非常有可能出现继发问题。这些患有行为障碍的青少年如果不接受治疗，他们将无法适应成年后的社会状况，他们将不能维系正常的人际关系，他们无法正常维持住一个稳定的工作。他们常常会做违法的事，或者表现出反社会的行为。

导致儿童患行为障碍的因素有很多，这包括：大脑损伤，虐待儿童，遗传因素，课业成绩不好，生活经历创伤。

有关行为障碍的研究还强烈警示人们：行为障碍的问题并不纯粹由儿童本身体现出来，而是由外因或内因引发的。更为重要的是，行为障碍的出现通常是由其他疾病的出现，或缺少必需和没能获得及时的治疗而激发所致。研究人员提示人们，缺少及时的观察和治疗，正是发生在青少年中的行为障碍被认为是发生在儿童中的行为障碍问题更为严重的最根本原因。因为，最初的行为障碍没有得到有效识别和控制，就有机会发展成越来越严重的状态。研究表明，儿童行为障碍比青少年行为障碍要轻的多，因为儿童没有接触到促使他们产生社会问题的刺激因素，电脑游戏和电视都会成为促使儿童产生社会问题的因素。

还有很多种不同形式的心理障碍会与行为障碍并存。最常见到的两种是对立违抗性障碍和注意力缺陷障碍。

3 对立违抗性障碍

行为障碍被界定为发生在儿童和青少年身上的行为和情绪问题，而对立违抗性障碍则是攻击和有故意影响旁人倾向的结合。这种结合从心理学角度来看，对于那些受此困扰的人来说这个组合非常奏效：一个患有对立违抗性障碍的儿童因其违背社会行为受到“奖励”，然而一个青少年则用对立违抗性障碍做为一种驱动力，以一种心理满足的方式来故意与权威对抗。

有数据统计表明，美国儿童及青少年中大约有5%的人表现出某种形式的对立违抗性障碍行为。儿童心理学家们发现对立违抗性障碍几乎总是与行为障碍如影随行，这表明在行为障碍和对立违抗性障碍之间存在极大的关联性。研究还表明青少年比儿童更可能表现出这种行为障碍，这也说明行为障碍是对立违抗性障碍的先兆。但是也有大量证据表明无论是行为障碍还是对立违抗性障碍都存在着一些诱发因素，比如母亲在怀孕期间的吸烟行为。有资料显示：每日吸烟超过半包的孕期女性比那些孕期不吸烟的女性极有可能会生出患有行为障碍的孩子。

与行为障碍相似，那些患有对立违抗性障碍的人表现出下列征状：

① 经常发脾气；

② 经常与成年人发生争执；

③ 经常主动挑衅或拒绝服从成年人的要求或规定；

④ 经常故意激怒别人；

⑤ 经常因为自己的错误或不当行为而责备旁人；

⑥ 经常情绪激动或容易被旁人激怒；

⑦ 经常生气和恼怒；

⑧ 经常心存伤害和报复心理。

再者，那些从事此项研究的人强烈提示，一旦一名儿童或青少年被诊断为患有对立违抗性障碍，那么，就要对其进行心理异常的检查。如果该儿童的对立违抗性障碍没有获得及时诊治，无疑，在这名儿童身上将会出现其他的心理障碍，也必将导致其发展成同时患有多种行为障碍。Kuhne等的研究显示，多达40%患有对立违抗性障碍的青少年有某种形式的严重行为问题，即注意力缺陷多动障碍。

4 注意力缺陷多动障碍（ADHD）

注意力缺陷多动障碍在媒体上受到了显著关注，但对于注意力缺陷多动障碍的大量关注掩盖了行为障碍和对立违抗性障碍的存在，这样一来，非常有可能导致治疗专家和家长们努力治疗的是他们孩子的表征，而没有找到导致患病的诱因。众所周知，注意力缺陷多动障碍常常伴随有行为障碍和对立违抗性障碍的出现。那么，行为障碍和对立违抗性障碍被耽搁的时间越长，该儿童患上注意力缺陷多动障碍的可能性就会大大地增加。

《美国治疗注意力缺陷多动障碍DSM-IV诊断标准（2000）》提示人们：注意力缺陷多动障碍有多种表现形式，一般都可以从其呈现的不同寻常的行为而识别出来。这些行为可以是攻击行为、注意力不集中、或多动行为。在某个儿童身上所呈现出的注意力缺陷多动障碍主要取决于他的行为举止以及对他行为的限制程度。《美国治疗注意力缺陷多动障碍DSM-IV诊断标准》罗列出了注意力缺陷多动障碍的四个分类，它们是：

① 注意力缺陷多动障碍，注意力不集中型——在过去的六个月中满足注意力不集中标准；

② 注意力缺陷多动障碍，多动-冲动型——在过去的六个月中满足多动-冲动标准；

③ 注意力缺陷多动障碍，组合型——在过去的六个月中满足上述两者；

④ 注意力缺陷多动障碍，未特殊说明型——明显的注意力缺乏或多动-强迫表现不满足ADHD范畴。

研究人员对注意力缺陷多动障碍的研究非常感兴趣。从前，人们普遍认为患有注意力缺陷多动障碍的人通常是青少年居多。这表明注意力缺陷多动障碍不是一种即发型行为问题，而是基于各种心理问题，如行为障碍和对立违抗性障碍一直被忽视所导致的行为问题。也就是说在注意力缺陷多动障碍这一行为问题在孩童时出现的初期没能获得及时干预的情况下，一直持续发展到青少年时期的行为问题。但很明显，因为这种疾病在年轻人的身上表现更为突出，说明其或是由于注意力缺陷多动障碍最初发作时没能获得精准的预判，或是由于这种疾病是由其他因素导致而成。诸多研究人员归纳的结论为：注意力缺陷多动障碍越迟发作，就越表明各种社会因素如电脑游戏和电视，与ADHD之间有着密不可分的因果关系。

5 行为障碍对儿童和青少年的影响及解决方法

无论儿童还是青少年，心理障碍的逐步发展，如行为障碍、对立违抗性障碍和注意力缺陷多动障碍，都表明学校和家庭在对待这些孩子的教育方式方法上存在缺失。尽管研究人员到目前为止还没有下最后的定论，但仍然可以断定，如果行为障碍在初发期没能获得及时干预，将很有可能发展成其他行为障碍。

这类行为障碍最明确的迹象之一是其对儿童在学校的表现以及在其社会行为的影响。资料表明密切关注孩子的成长而且积极采取行动的家长是不会允许任何一种行为障碍持续发展的。早期的行为问题表现形式为行为障碍，这种行为问题通常会被家长捕捉到。较为恶劣的情况是校方将此孩童的问题转达给家长，希望家长引起足够的重视。然而令人咋舌的是，更多的情况是，行为障碍和对立违抗性障碍常常被忽略，而导致其一直延续到青少年时期。

就行为障碍和对立违抗性障碍，以及青少年的注意力缺陷多动障碍而言，人们呼吁教育系统应该注重分析学生的行为举止，并且还要评估他们是否具有行为问题的表征。学校咨询师捕捉学生行为问题的话题似乎已是老生常谈：通常人们普遍认为教育系统应该为学生的行为负责，因为那是孩童和青少年所处的环境，在此环境中，他们会接触到某种形式的校园暴力。可以通过很多方式，学校应该召集校方咨询师来处理、讨论这个学生的家教问题。非常明显，在诸如行为障碍这类行为问题，对孩子密切关注的家长应该具有识别这些行为问题的能力。更为重要的是，家长应该充分了解他们的孩子，以便及时捕捉孩子的这些严重的行为问题。很多对学校持批评态度的人士认为最大的失败是人们普遍认为学校系统应该为捕捉家庭教育问题的疏忽而负责任。然而，在现代教育体制的实际操作中，对于谁应该为学童和青少年的行为问题负责任这个问题的争论的结果是开放式的。校方咨询师应该承担测评学童或者青少年在学校的表现的角色。

学校心理专家不必对那些他们认为可能有严重行为障碍的学生的治疗负责。学校心理专家要提供学生的行为报告，并将寻求治疗和实施方案的建议提交给学校董事会和学生家长。学生的行为报告应该包含由《美国治疗注意力缺陷多动障碍 DSM-IV 诊断标准》提出的指南，还应该包括学校心理专家针对此学生行为问题的个人意见。这份报告应送交专业的心理专家或精神病专家。之后该学生和家长将与学校心理专家、职业第三方咨询师和校方一起共同制定方案来指导学生获得期望的行为。

就已经证实行之有效的规范行为问题的治疗方案而言，针对某一特定行为问题，治疗方法是多种多样的。推荐给家长的实际治疗方式必须根据学生的年龄以及其行为问题的严重性而制定的。通常治疗的目的是促进学生接受社会行为标准。使用药物来治疗注意力缺陷多动障碍目前已经是很普遍的方法。尽管治疗这些行为问题有诸多的方式方法可选，家长仍需意识到解决行为问题没有什么简易的方法，只有不间断的关注才能逐步减少该学生的不好的行为举止。孩子越大，这些不好的行为问题就会也根深蒂固，因此非常有必要有针对性地将这些问题解决，才不致其将这些行为问题带到成年时期。

参考文献

[1] American Psychiatric Association. Diagnostic and Statistical Manual of Mental Disorders [M]. Washington, DC: Author, 2000.

[2] CQS. Prenatal smoking linked to conduct disorder in boys [EB/OL]. http://www.cqs.com/smokaspd.htm.

[3] DEGRANDPRE R. Ritalin nation [M]. New York: W. W. Norton & Company, 1999.

[4] HOZA B, et al. Academic task persistence of normally achieving ADHS and control boys: performance, self evaluations, and attributions [J]. Consulting and Clinical Psychology, 2001, 69 (2).

[5] KUHNE M, et al. Impact of co-morbid oppositional or conduct problems on attention-deficit hyperactivity disorder[J]. Acad Child Adolesc Psychiatry, 1997, 36(12).

[6] LEFEVER G B, et al. The extent of drug therapy for attention deficit-hyperactivity disorder among children in public schools[J]. Am J. of Public Health, 1999, 89.

[7] RENAULD J, BIRMAHER B, et al. Suicide in adolescents with disruptive disorders [J]. J. Am. Child Adolesc. Psychiatry, 1999, 38(7).

[8] SHORT R J, SHAPIRO S K. Conduct disorder: a framework for understanding and intervention in schools and communities[J]. School Psychology Review, 1993, 22(3).

从政府工作报告看政府话语策略
——以所有制经济为例

刘红艳　李婧暄　杨　凯

摘　要：我国国有企业改革从1978年至今已经走过了三十多年的历程，经历了“初步探索”“制度创新”和“纵深推进”三个改革阶段，取得了巨大成就。在国企改革进程中，政府作用不可小觑。本研究以我国1954年至2015年（期间有16年未召开全国人民代表大会）的政府工作报告微型语料库为研究对象，探究“所有制经济”在国企改革大环境下的相关搭配词使用情况及话语特征，从而为分析政府对所有制改革及国企改革的话语使用策略及态度奠定基础。

关键词：语料库；政府工作报告；所有制经济；国企改革；政府话语使用策略

1 引言

近年来，国内学者多选取一年或多年政府工作报告进行不同领域的研

项目/基金：本论文是北京工商大学国有资产管理协同创新中心项目“基于语料库的国有企业组织话语研究”(批准号:GZ20131301)，和2014年度北京工商大学研究生创新基金项目“国有企业变革与组织话语研究”的部分成果。

作者简介：刘红艳，女，山西太原人，北京工商大学外国语学院教授，硕士生导师。李婧暄，女，北京人，北京工商大学外国语学院2013级国际法商英语专业研究生。杨凯，女，河北人，北京工商大学商学院2012级本科生。

究，将政府报告视作能传达政府意愿的重要工具而给予高度重视。政府工作报告由各级政府的办公机构拟稿，如国务院办公厅、省（自治区、直辖市）政府办公厅、市政府办公厅等，交由政府领导审阅后，正式在“两会”上由政府正职领导人宣读，具有权威性高的特点。经文献阅读发现，对于政府报告的研究，大多集中在翻译领域及语言与社会的辩证关系等，而对政府自身对于体制改革发挥的作用或者其如何影响制度改革、经济发展以及企业改革的研究相对匮乏。本研究基于自建的政府工作报告语料库，分析国企改革进程中与所有制经济相关的搭配词，分析政府在影响所有制经济的发展以及国企改革进程所使用的话语特点，话语正是反映政府态度的有效工具，因此该研究具有实际意义。

2 文献回顾

所有制改革对所有制经济以及国企改革产生的影响不言而喻。对于我国所有制改革的问题，学者们从不同方面作过研究。李敏华发表过对深化国企改革与我国所有制两者关系的看法，认为我国国企改革能否导致私有化的这个思想疑虑决定着改革能否深化。因此需要深化对国企改革与我国所有制关系的认识。李敏华从国企产权结构调整看国企改革与所有制关系时指出传统单一的公有制不能形成真正的市场主体，市场配置资源功能不能有效地发挥，导致国民经济不能持续稳定增长。并得出结论说国企股份制、出售等项改革，符合我国所有制并存要求，国企大规模股份制改革亦不会动摇“以公有制为主体”的基本经济制度。就产权结构改革而言，所有制为国企改革指明了方向；国企改革是所有制的体现而不是冲击。

在《国有企业混合所有制改革探讨》一文中，于冰提到，国有企业大力发展多种资本相互融合的混合所有制经济，有助于改善国有企业的产权结构，建立规范的企业制度，激发组织活力，以及优化资源配置等众多裨益。这种观点正与李敏华所提到的所有制为国企改革指明方向相呼应。秦晓也曾在其文章里提到了要推进国企“混合所有制”的必要性。可见所有制改革是国企改革的内在需求。

对于所有制经济方面的研究，如混合所有制经济的必要性，学者们有所涉及。方玉梅在《公有制与非公有制经济关系特点研究》一文中指出，公有制经济与非公有制经济相互补充、相互借鉴、相互合作、相互竞争，且统一于社会主义现代化建设进程中。杨娟提到，国企改革中发展混合所有制经济的对策时引用了十八届三中全会所提到的“集体资本、国有资本以及非公有资本等都是基本经济制度的重要实现形式”，并表明坚持和发展混合所有制经济是为进一步搞活经济、应对日益激烈的国内外竞争态势的大势所趋。

3 语料收集与统计

为了客观分析建国以来国企改革背景下所有制经济的发展历程，本研究搜集整理了1954年至2015年共47年的政府工作报告（期间有16年未召开全国人民代表大会）。根据经济体制改革和国有企业改革的阶段，语料可分为4个阶段：1954~1978年，1979~1992年，1993~2003年，2004~2015年。因所有制经济的发展离不开所有制改革的大背景，所以本研究首先对各类所有制进行检索，以对各类所有制这些年在政府报告中出现的情况有个大致了解。运用Powerconc软件，对各类所有制分别进行检索统计出频数如表1所示。

表1　各类所有制在政府工作报告中出现的频数及年份

所有制类型	累计频数	出现年份或时间段
公有制	87	1957，1978，1981，1982，1986~1990，1992，1993，1996~2015
非公有制	47	1996，1998~2000，2003~2015
全民所有制	40	1955，1959，1960，1964，1978~1980，1982，1985~1993
集体所有制	20	1955，1959，1960，1964，1979~1983，1991，1993
各类所有制	13	2002~2004，2006，2012，2014，2015
多种所有制	11	1986，1991，1998，2002，2003，2005，2009~2012
私有制	7	1955，1957，1981，1983
混合所有制	4	2002，2003，2014，2015

续表

所有制类型	累计频数	出现年份或时间段
三级所有制	3	1960
城镇集体所有制	2	1980，1983
个体所有制	2	1959
公社所有制	2	1960
社会主义集体所有制	2	1959
资本家所有制	2	1955
城乡集体所有制	1	1981
多种形式的所有制	1	1988
非全民所有制	1	1989
其他所有制	1	1998
社会主义的集体所有制	1	1959
社基本所有制	1	1960
生产队的所有制	1	1960
生产资料的集体所有制	1	1959
生产资料私人所有制	1	1957
资本家的所有制	1	1955
资产阶级所有制	1	1959

表1客观反映出1992年十四大提出的“公有制为主体，多种所有制经济共同发展”的我国基本经济制度。从数据统计可知，“公有制”累计出现87次，明显占据主导地位。而“非公有制”从1996年的政府工作报告才开始出现，累计出现47次，相比其他所有制类型出现的频数也相对较高。“全民所有制”“集体所有制”出现较频繁的初始年份与“公有制”类似，但从1993年之后就逐渐淡出政府报告提及范围了，可见1993年之后全民所有制和集体所有制不再是政府关注的重点了，其他所有制类型相继出现并凸显地位。这也可作为解释“非公有制”后来频繁出现的原因。

4 政府话语策略

基于不同类型的所有制经济在语料库中的频数及其出现的时间段，我们进一步关注与“所有制经济”相生相伴的搭配词，进而客观呈现其搭配特点。通过对这些所有制经济的搭配词的研究，探索政府话语特点，进一步观察政府在影响所有制经济发展这一国企改革大背景的过程中持何种态度以及怎样发挥作用。

为便于观察分析，笔者首先将索引词及相应搭配词进行整理，以不同类型的所有制经济为索引词进行搜索，整理出与之相关的搭配词，并且对这些动词表达出现的频数以及时间段作出统计。整个表格记录了对“多种所有制经济”“非公有制经济”“个体经济”“混合所有制经济”“集体所有制经济”“公有制经济”等12种经济类型的搜索结果。

统计结果显示，非公有制经济的搭配词种类最多，包括“鼓励”“支持”“鼓励和引导”“鼓励、支持和引导”等19种，且出现的时间段主要集中在2004~2015年，也有个别出现在1993~2003年。这清楚地反映出我国政府对非公有制经济越来越重视的趋势，从宏观层面不断鼓励、支持和引导非公有制经济的发展，完善并落实促进非公有制经济发展的各项政策措施，微观层面各级政府也通过清理和修订限制非公有制经济发展的法规和政策配合国家政府工作。不管是从宏观还是微观上看，政府都在对非公有制经济的发展起到推动作用并严格落实已制定的政策。

对应表1来看，除了“非公有制”出现最频繁外，“全民所有制”“集体所有制”相对于其他所有制类型也出现较多，上述统计结果与表1显示结果并不对等。“集体所有制经济”的搭配词以“大力发展”的表达形式在1980年出现过一次，以“积极发展”的表达形式出现在1981年的政府报告中，且并未搜索出“全民所有制经济”的相关搭配词。由此可见对于集体所有制经济的发展，尽管政府也强调要大力发展，可重视程度已不再加大，这个结果也与表1反映出的1993年以后“全民所有制”“集体所有制”出现的频数下降相呼应。

5 结语

本研究从一定程度上客观反映了所有制经济发展过程中政府所使用的话语特征，为进一步研究政府如何推动国企改革的进程起到铺垫作用。不可否认，本研究也存在不可避免的局限性和困难。例如无法做到筛选搭配词时毫无遗漏，因为数据统计软件只能根据研究者有针对性的搜索得到对应的搜索结果，但具体选取哪些数据进行研究，还需要研究者基于对语料的仔细观察和大量文献回顾做出客观选择，此过程耗时很长且有一定局限性。此外，此领域研究相对匮乏，研究者可以借鉴的研究成果局限性大，但这也标志着该领域具有更广阔的研究空间，值得进一步研究探索。

参考文献

[1] 安格斯·麦迪森. 世界经济千年史[M]. 北京:北京大学出版社,2003.

[2] 方玉梅,袁小雪. 公有制与非公有制经济关系特点研究[J]. 学理论,2015(19).

[3] 郭毅,王兴,章迪诚,朱熹. “红头文件”何以以言行事?——中国国有企业改革文件研究(2000~2005)[J]. 管理世界,2010(12).

[4] 胡鞍钢,唐啸,鄢一龙. 中国经济体制改革十年(2003-2012):进展与评估[J]. 国家行政学院学报,2013(5).

[5] 黄速建. 中国国有企业混合所有制改革研究[J]. 经济管理,2014(7).

[6] 蒋珍莲. 中国高等教育改革与发展重心的历史变迁——基于政府工作报告的分析[J]. 高教论坛,2013(3).

[7] 康芒斯. 制度经济学[M].北京:商务印书馆,1997.

[8] 李敏华,仲伟良. 论深化我国国有企业改革的两个突破点——国企改革与所有制关系及其法制化的深化问题[J]. 学术交流,2004(6).

[9] 林春宇. 中国政府工作报告的话语分析——从高频词看中国政府工作的延续性与时代性[J].山西青年,2013(7).

[10] 彭庆. 从政府工作报告的文字表述看我国多边外交政策:1986~2005[J]. 外交评论:外交学院学报,2005(8).

[11] 钱毓芳,田海龙. 话语与中国社会变迁:以政府工作报告为例[J]. 外语与外语教学,2011(3).

[12] 宋志平. 我的企业观[M]. 北京:中信出版社,2014.

[13] 唐任伍,马骥. 中国经济改革30年[M]. 重庆:重庆大学出版社,2008.

[14] 吴敬琏. 当代中国经济改革[M]. 上海:远东出版社,2004.

[15] 项启源,何干强. 科学理解和积极发展混合所有制经济——关于改革和加强国有企业的对话[J]. 马克思主义研究,2014(7).
[16] 于冰. 国有企业混合所有制改革探讨[J]. 财经界,2015(12).
[17] 杨明文. 混合所有制经济发展与新一轮国企改革[J]. 人民论坛,2014(26).
[18] 邹东涛,欧阳日辉. 中国所有制改革30年[M]. 北京:社会科学文献出版社,2008.

The Poor Educational Quality in Rural Schools

艾丽娜

摘　要：中国有全世界最庞大的农村教育系统，农村教育质量差是大家对中国农村教育的普遍观点。作者分析了农村教育发展的障碍，批判了“考试分数决定一切”的教育评价系统，并探索在农村实行切实可行的教育评价系统。

关键词：restriction；backwash effects；assessment

1 Introduction

China has the largest rural education system in the world. By the end of 2014, there were 94 510 651 primary school students, and about 43 846 300 enrolled at secondary level. In this paper, the author will analyze educational quality in rural schools, which is a main theme in rural education. Since people equate examination results to educational quality, the backwash effects of examinations on rural children are also discussed. Finally, the restrictions on educational quality are analyzed. It is concluded that educational quality depends on the relationship of teaching and learning and its supporting context.

Even though the term *educational quality* has not been defined precisely, it is a topic of common concern. All countries are engaged in improving educational quality. The intrinsic disparity between urban and rural areas is apparent in China.

作者简介：艾丽娜，辽宁沈阳人，英国约克大学硕士研究生毕业，北京工商大学外国语学院讲师，研究方向为比较教育。

Furthermore, China has pursed a policy of decentralization since 1980s. Many responsibilities and rights have shifted from central government to provinces, cities and local governments. Therefore the input and processes of education are poor in economic backward areas, especially in rural areas. It is not in doubt that the output and outcomes of schooling are poor. Inevitably, the educational standards of poor areas fall behind richer areas. In 1997, the Asian Development Bank conducted a study in eight countries (Indonesia, Kyrgyz, Nepal, Pakistan, Philippines, Papua New Guinea, China and Vietnam) to evaluate the trends and issues in education. The Chinese situation was summarized as too much emphasis on examinations, heavy teaching schedule of teachers, low salaries of teachers, and inadequate supply of teaching materials. Of course, this conclusion reflects the trends and issues in the whole country. There are local characteristics in each different research locality.

Some writers concentrate on the analysis of educational quality. In Chapman and Adams' view, educational quality examined in context may refer to input (number of teachers, amount of teacher training and number of textbooks), processes (amount of direct instructional time, lecture versus other means of presentation), output (test scores) and outcomes (ability to perform well in subsequent employment). In brief, educational quality=input + processes + output + outcomes.

2 The Restriction on Educational Quality in Rural Schools

Firstly, the curriculum issues are most prominent in efforts to improve educational quality. There is a gap between the National Curriculum and the daily life of rural children. Pupils cannot understand curriculum contents, but they have to memorize them mechanically under the examination-oriented education. In this circumstance, teachers are required to relate academic knowledge with pupil's rural life in order to achieve good results. Taylor and Mulhall argue that rural-oriented teaching methods have to be introduced into rural schools. They provide a new method: linking the formal school curriculum with the life experience of pupils. However, the new method does not suit all subjects and teachers. On one hand, in some subjects it is difficult to carry out relevant teaching. For example, it is impossible for English teachers to relate *cheese* and *butter* with familiar things for rural children (unlike in Britain, cheese and butter are not consumed in rural China). On the other hand, some teachers do not bother to use this method since the teaching is for examinations. Under the two circumstances, the educational quality is doomed to be poor.

Chapman and Adams argue that improving national testing systems is an important strategy to improve educational quality. They argue that tests do not assess some important areas of student growth. The content and type of items on national examinations do not change quickly. Therefore introduction of new materials or teaching practices in the schools can throw instruction out of alignment with these tests, which is to the disadvantage of the students.

Secondly, students having no interest in study are a bottleneck in improving educational quality. Teachers complained that some students have no interest in study, which demoralizes the teachers.

Finally, there is the issue of rural traditional culture and family environment. The majority of teachers mentioned that rural social environment and family influences are the origins of demotivation and poor educational quality. Peasants are the backbone of rural areas. They live on land. Most rural areas are remote and economic backward areas in China, which leads to conservative views. They have resisted new issues over several thousand years, and their way of life is little changed. Each year, peasants are engaged in farming for only two months, so they are idle for long periods. Occasionally they do casual or part-time jobs. This kind of cultural atmosphere in rural areas influences the children's thoughts.

There is no doubt that families influence pupils directly. Most of the parents in rural areas received a five-year schooling under the restriction of various conditions. During their lives, they gradually feel the importance of knowledge. Therefore all the parents expect their children to learn much knowledge. It seems there is a strong belief towards pursuing knowledge in their minds, but they have no activities to support the belief. Most parents have never been to school or spoken to teachers to inquire into their children's study. Similarly teachers rarely go to visit families or call parents (the telephone fee is paid by teachers). The majority of parents are illiterate, so they do not know how to educate children. They are not willing to co-operate with teachers.

Parental involvement in schooling has become an emerging research agenda. It has been defined as any interaction between a parent and child that may contribute to the child's development or direct parent participation with a child's school in the interest of the child's. Student success is the basic aim in involving parents in education. Parental involvement stems from the 1960s in some developed countries, such as England and Wales, United States, Australia and New Zealand. Some governments fund programs to encourage parents to become involved in schooling.

In China, parental involvement is not a popular research topic. Parents are not given the right to be involved in daily issues in schools. The educational system in China is different from that in other countries, such as the United Kingdom or United States. The school management is centralized, and the head teacher is in charge of a school. Especially, since the decentralization policy in the 1980s, the responsibilities and rights are shifted from central to local schools. The head teacher takes responsibilities for all the issues in the school. Therefore parents are not strong enough to form a force to be involved in school. Moreover, rural parents have no awareness of how to participate in school activities; they think it is the responsibility of school to educate their children.

In rural areas, lack of transfer of information between school and home is an important reason leading to demotivation and poor student achievements.

3 The Backwash Effects of Examinations

In China, the educational emphasis is still laid on selection, which is induced by competition to climb the education ladder. Dore argues that, in developing countries where college entrance examinations act as gatekeepers to a relatively tiny number of privileged civil service and modern-sector urban jobs, the entire education system inevitably becomes oriented to the examinations. The result is rote learning of scholastic material that is of little intrinsic value even to those few who pass the examinations and worth even less to the great majority who do not. A compulsive focus on college examinations stifles real learning and particularly devalues the practical application of knowledge, including that pertinent to rural development. Despite the meritocratic ideas of equal access and social mobility that underpin examination-governed education hierarchies, the rural majority are typically excluded or eliminated in the early stages of the competition. There have been few opportunities to actually evaluate the effectiveness of rural-oriented education.

Under the influence of examination-oriented education, the schools intent to promote as many pupils as possible into higher schools, so students from very early years of study see education as the memorization of facts in order to pass classroom tests that are preparations for the all important selection examinations for higher-level schools. A selection system through exams has been popular for more than 2000 years in China, so the idea of learning for examinations is firmly rooted in pupils and teachers' minds. Sometimes, teaching and testing are separate activities. Teaching is the responsibility of the teacher, whereas testing is the responsibility of the testing expert. The demand for objectivity and fairness in testing, and a high level of standardization where important decisions are to be based on test scores stimulate these experts. The teacher concentrates on researching examination questions, examination emphasis and criteria for marking. The teaching emphasis is determined by examination. It is not surprising that examinations dominate the curriculum, restrict teachers' pedagogy, and hinder students' abilities. Dore argues that: all learning is ritualized, that curiosity is devalued, that no one is allowed to stray from the syllabus, that no one inquires about the usefulness, the relevance, or the interestingness of what is learned. Passing exams has become the direct goal and the most important task. Confronted with this issue, teachers have no choice but to obey the exams.

Under the command of exams, those subjects which are less crucial to examination success are devalued, even abandoned. The majority of students think non-examination subjects are useless. Teachers who teach non-examination subjects feel no pressure.

4 Assessment Culture

In view of the backwash effects of examination on teaching and learning, some assessment experts considered introducing new measures to improve learning. They call this "assessment culture". They argue that in the traditional testing culture, teaching and testing are separate activities. The assessment culture emphasizes the integration of teaching and assessment. Students' roles change from being marked by teachers to self-evaluation. In the assessment culture, the teacher is not a person who transfers knowledge, but a mentor who provides opportunities for learners to use the knowledge and skills they already posses in order to understand new topics. Some authors claim that sound assessment can improve teaching.

It has to be paid attention that the new methods provided by assessment specialists are western-oriented. They cannot be transplanted to Chinese context. Assessment and selection have always been central issues in Chinese educational development. To reform the examination-oriented educational system might lead to confrontations with some obstacles in China. Firstly, the Confucian education tradition and examinations have existed for more than 2000 years in China. To select an elite through examinations has deep roots in people's minds. It is not easy to abandon the tradition. Secondly, according to the detailed Chinese situation, job opportunities are very few compared with the large population. No better method to compete in the society except for examination has been devised. Thirdly, China has eliminated examinations during the Cultural Revolution (1966~1976). People still flutter with fear about the disastrous effect resulting from it. Even though there is no attempt to reform the examination-oriented education, some Chinese exam specialists try to avoid the backwash effect of examinations. For instance, examination contents are inclined to be more flexible than before. Many questions aim to examine the students' understanding ability instead of memorizing ability. On the whole, there is a long way to go to reform the examination system in China.

5 Conclusion

The discussion in this paper articulates that educational quality is the result of the relationship of teaching and learning and the relevant supporting context. The factors influencing quality in rural schools are analyzed in this paper. From the education itself, the curriculum and examination separate from reality, which leads students to lose interest in study. Some other external factors, such as the low salaries of teachers, the drain on excellent students and teachers, rural social and family environment, also hinder educational development in rural schools. The backwash effects of examination on rural pupils are revealed in this paper. Finally, in concluding this paper I briefly explore the new assessment methods in Chinese contexts.

Bibliography

[1] China statistical yearbook 2014[EB/OL]. http: // www.stats.gov.cn.

[2] CHAPMAN D W, ADAMS D. The quality of education in Asia: the perennial prioritye[J]. International Journal of Educational Research, 1998, 29: 643-665.

[3] TAYLOR P, MULHALL A. Linking learning environments through agricultural experience [J]. International Journal of Educational Development, 2001, 21: 135-148.

[4] DIMMOCK C, O'DONOGHUE T A, ROBB A S. Parental involvement in schooling: an emerging research agenda[J]. Compare, 1996, 26(1): 5-20.

[5] FILIP J R C, MCDOWELL L. Assessment as a tool for learning[J]. Studies in Educational Evaluation, 1997, 23(4): 279-298.

浅谈思辨思维能力的概念与意义

范燕燕

摘　要：思辨思维是一种审慎的思维方式。这个概念并非西方文化的“专利品”，但对于开展大规模的思维训练的倡导和实施，西方人做的有可借鉴之处。倡导并培养思辨思维能力，有利于开拓更有意义的人生和建设更加民主和公正的社会环境。

关键词：思辨思维；思维训练；民主公正

1 什么是思辨思维能力

思辨，顾名思义，思是进行思考，辨，是两个罪人持刀争执，需要裁断。辨，还有“判别”“区分”和“辨别”之意。“critical thinking”的概念，开始流行于美国20世纪中叶。中国有人将之翻译为“批判思维”。字典对于“critical”的解释，除了“批判”，还有“审慎”“有判断力的”和“公正的”等解释。因此，有专家认为将其译为“审慎思维”或“思辨思维”更为妥帖。美国教授和大学管理者彼得·法乔恩（Peter Facione）出版的一本《批判性思维：思考让你永远年轻》，通俗易懂，可以帮助人理解什么是critical thinking。

思辨思维对于中国人其实并不是全新的概念。中国传统文化典籍《礼记·中庸》第十九章中对于这样的思维方式早有所云：“博学之，审问之，慎思之，明辨之，笃行之。”这里说的是为学的几个层次。这简短的论述，

作者简介：范燕燕，北京工商大学外国语学院讲师，研究方向为教学法和跨文化交流。

与西方的“critical thinking”的概念说的是一回事。而且更可贵的是，博学这种思维方法的基础，被放在了首位。有研究表明，在大脑机能正常的情况下，人的判断能力随着年龄和阅历的增长而增长。“博学”的前提是好奇心和对于世界的包容心。缺少了包容，也就失去了兴趣，因此，一个博学的人应该是具有开放胸襟的人，也就是具备英文里提到的“open-mindedness”。可见，一种思维方式的养成，首先是以一种心态作为基础。“审问”，就是质疑。好奇心启动思维功能，然后进行观察和分析。第四阶段的“慎思”，要辨别知识是否符合事实真相，适用性如何。不进行审慎的思考，博学来的知识就会是些半成品或废品，甚至危险品，造成所知障。“笃行”是为学的最后阶段。既然学有所得，就要努力实践，使所学到的知识有所落实，做到“知行合一”。“笃”就是坚持不懈和一心一意。只有通过理智思考做出的决定，才可以确定明确的目标，发挥人的坚定意志力，成就该做的事。

中西文化贯通的学者胡适先生提出过一个口号：“大胆假设，小心求证。”这也与思辨思维的概念有关。虽然对此提法褒贬不一，然而“大胆假设”代表了一种打破旧有观念的束缚的魄力。“小心求证”，要求人们不能停留在假设或模糊的思想上。要用辩证思维的方法，进行证明其可行性。这个口号一方面反映了求新精神与求实态度的矛盾，另一方面也是一种结合，为人们解决问题提出了一种新的思路。

对于“critical thinking”的概念定义，众说莫一，然而对于概念所包含的某些内容，以及理想的具有思辨思维能力的人的特征，专家已经达成共识。美国研究思辨思维能力的专家皮特恩·法喜奥尼在他的《思辨思维的内涵与意义》一文中对这种共识进行了总结。思辨思维是借助解释、分析、评估和推断等手段，进行有目的和自我监管的判断，还包括通过诸如对证据性的、概念性的、方法性的、标准性的或者语境的上下文关系方面考虑的解释来达成。思辨思维是探究问题的必要工具，是教育领域里一股自由的力量，也是个人生活和社会生活的动力源泉。思辨思维虽然不能等同于完全的思维模式（good thinking），但它是一种具有普遍用途的，可以自我纠偏的人类现象。一个理想的具有思辨能力的人一般习惯于问询和质疑，知识储备丰富，相信理性思维，思想开明，灵活变通，在评估中主持公正原则，面对个人偏见有诚实的态度，判断时态度谨慎，乐于反复思考，对问题有清醒的认识，对复杂事务条理清晰，孜孜不倦求索相关信息，选择评价标准理智，专注于探究，坚定不移追求在主观与客观条件允许下的精确结果。因此，培养思辨思维能力强的人意味着朝着这个方向努力。这个教育过程要把发展技能和培养那些能够产生有价值的洞察力素质的人，以及利于营造理性的和民主社会的素质的人的目标结合起来。

美国教育家本杰明·布鲁姆把教育目标分为：知识—理解—应用—分析—综合—评价六大类型。洛林安德森和大卫克拉斯沃尔把以上目标分类进行修改，把认知技能分为记忆—理解—应用—分析—评价—创造，由此形成了布鲁姆安德森认知能力模型，这一教育目标分类，为西方国家学校课程设置和教学目标提供了科学依据，也是培养学生思辨思维的可以参照的一种模型。现在我国在制定教学大纲的时候也参照此模型。

2 思辨思维能力培养的现实意义

虽然思辨思维在中国文化中并不是全新的概念，但在如何培养这种思维方式方面，没有一个完整的体系和方法，更没有深入人心。西方教育对此在研究与实践方面做得更好。培养思辨思维已经成为西方大学教育的一种使命。众所周知，哈佛和剑桥等世界名校在教育理念上倡导探索和思辨能力的培养，鼓励学生质疑。美国研究思辨思维能力的专家皮特恩·法喜奥尼在《思辨思维的内涵与意义》一文中引用了“加里福尼亚州思辨思维技能测试”研究统计数字，表明思辨思维能力与学生取得的JPA数值成正比关系，同时也证明，这种思维方式是可以学习的。进一步支持这种假设的是，思辨能力与阅读理解能力成正比。从专家对教育方面的见解中也可窥见西方国家对于培养思维能力的重视。美国密歇根州立大学哲学博士，作为著名教授和大学管理者，他提出：教育就是要让学生学会思考。如果说大学教育最重要的是素质教育，那么在智力范围的素质就是一种思维能力，这种能力无论在那个领域和位置，处理什么样的问题，都可以被转换。由此可见，学校对学生最有用的教育是一种思维能力的培养。

显然，思辨思维能力的培养的价值不仅仅在于学生取得更好的学习成绩。学校是培养走向社会的人才的加工厂，这些人才的素质，决定社会的人文状况。思维训练似乎更依赖于文科教育。文科在英文里是“liberal education”，这里“liberal”的解放之意，是否可以理解为从教授灌输的思想束缚中求得自由思考的能力呢？培养思辨的精神并不仅仅是一种达到目的的手段，而是目的一部分。一个人的学历无论有多高，如果缺乏了思辨思维的能力和精神，不足以被认为是受过人文教育的人。从这个意义上来讲，思辨思维的培养关系到是否可以营造一个民主和公正的社会，牵扯到一个国家的利益。北京外国语大学孙有中校长在2015年8月举办的《外语教学思辨思维能力培养研修班》的开幕讲话中提到：国家制度的改革和国民素质的提高应该是并行的。培养思辨思维能力就是在培养具有健全心智的公民。大学对于思维能力的训练被提到了一个国家政治的高度。

随着国内英语教育改革的深入，对于培养学生思辨思维能力的要求已经被写入教学大纲，因此应该引起教师和学生的重视。在2008年公布的《普通高中英语教学标准（实验）》和2007年公布的《大学英语课程教学要求》中都明确指出了对高中生和大学生英语“分析”“综合”“评价”和“创新能力”的培养的教育目标。在《高等学校外语专业本科教学质量国家标准》里，把培养“思辨能力”“研究能力”和“创新能力”等，明确地列出。

因此，作为英语教育工作者，我们必须要开始重视培养学生的思辨思维能力了。

参考文献

[1] 牛津高阶英汉双解词典(第六版)[M]. 北京:商务印书馆,2004.

[2] PETER A F. Critical thinking: what it is and why it counts[J]. Insight Assessment,1992(2).

[3] 徐苏. 高考英语改革与师范院校英语专业课程设置的思考[J]. 延边教育学院学报,2014(8).

体裁分析在大学英语教学中的应用

周纳新

摘　要：随着体裁分析的发展，体裁（genre）概念和体裁分析（genre analysis）方法被越来越多地应用于语言教学领域，形成了称作“体裁教学法”（genre-based approaches）的课堂教学体系。在对其进行理论探索和教学实验阶段，国内外语界表现出极大的关注和广泛的重视。随着新形势下大学英语教学目标的提出，教学手段和内容也要相应进行调整。提高学生的文体学意识有利于他们在实际工作和社会交往中更加正确有效地使用英语，满足大纲的要求。因此在大学英语教学中科学地进行文体学知识渗透、运用体裁分析手段培养学生阅读和写作等技能具有十分重要的现实意义。

关键词：体裁分析；文体学；体裁教学法

1 概念及理论简介

对于语言使用价值的研究是近年来语言学研究的重点。文体学的新兴就是由此而生的。在不断的研究探讨中，其前景意义越来越被重视，研究成果的推广也逐渐进入到语言研究与教学的各个领域。在专业英语教学中，文体学的重要地位已确立，但是，在大学英语教学中，文体学知识的作用虽然已被广泛认识，在教学中仍处于探讨和试验阶段。体裁教学法就是把文体学概念和体裁分析方法自觉地运用到课堂教学中，围绕语篇的图式结构开展教学

作者简介：周纳新，中国文体学研究会会员，北京工商大学外国语学院讲师，主攻英语语言学、文体学研究。

和学习活动。它的实质在于利用体裁分析的成果使学生了解不同体裁语篇的结构和目的，并把这些知识应用到其语言学习方面，从而使他们认识到语篇不仅是一种语言建构（1inguistic constructs），还是一种社会的、意义建构（social，meaningful constructs），使他们不仅能够掌握语篇的图式结构，而且能够理解语篇的建构过程，从而帮助学生理解或创作属于某一体裁的语篇。通过教学实践中实验性的文体学知识讲解和运用，利用体裁分析的方法进行阅读和写作的训练，能够收到很好的教学效果。

2 体裁教学法的目的和意义

在大学英语教学中，往往有一些无意识的文体学知识传授，比如修辞手法的讲解、词语和结构正式或非正式用法的比较、口语表达和书面语体的区分等，但是这样单纯的讲解和举例很难让学生有具体感性的认识，在他们“输出”的语言表达中，很难看到文体一致有序、词句恰如其分的安排，而且经常是错误百出。原因是学生缺乏对语言表达效果的认识，即文体学所强调的：在适当的场合，对适当的对象，使用适当的语言，达到交际的最佳效果。语言的“正确性”并不只是语法方面的，还应该包括语言交流效果的“适合性”。我们决不可设想以一种文体表达各种各样的感情，应付各种不同的需要。要使学生清楚这一点，就要求我们在英语教学的过程中不仅仅训练学生听、说、读、写方面的能力，还要向他们讲授一些文体学方面的知识，使他们了解英语各种文体的语言特点，熟悉各类英语的功能，在正确使用英语语言的基础上，能用恰当的方式表达自己的思想。

怎样才能让学生体会到语言的正确表达应该胜过语法的正确使用呢？我们有很多问题需要解决，这些不是无关紧要的问题，是语言本质对于我们工作的要求，是我们对语言教学中更高目标的追求，也是我们必须认真想办法才能完成的任务。解决上述问题有很多方法值得尝试，都离不开对于不同体裁的文章进行综合的文体分析和比较。首先讲解文体学基本概念知识，然后选择有代表性的材料进行对不同文体的分析，提高学习者对这门外语的不同文体差别的敏感度，加强他们“语言适合性”的意识，使他们无论在交谈还是在书写中，都能有意识地选择最准确的词汇，运用恰当的修辞手段和其他语言表达形式，准确地传达思想，达到交流的最佳效果。

通常，人们对本民族的语言的文体差别往往是很敏感的。而在语言的运用方面，文体学强调必须适合特定场合的要求。在阅读或对话中，如读到或听到一个十分优美的句子，甚至一个文雅的词，本族语者都能立刻觉察得到。对于外语学习者来说，要做到这一点需要对目标语言和文化环境有长期的接触。

在英语教学中，我们强调培养学生的听、说、读、写方面的能力。虽然不少学生在这几个方面打下了较牢固的基础，但在实际运用中，在说话或写文章时他们往往不能恰当地表达自己的思想，甚至有时语言很不得体。例如谈生活琐事却用书卷气的正式词汇，写正式文或翻译公文却用过分的俚俗语。还有的学生在写文章或在与人交谈时，俗语、雅语不分地乱用一气，结果闹出不少笑话。实际在课堂上，无论有意识，还是无意识，我们已使文体学深入到了教学中。只是我们目前还没能使这门学科如同词汇、语音、语法、文学、翻译等课程那样引起足够的重视。无论怎样，我们不能否认外语教学离不开文体学。不仅如此，我们还要认识到，文体学在教学中所起的作用是多方面的。

2.1 培养学生在不同的语言环境中运用得体的表达方式及英语修辞手段

中国人学英语，往往只注重运用语言的“正确性”，而忽视其“适合性”。使用英语当然要做到准确无误，然而这并不意味着正确的英语都是得体的英语。在适当的场合使用适当的英语是文体学讨论的一个中心问题。让学生学习英语文体学知识，他们在英语语言的表达能力上和语言的修辞能力上都能得到提高。

2.2 提高学生对英语不同文体作品的分析、理解能力及欣赏水平

文体学能帮助学生了解英语各种文体的语言特点，熟悉并学会分析英语的功能及不同的表现风格，区别其中音调、韵律、句法、词汇、结构上的不同。通过对作品的分析，对语言各种功能的了解，使他们能深入、全面地理解其内容。在理解的基础上，提高学生对英文作品的欣赏是外语教学不可忽

视的一个环节。文体分析过程可以帮助学生了解语言的特征与艺术效果，了解作者是通过哪些语言手段增强了表达效果。也就是说，在阅读作品时，学生不仅要知道作者要说些什么，而且更重要的是要知道作者是怎么说的。从而使学生在比较和评论的过程中，提高对英文作品的鉴赏能力。

2.3 学习各种文化知识，提高文化修养

不同国家有着不同的文化背景。生态环境、物质文化环境、社会文化环境和宗教文化环境的不同，导致了语言文化的不尽相同，语言中的某些成分被约定俗成地赋予一定的文体色彩。学生只有了解这些语言中的文体功能才能理解其文化含义。通过文化背景知识的学习和掌握，学生对英语社会有了较深的了解，从而知识结构发生质和量的变化，文化素质也随之大大地得到提高。

2.4 激发学生的学习热情

文体课既是一门重要的理论课，又是一门能帮助学生学好英语的实践课。通过对英语各种文体的了解，学生们可根据不同的交际方式、内容、对象和场合去选择适当的言语风格，实现交际的目的。成功的交际增添了他们学习英语的信心，激发了学习英语的积极性。

3 体裁教学法的实践过程

3.1 教材的分析和比较

大学英语的教材选编注重文章主题的丰富性和体裁多样性，话题涉及日常的生活、学习和社会经济、历史文化、科技发展等深层问题。课文多选自近年出版的英美报刊书籍，其中不乏经典名篇和上佳时文，文章的风格或睿智幽默，或严肃尖锐。在学习语言技能的同时，学生也开阔了视野、丰富了认识、提高了对英语的鉴赏力。教师在讲解课文的同时，需要注意将不同文体的材料进行分析和欣赏，并将分析结果进行比较，找出不同文章、各类文体最突出的一些特征，即某一种体裁的原型特征（prototypical features），并将不同文体的原型特征进行对比，分析它们在词汇、句法、语义、语境层面

的不同。也就是利用文体分析的过程来进一步了解课文的语言，使得正确恰当的语言表达深入人心，从学习中鉴赏语言，通过鉴赏来提高和巩固认识，提高学习目标，丰富学习活动形式，提高学习的热情和兴趣。

3.2 技能的应用和训练

为了不断加深学生对文体理论的认识，更熟练地掌握文体规律，必须对学生进行有意识、有目的的语言操练。操练的形式是多种多样的，而且应该包括听、说、读、写各项技能全方位的语言实践训练。比如在进行课程要求的阅读、写作和听、说练习时，应该补充说明所涉及语言材料所处的语境。在明确了语言环境和对象以及表达形式的情况下，考查学生选择语言（语素）、进行写作或对话的能力。

在做翻译练习时，将目的语和本族语中同一语体进行对照，在该语体基本特征的指导下，用对本族语的准确把握来带动目的语水平的提高。在阅读练习中，注重让学生把不同文体的文章，尤其是正式与非正式文体，在语言特征上进行分析、对比。为了培养学生对不同文体的敏感性和洞察力，教师还可以把几种不同文体的例句混合在一起，让学生选择和辨认。通过课堂讨论，学生最终会认识到文章的不同词汇和句法等文体特征，以及这些特征如何表达了不同的语言效果。

4 总结

实际上，无论我们采取哪些方法提高学生的文体认识，其过程都是我们正常语言教学中的自然活动，不会增加我们讲课的负担，相反这一目的的加入会令我们的教学手段更加生动有趣，使学生的学习兴趣更加浓厚，学习效果更是不言而喻。但是我们必须清楚，“体裁教学法”即文体分析教学法，在课堂教学中的应用仍然处于探索、总结阶段，还有进一步的探讨和实验的价值，本文所提出的观点和方法也希望获得关注和讨论。

参考文献

[1] BATIA V K. Analysing genre: language use in professional settings[M]. London: Longman, 1993.

[2] MARSHALL S. Genre-based-approach to the teaching of report-writing[J]. English for Specif Purposes, 1991, 10(1).

[3] 秦秀白. 文体学概论[M]. 长沙:湖南教育出版社,1986.

[4] 刘宓庆. 文体与翻译[M]. 北京:中国对外翻译出版公司,1998.

[5] 胡曙中. 英语修辞学[M]. 上海:上海外语教育出版社,2002.

[6] 刘世生. 西方文体学论纲[M]. 济南:山东教育出版社,1998.

[7] 钱敏汝. 篇章语用学概论[M]. 北京:外语教学与研究出版社,2001.

[8] 钱瑗. 英语实用文体学(上)[M]. 北京:北京师范大学出版社,1991.

[9] 王佐良. 英语文体学论文集[M]. 北京:外语教学与研究出版社,1980.

英语写作中汉式英语的问题分析

刘江红

摘　要：学生在英语写作过程中，由于受到汉语特点和文化背景因素的影响，经常会出现汉式英语的语言错误，影响了文章的可读性。本文分析汉式英语的表现形式、产生的原因和应对的策略，旨在引起大家对此类问题的关注，提高自己的英文写作水平。

关键词：英语写作；汉式英语；文化因素

大学英语课程要求学生能够就熟悉的话题流利地用口语交流，并且写出符合英文表达方式的文章。但是由于受自身英语表达能力的限制以及汉语特点和文化背景的影响，学生在写作过程中经常会把要表达的意思逐字逐句地翻译成英文，从而出现了大量的汉式英语。虽然汉式英语曾被美国语言学家Larry Selinker称为"中介语"，是从母语到目标语的一种过渡语言，在写作过程中不可避免，但它终究是一种错误语言，影响了文章可读性，削弱了书面交际的效果。

1 汉式英语的表现形式

通过对学生写作样本的分析和英汉语言的比较研究，发现学生写作中的汉式英语主要表现在词汇的选择和搭配错误，句子的语法问题和无规范性以及语篇的松散和无逻辑性等几个方面。

作者简介：刘江红，河北保定人，北京工商大学讲师。

1.1 词汇层面的汉式英语

词汇层面的汉式英语体现在选词和搭配两个方面。学生在选择词汇时，经常会英汉对照，把和汉语意思对应的英文词直接搬来用，并没有真正了解该词汇的意思和用法。比如把“黑眼睛”（dark brown eye）译成“black eye”（黑眼圈），“一次性筷子”（disposable chopsticks）译成“one-time chopsticks”。在表达“我们可以从网络中获得最新新闻”时，某位学生译写的“We can get fresh news from the internet”，完全是英汉词汇的“对号入座”：“fresh”表示“新的，新鲜的”，通常是用来修饰空气、水果等；修饰“new”可以用“latest，up-to-date”，表示最近的新闻。在表达某些游客的不文明行为时，有的学生译成“Some people break the traveling sights just to make themselves happy”。在英文中“break”和“travelling sights”是不会搭配在一起的。“破坏旅游景点”中的“破坏”可以选择“damage”或“spoil”。词汇层面的另外一个问题是选词空泛，如“We can obtain all kinds of things from internet”。由于词汇量不够，不少学生用“thing”来覆盖所有的东西，这种表达会让文章的意思很模糊，而且没有语言上的亮点。在本句话中，可以根据上下文的意思，选取information、knowledge、data、news等来代替things，这样会更具体，更有针对性。

1.2 句子层面的汉式英语

有时候学生写出的英文句子没有语法问题，但不合乎规范，带有浓重的汉语色彩，不是地道的英文表达方式。比如在表达“这件外套价格很贵”时会写成“The price of the coat is expensive”，而地道的英文是“The price of the coat is high”，或者“The coat is expensive”。在表达“体育运动能让我们身体健康”时，有的会直接翻译成“Sports can make our body healthy ”。“body”在英文中表示人的“躯干、尸体”，并没有汉语中暗含“身体健康情况”的意思，所以这句话翻译成“Sports can make us healthy”就可以了。

下面是学生在写作中出现的一些汉式英语的例子，隐现了汉语思维的痕迹。第一句是汉式英语（CE），第二句是规范英语（IE）。

（1）His writing and translating levels are very high.　（CE）

He has very good writing and translating skills. （IE）

（2）Thank you for your goodwill. But I can go home on foot. （CE）

Thank you for your offer，but I can walk home. （IE）

（3）He gave me a job to do. （CE）

He offered me a job. （IE）

（4）Please use this kind of cosmetics. The effect will be absolutely different. （CE）

Please try this kind of cosmetics. I bet it will make a big difference. （IE）

从这些例子可以看出，在写作时学生会按照汉语思维的习惯，把要表达的意思生硬地翻译成英文，虽然没有语法错误，但很难让以英语为母语的人看懂，从而影响了交际效果。

1.3 语篇层面的汉式英语

从语篇角度来讲，英语的语言表达注重“形合”，句子之间逻辑关系紧密，衔接词和过渡词必不可少。而且在书面表达中，习惯使用主从句，复合句等高度凝炼的句子。而汉语注重“意合”，结构松散，只要意思连贯通顺即可。这就致使有些学生在写作中经常出现粘连句，即句子之间只用逗号隔开，没有任何过渡词或衔接词，并列或主从句的小句之间也没有并列或从属连词。

例如在四级英语写作中，有一篇对漫画的描写是这样的：

The picture shows obviously，a teacher is teaching the multiplication table，pupils are in the math class，they question its use. Will the table be out of date when get employed.

从例子中可以看出，由于受汉语思维的影响，这段描写缺少衔接词，致使逻辑关系混乱，内容不清晰，让人费解。修改如下：

It is apparently depicted in the picture that while a teacher is teaching the multiplication table，pupils in the math class question its future use by inquiring whether that stuff will be out of date when they get employed.

2 汉式英语产生的原因

2.1 语言因素的干扰

除了语法错误，学生在写作中的选词问题比较复杂，主要在于英语词和汉语的某一个看似对应，但其实搭配、褒贬义和感情色彩都不同。

某些英语词与汉语中的某个词有一定的对应关系但并不是绝对的。如汉语中“看”在英语中就有很多词与之对应，在不同的情景中要酌情选择。“看书”是“read a book”，“看电视”是“watch TV”，而“看电影”则是“see a film”。如果学习者不清楚这一点，就不能快速准确地传达信息。

除了不同的对应关系，汉语词和英语词还存在不同搭配的问题。以“dress”和“suit”为例，汉语都可以译为“套装”，“dress”是女式连衣裙，“suit”是男西装或女套装。但在表示“她的生日礼服非常漂亮”时，只能是“Her birthday dress is very beautiful”，而不能用“birthday suit”，因为“birthday suit”是戏谑语，表示（像出生时）光着身子，赤身裸体的样子。

2.2 文化背景因素的干扰

语言是文化的载体，反映了目的语国家的生活习惯、民族心理和文化背景。因此学习英语不仅要熟悉语言本身，而且要了解英语国家的生活习惯、心理特点等，这样才能做到无障碍交流。比如80岁高龄的John成功地指挥了音乐会，获得一致好评。一位中国友人向他表示祝贺：“Congratulations! This is a perfect concert! You must be tired and just take a seat.”在我们看来关心老人健康没有什么不妥，但却让John很不悦，因为西方人会把这种“关心”视为一种轻视，其暗含的意思是“你身体不好，赶紧歇着吧”。由此看来，如果不了解目的语国家人们的心理特点，有时候会弄巧成拙，甚至造成误会和冲突。

语言受文化的影响，反映了文化的特点和差异。尤其是语言中的谚语、俗语、成语等，带有鲜明的文化痕迹。学习者若只按照其字面意思理解，不了解其含义和渊源，就会闹笑话。比如刚去美国的Mark和朋友联欢，大家玩得很开心，一位美国朋友向Mark伸出手说“Give me five!”（击掌庆祝一下吧!）。Mark很疑惑，难道联欢会在筹钱吗？于是他摊开手说：“Sorry, I have no five-dollar bill. How about 10 dollars?”美国朋友愕然，片刻后大笑起来，当天晚会中Mark成了最红的人。

3 减少和避免汉式英语的对策

通过读、听等方式增加词汇量，不仅要掌握单个词汇的意思，还要熟悉其用法、搭配、使用范围、语意色彩等。词汇是一切写作的基础，只有大量扎实的语言输入，才会有地道的语言输出。

在写作过程中，可以围绕课文的主体，运用新学的词汇和句子结构进行写作练习，对于非常熟悉的词和句式，学生就不会再用汉语作为媒介进行写作。这样不仅巩固学过的知识，还可以让学生逐渐熟悉用英语的思维进行写作，避免汉语表达方式的影响，从而提高英语表达水平。写作是一个日积月累的过程，也可以多维度进行练习，和读、听、说结合起来，如对阅读的文章进行归纳总结，复述口语中的话题等。也可多看范文，进行模仿练习，以熟悉其写作方法，提高表达能力。

熟悉英语背后的文化背景知识，了解其民族情感、生活特点和传统习俗。在书面交际时，不仅是语言的沟通，也是情感的交流和互动。多了解跨文化交际的知识，多向身边的外国朋友或外教请教，学习地道的英语表达，同时学习西方的文化，了解中西文化差异，减少写作中由于文化因素造成的问题。

4 综述

汉式英语写作的问题不是一朝一夕所能解决的。它需要学生对所产生的问题做出分析，并进行整理积累。平时多读、多听，从范文中学习英文地道的表达方法，并勤加练习。熟悉英语国家的生活习惯和民族特点，会帮助学生更好地学习英语，提高语言运用的能力。

参考文献

[1] 陈立平. 新编英语写作教程[M].西安:西安交通大学出版社,2002.

[2] 刘辰诞. 教学篇章语言学[M]. 上海:上海外语教育出版社,1999.

[3] 陶嘉炜. 写作与文化[M]. 上海:上海外语教育出版社,1998.

[4] 黄建华,蒋戴丽. 英国国家概况与文化[M]. 武汉:华中科技大学出版社,2010.

[5] 严明. 大学英语跨文化交际教程[M]. 北京:清华大学出版社,2014.

[6] DAVID A T. 美国人教你学习语[M]. 北京: 新世界出版社,2002.

浅析大学英语四、六级写作训练技巧

颜　昆　刘明宇

摘　要： 虽然写作是大学英语四、六级考试的重中之重，但是在历次英语考试当中写作成为了考生得分最低的题型。考生缺乏应对四、六级英语考试写作题型的训练技巧，是导致写作题型难以得高分的主要原因。本文以大学英语四、六级写作训练技巧为研究对象，分析了大学英语四、六级写作题型得分较低的原因，针对考生存在的问题提出相应的对策。

关键词： 大学英语；四、六级写作；训练技巧

1 引言

大学英语四、六级对于大学生的重要性毋庸置疑，其不仅关系到大学生能否顺利得到学位，同时也是招聘单位衡量人才的标准之一。写作在英语四、六级考试中所占分数比例较高，但考生往往在写作题型上失分较多。大学英语教学课程中对英语四、六级写作缺乏专项练习，学生难以将课上所学知识转化为得分能力。许多英语水平较高的学生在应试中往往难以发挥出应有水平。因此，只有找到考生在四、六级写作得分较低的原因，并找到提高写作分数的对策，才能切实提高考生的英语写作水平，轻松应对英语四、六级考试。

项目/基金：本论文为2015年北京市级大学生科研与创业行动计划项目的成果，项目编号为SJ201502069。
作者简介：颜昆，女，北京工商大学外国语学院讲师。刘明宇，男，北京工商大学外国语学院讲师。

2 四、六级写作难以得分的原因

大学英语四、六级写作难以得分的原因主要包括以下三个方面。

首先，考生对四、六级考试写作命题规律不熟悉，考前盲目押题，导致四、六级写作偏离主题。大学四、六级考试的主要命题人一般为我国各个高校的资深学者，其对四、六级写作命题有深入的研究和精准的把握。四、六级写作题型一般不会选择当年的热门话题，也不会考冷僻话题，而是会选择次热门或者中性话题，其目的在于用逆向思维进行反押题。

其次，考生对四、六级考试写作阅卷规律不明晰，严重依赖模板导致写作得分较低。四、六级写作阅卷老师大多数为大学英语系教师以及英语系研究生。阅卷人只需要快速浏览即可洞悉考生的真实英语水平。众多阅卷老师反映，如果简单套用模板，写作功底薄弱，那么写作分数将直接被归入低分挡。而很多考生平时不重视写作，指望考前突击总结、背诵写作模板就能拿高分，这直接导致了考生英语写作分数低。

最后，考生自身因素也是导致大学四、六级写作低分的原因。例如考生对英语写作存在心理障碍，遇到写作题型就感到心里紧张。一些考生平时掌握的英语词汇较少，考试时经常出现“提笔忘词”的现象。还有些考生英语基础不错，但是难以将平时所学的英语词汇以及英语句型运用到四、六级考试的写作当中。上述问题皆是导致考生在四、六级写作当中难以拿到分数的重要原因。

3 提高四、六级写作分数的对策

提高英语四、六级写作分数的根本途径在于切实提高考生的英语写作水平。近些年来，针对英语四、六级写作的培训层出不穷，多是打着传授英语四、六级写作技巧的名号押题、兜售写作模板，殊不知这正是导致考生写作低分的症结所在。因此，英语四、六级写作训练并无捷径可走，考生只有将英语写作水平真正提高上去，写作分数才能随之提高。

笔者结合多年英语教学经验，总结出英语四、六级写作备考的三种方法：背诵、默写、仿写。首先，背诵是提高英语四、六级写作水平的基础。背诵不但可以提高英语写作水平，也是真正提高英语综合实力的必经之路。

在背诵范文时切忌死记硬背，务必结合中文译本背诵英文原文，理解之后再进行背诵。对于英语基础薄弱的考生，可以先背诵中文译本，然后根据中文译本背诵英文原文。或将中文译文与英文原文逐句抄写下来，彻底搞懂每个词汇、词组、句子结构之后再进行背诵。由于英语基础不同，背诵的速度也因人而异。但是，许多考生虽然考前背过很多范文，在考场上却不知道如何使用。这主要是由考生背诵范文不熟练以及考前从未主动运用过范文内容造成的。因此，建议考生在考前每天抽出半小时以上的时间背诵考研写作范文，在考试时会产生较好效果。

其次，考生背诵范文之后，需要经常计时默写范文。许多考生平时只知道背诵范文，却从不默写范文，结果考场上错误百出导致写作低分。因此，考生需要对已经背诵的范文进行默写，可以在每天晚上睡觉之前默写一篇范文，每隔半个月左右重新默写一次，这样符合人脑的记忆规律。每次默写之后，仔细对比原文，发现自己的写作弱点，并对每篇默写进行批改，找到默写中存在的拼写错误以及语法错误。经过不断的默写，考生的语法水平可以逐渐得到提高，而每篇默写所用时间控制在10分钟到15分钟为宜。

最后，经过背诵范文以及默写训练之后，考生需要通过仿写来提高英语知识的运用能力。考生可以运用刚背过的一篇范文去写另外一道主题相近的写作题目，并尽量使用刚刚背过的词汇、词组和句型。英语基础薄弱的同学刚开始可能不会仿写，但是通过不断的背诵、默写，英语实力以及写作水平会不断提高，逐渐能够仿写一些相近的题目。如此，便可以解决考生不能将背诵、默写过的范文运用到写作中的问题，同样可以提高考生的应试能力。

4 结语

提高英语四、六级考试写作题型分数并无捷径可走，唯有切实提高考生的英语写作水平，才能在英语四、六级考试写作题型上得到较为理想的分数。笔者从事英语教学多年，总结出背诵、默写、仿写的大学英语四、六级写作训练技巧。该训练技巧简单易行，在多年的教学实践中得到了肯定和验证，希望能够为广大参与大学英语四、六级考试的考生提供帮助。

参考文献

[1] 杨继生. 中考英语作文写作技巧——如何写日记[J]. 新课程学习(上),2013(2).

[2] 陈文烨. 高中英语表格作文写作初探[J].考试周刊,2013(43).

[3] 杨燕. 图画式作文写作指导[J]. 高中生,2013(8).

[4] 易保树. 三段法攻克四、六级作文写作[J]. 海外英语,2008(7).

[5] 陈晓静. 英语开放式作文写作例谈[J]. 写作,2009(14).

关于高校实践教学管理问题的分析及对策

张霁雯

摘　要：实践教育是高校教育中的重要一环，而实践教学管理水平则直接决定着高校实践教学质量。近些年来，我国高校实践教学管理取得了长足的进步，但是仍然处于发展的初期阶段，还存在着诸多问题。本文着重对于我国高校实践教学管理中存在的问题进行分析，并针对高校实践教学中存在的问题提出相应的对策，以期为我国高校实践教学管理的发展提供借鉴。

关键词：高校；实践教学；教学管理

1 引言

实践教学在高校教学中发挥着重要作用，它是连接课堂知识和社会实践的桥梁。不仅能够锻炼学生的实践能力，而且可以培养学生的创新意识，为学生毕业之后的职业生涯打下坚实的基础。因此，对高校实践教学的管理已经成为了衡量高校管理水平的关键指标。虽然高校对实践教学的重视程度逐渐提高，但是高校对教学实践管理的效果还不理想。多数高校的实践教学管理依然存在着诸如重视程度不够、教学方法陈旧、实践教学团队专业水平低、就业与实践教学缺乏协调等问题。只有将这些问题妥善解决，才能使实践教学发挥出应有的作用。

作者简介：张霁雯，女，北京工商大学外国语学院研究生教学秘书。

2 高校实践教学管理中存在的问题

2.1 重视程度不够

高校对实践教学缺乏重视主要体现在以下两个方面：其一，由于长期受到应试教育的影响，实践教学被视为理论教学的补充，而不是与理论教学并重的一种教学模式。高校对于教师以及学生的评价往往以其理论水平以及学术成为为主，忽视实践性教学在高校教育中的重要性。其二，做好实践性教学管理对教师以及管理者的综合能力要求较高，因此教师以及管理者对实践教学存在着畏难情绪，不愿将主要精力放在实践教学上。上述两个原因造成了实践教学在高校中缺乏重视的问题。

2.2 教学管理方法不当

高校实践教学管理方式不当是高校实践教学管理中存在的另一问题。大多数高校的实践教学管理要么过于僵化，没有给学生足够创新空间，打击了学生在实践学习中的积极性。要么对学生放任自流，没有为学生提供有效的教学引导，使得实践教学变成了走过场，学生无法从实践教学中提高实践能力，反而浪费了宝贵的学习时间。不当的教学管理方法严重影响了实践教学的效果，甚至使实践教学变成了高校教学中的“鸡肋”。

2.3 实践教学管理团队专业水平低

实践教学团队专业水平低也是我国高校实践教学管理团队中普遍存在的问题。大多数从事实践教学管理的教师缺乏实践教学经验，自身创新意识不足难以产生实践教学成果，甚至少数实践教学管理者因为其专业水平不足反而成为了实践教学中的阻碍。例如，高校中实验技术人员得到进修、培训的机会较少，导致其专业知识较为陈旧，专业水平较低，总体上影响了实践教学管理的水平。

2.4 就业与实践教学缺乏协调

高校实践教学一般安排在大学最后一个学期，但是这学期也是学生忙于查询人才供求信息、参加人才交流会，供需见面会、签约、面试等各种就业活动的时候。所以，学生对于实践教学往往存在着消极应付的心态。而考虑到毕业生的就业压力越来越大，高校对实践教学的要求也逐渐放松。就业与实践教学之间缺乏协调，也在一定程度上使得实践教学变得形式化，失去了本来意义。

3 针对高校实践教学管理中问题的对策

3.1 转变观念提高实践教学重视程度

实践教学既是现代经济社会发展对人才培养提出的客观要求，又是我国高等教育更深层次改革与发展的内在要求，更是高校人才培养目标的迫切需要。因此高校管理者要解放思想，更新观念，提高认识，结合本学科的实际，不断完善改进，提高实践教学的质量和效果。只有转变高校管理者对实践教学的看法，切实提高实践教学的重视程度，高校实践教学以及教学管理水平的提高才获得了坚实的基础。

3.2 建立新型实践教学体系改革教学方法

改革教学方法建立新型实践教学体系，是解决实践教学管理方式不当问题的最佳路径。新型实践教学体系包括纵向体系和横向体系。纵向体系是一个学校、学院、学科的三级管理层次。横向体系是由课程实验、专业实习、毕业实习、暑期社会实践、社会活动、科研创新、各类竞赛组成。同时，教师在教学时应当给予学生的认知规律以及个性以充分的尊重，培养学生的独立思考能力以及创新精神。

3.3 产、学、研结合打造专业实践教学管理团队

实践教学管理团队应当从具有丰富实践经验的教师中遴选，力求做到产、学、研相结合。通过实践教学工作量津贴，实践教学成果奖励，实践教学工作考评，职称评审及教学改革与科学研究等机制充分调动教师参与实践教学的主动性、积极性和创造性。提高实践教学管理团队的整体管理水平。

3.4 科研创新与毕业实习相互结合

高校可以通过建立学生科研创新基金，加强学科竞赛活动，构建大学生创新基地，创办大学生创业中心，开展各类创业大赛活动，让学生创办各种公司等，鼓励学生搞科研创新。同时，在学科内尝试由导师—博士—硕士—本科生组成的科研创新小组，形成研究梯队，产、学、研结合，引导学生尽早参加科研创新小组，并把部分研究作为毕业论文的一部分，提前完成毕业实习的教学实践环节，解决毕业实习与就业的矛盾。

参考文献

[1] 许世华,李耀宏. 对地方高校教学管理队伍建设的认识与思考[J]. 教育与职业,2009(26).

[2] 刘卫萍,叶泽. 教学管理队伍构成指标内涵质疑[J].高教发展与评估,2008(5).

[3] 顾健辉. 高校教学管理队伍专业化建设分析[J].广西社会科学,2008(2).

[4] 张莉娜,虞海珍,潘学松,梁玉玮. 高校实践教学管理存在的问题及对策浅议[J]. 高等理科教育,2008(5).

[5] 庞洪芬,张艳霞. 市场营销专业实践教学的研究现状与对策[J]. 中国校外教育(理论),2008(S1).

素质教育视域下的教学管理工作

韩佶彤

摘　要： 素质教育是以提高学生综合素质为目的的教育模式。素质教育这一理念一直是我国教育界的重要课题。《关于当前积极推进大中小学实施素质教育的若干意见》中明确提出，将提高学生的综合素质作为教学的目标。但是，我国长期以来以应试教育为主，素质教育虽然得到了教育界乃至全社会的广泛关注，但是素质教育的实施并不顺利。发展素质教育的阻力是多方面的，其中教学管理工作的偏差是导致素质教育难以在我国真正实施的重要问题。本文以素质教育的教学管理作为问题的出发点和落脚点，分别从素质教育的教学管理原则，以及素质教育的教学管理发展方向两个角度入手，探讨如何在素质教育的大前提下开展教学管理工作。为我国素质教育的发展进行有益的探索。

关键词： 素质教育；教学原则；教学管理

1 引言

素质教育是在遵循社会发展的需要以及人自身的认知规律的基础上开展的教育，旨在整体提升学生自身的综合素质。素质教育不仅注重对学生应试能力的培养，而是将提高学生的身心素质、创新精神、独立思考能力放在首位。随着素质教育逐渐被社会各界广泛认知，我国各级高校也在不同程度上

作者简介： 韩佶彤，女，现任北京工商大学外国语学院研究生教学秘书。

开展了素质教育，并在近年来取得了一些成果。但是，从我国总体的教育模式看，应试教育依然是当今教育界的主流。许多学校对素质教育的认识还仅仅停留在增加学生的课余活动，减少学生的课堂作业等浅显层面。甚至有些学校只是以素质教育之名，行应试教育之实。学生的综合素质并没有得到真正提升。教学工作是教育的核心内容，唯有确定教学管理工作的管理原则，准确把握教学管理工作的发展方向，才能保证教学不偏离素质教育的轨道。本文仅就这两个方面对素质教学视域下的教学管理工作进行探讨。

2 素质教育视域下教学管理的发展方向

2.1 继续深化教学改革

继续深化教育改革是我国素质教育发展的总体趋势。教学改革的目的在于切实提高学生的综合素质，课程改革是教学改革的核心内容。课程设计应当以时代性、使用性、多样性为标准，将综合发展课以及活动课作为基础课的补充。使课程更为贴近学生生活，不仅开发学生的智力，培养学生的应试能力，更能够塑造学生的创新精神、团队协作能力以及独立思考能力。

2.2 工作评价标准科学化

科学化评价教学管理工作也是素质教育发展的方向之一。应试教育强调教师提升学生考试分数的能力，仅将学生的考试分数作为评价学生的唯一标准。但是素质教育则应当对教师、学生进行综合化、科学化评价。学生参加活动课以及综合发展课中的表现应当列为学生的评价标准。而对教师的评价应当将教师对学生人生观、价值观的培养确定为评价标准。真正形成科学化、规范化的教学评价体系。

2.3 切实减轻学生课业负担

减轻学生的课业负担是素质教育下的教学管理发展的必然趋势。我国各级院校中普遍存在着学生课业负担沉重的现象。而沉重的课业负担也是我国实现素质教育的主要障碍。学习时间过长、作业量过大、考试过多等问题远没有得到解决，反而愈发严重。有些学生的在校学习时间甚至达到了每天12

小时，而且在周末的课余时间还要参加诸多辅导班。学生们在沉重的课业负担之下苦不堪言。这些问题归根结底是应试教育造成的恶果。只有改变应试教育模式，才能切实减轻学生的课业负担。

3 素质教育视域下的教学管理原则

3.1 教师与学生互动原则

教师与学生互动原则应当作为教学管理原则之一。教师在授课过程当中应当运用提问法、谈话法、讨论法以及演示法等教学方法，使学生与教师在课堂上能够充分地交流互动，在讨论和探究中推进教学。互动教学不仅能够活跃课堂气氛，提高学习的探讨性和自主性。同时也拉近了学生和教师之间的距离，使教师对学生的思想和学习情况更深入地了解，并针对学生存在的问题进行改进，培养学生的个性思维。

3.2 智力因素与非智力因素结合原则

影响学生认知的因素包括智力因素和非智力因素。在教学以及教学管理中，教师应当将智力因素与非智力因素相结合，充分发挥二者的作用。力求做到智力因素引导非智力因素，非智力因素促进智力因素的发挥。只有将智力因素与非智力因素有机结合起来，才符合学生的认知规律。应试教育将重点主要集中在智力因素上，然而非智力因素往往在学生的长期学习中起到至关重要的作用。因此，只有真正做到智力因素与非智力因素结合，才能真正提升学生的综合素质。

3.3 过程教学与结果教学并重原则

过程教学与结果教学并重是素质教育下教学管理的重要原则。注重结果教学是应试教育教学管理的特点。素质教育则将过程教学与结果教学视为同等重要的教学环节。过程教学注重学生在学习过程中对知识的理解和形成。教师需要通过对学生进行引导和启发实现学生对所学知识的消化掌握。过程教学和结果教学并重，可以激发学生的学习积极性，养成学生的探究精神。从而达到素质教育培养学生创新精神和独立思考能力的目的。

参考文献

[1] 李志义,朱泓,刘志军. 我国本科教学评估该向何处去?[J]. 高教发展与评估,2011(6).

[2] 郝文武. 课程教学公平的本质特征和量化测评[J]. 教育研究与实验,2011(5).

[3] 王小红,杜学元. 学校规训教育与人的异化——福柯规训理论透视[J]. 教育研究与实验,2011(5).

[4] 金保华,罗建河. 西方自然连贯主义教育管理伦理观及启示[J]. 现代教育管理,2011(10).

[5] 龙兴海. 现代性道德谋划:中国背景下的探讨[J]. 道德与文明,2011(5).

翻译研究

语言学与教学研究

外国文学与文化研究

教育、教学探讨与实验教学研究

听歌识文学
——解读英文歌曲《Hallelujah》中的圣经故事

王秀贞

摘　要：课堂之外，学习英语的途径也多种多样，听原版录音、看英文电影、读原版小说、看美剧、听英文歌曲等，都是很好的大量接触原汁原味英语的方式。有的歌曲，文学色彩极为浓厚，不仅抒情，还讲故事。《Hallelujah》这首歌曲，基于圣经故事而创作，用典丰富，感情表达浓烈，是不可多得的学习英语和了解文学故事的材料之一。本文试图从英语学习者的角度，解读歌中所述圣经故事，品味其中的文学色彩。

关键词：《Hallelujah》；圣经典故；大卫王；力士参孙

1 歌曲简介

歌曲《Hallelujah》，最初是由被称为“游吟诗人”“民谣歌手”的加拿大音乐人莱纳德·科恩（Lenard Cohen）创作的。在出唱片之前，莱纳德·科恩写过小说，也出版过诗集，还被誉为加拿大有史以来最重要的作家之一。虽然大学肄业，但英语文学的专业背景对他的歌曲创作有着显著的影响。

《Hallelujah》是收录在其1985年发行的专辑《Various Positions》中的一首歌曲。这首歌从发行以后，除了莱纳德·科恩本人后来又改编过之外，亦

作者简介：王秀贞，女，山东安丘人，硕士，北京工商大学讲师，主要研究方向为英美文学。

有众多其他歌手翻唱过，据统计至今已有两百多个版本。同一首歌，被不同风格的歌手演绎之后，显现出不同的格调，诠释出不同的情感。

《Hallelujah》这首歌，莱纳德·科恩本人就有三个不同的版本：录音室版、现场版和全球巡演版，主要区别在于歌词的较大变动，甚至是整段歌词的替换。后来不同的歌手在改编的时候，对歌词也有不同的取舍与组合。笔者以为Jeff Buckley的翻唱版本为最佳，故以下讨论均以此为据，解读其中较为突出的圣经故事。歌词全文如下：

I've heard there was a secret chord/ that David played and it pleased the lord/ but you don't really care for music, do you?/ it goes like this the fourth, the fifth/ the minor fall and the major lift/ the baffled king composing hallelujah/ hallelujah, hallelujah, hallelujah, hallelujah...

Your faith was strong but you needed proof/ you saw her bathing on the roof/ her beauty and the moonlight overthrew you/ she tied you to her kitchen chair/ she broke your throne and she cut your hair/ and from your lips she drew the hallelujah/ hallelujah, hallelujah, hallelujah, hallelujah...

Baby I've been here before/ I've seen this room and I've walked this floor/ (you know)I used to live alone before I knew you/ I've seen your flag on the marble arch/ and love is not a victory march/ it's a cold and it's a broken hallelujah/ hallelujah, hallelujah, hallelujah, hallelujah...

There was a time when you let me know/ what's really going on below/ but now you never show it to me, do you/ but remember when I moved in you/ the holy dove was moving too/ and every breath we drew was hallelujah/ hallelujah, hallelujah, hallelujah, hallelujah...

Maybe there's a god above/ but all I've ever learned from love/ was how to shoot somebody who outdrew you/ and it's not a cry that you hear at night/ it's not somebody who's seen the light/ it's a cold and it's a broken hallelujah/ hallelujah, hallelujah, hallelujah, hallelujah, hallelujah, hallelujah, hallelujah, hallelujah, hallelujah, hallelujah, hallelujah, hallelujah...

2 歌曲中的圣经故事

2.1 David（大卫）和Bathsheba（拔示巴）的故事

歌曲开头便是：I've heard there was a secret chord/ that David played and it pleased the lord... the baffled king composing hallelujah.（我曾听闻一曲神秘的旋律，是大卫取悦上帝的赞颂……不知所措一世尊荣的大卫王，五味杂陈地谱下哈利路亚。）这其中的"David"和"the baffled king"指同一个人，那就是大卫王。大卫王是谁？他又为何要弹奏一曲来讨好上帝呢？

大卫容貌俊美，英勇善战，能赋能歌，战胜巨人哥利亚，被上帝选为以色列的国土。在年轻时就尽展才华的他，却在登基十年的时候，在平安顺利的环境中迷失自我了。他不再持守黎明的敬拜，直到日头平西时才起身。一日，在皇宫的屋顶上闲逛时，他偶然看见一个女人在屋顶洗澡，因此而动了淫念。正如歌词所唱："your faith was strong but you needed proof/ you saw her bathing on the roof/ her beauty and the moonlight overthrew you."（你百胜沙场的信心虽坚定，却在这件事上犯罪，需要验证对上帝的忠心。在楼顶上，你窥见了她沉鱼落雁的出浴；惹祸的月光，加上她令人屏息的美丽，彻底攻溃了你的心。）之后，本就有几房妻子的大卫，便派人四处打听此女子，想要知道她的芳名。原来，这个迷人的女子名叫Bethsheba（拔示巴），是大卫的一位部将Uriah（乌利亚）的妻子。大卫不禁心生占有拔示巴的欲望，于是让人将拔示巴接入宫中，此时乌利亚还在前线战场上冒死作战呢。大卫与乌利亚的妻子拔士巴同房，并致其怀孕。为了掩盖这个罪行，他派人把乌利亚从前线召回来，企图让他回家与妻子团聚而造成他们夫妻自然怀孕的假象。但这个乌利亚却实在是对君王有着忠心不二的心，想着前方将士还在浴血奋战，他怎能与妻子共度温柔乡呢？所以他宁愿在王宫外席地休息，也不回家与妻子团聚，并要求大卫将自己重新派回到战场上。大卫此时便顺水推舟，并写成密信一封，让乌利亚携信到大将军约亚那里。信中大卫指示约亚将乌利亚派往最为危险的战场。果然不几日就传来了乌利亚的死讯，拔士巴为丈夫守丧期刚满，大卫就将拔示巴迎进自己的后宫，名正言顺地占有了拔示巴。占有拔示巴的大卫并不快乐，他白天对着众人强颜欢笑，夜晚就成为自己罪过的奴隶，受尽折磨。然而，这件事情并没有就此结束，因为神的追讨立刻随之而来。追讨从先知来向大卫讲故事开始，大卫被先知所讲的故事所激怒，说那个霸占他人心爱之物的人当死。先知勇敢地告诉他，你就是那个人。大卫在这个审判面前醒悟过来，认识到自己的罪行，便写下51篇忏悔书，歌与上帝，祈求宽恕。

2.2 Samson（参孙）和Delilah（达利拉）的故事

第二段歌词中唱道："She tied you to her kitchen chair/she broke your throne and she cut your hair."（你犹如大力士参孙，束手无策地被捆缚在她家的餐椅上；她击碎了你的宝座，并剪掉了你的头发。）

此处运用了Samson（参孙）和Delilah（达利拉）的故事作为典故。力士参孙的故事出自《圣经·旧约全书》的《士师记》，虽然篇幅不长，但故事结构完整，人物鲜明，情节曲折，包含了爱恨交织的丰富情感。

以色列在被非力士人统治的时候，族中有个大力士，名字叫参孙，上帝赐予他空手撕裂雄狮的神力，这使得非力士统治者颇为惧怕。但是，参孙有个弱点：上帝与其约定——不得剪发，否则神力尽失。参孙爱上了一位非力士族的姑娘，名叫达利拉。非力士统治者赐予达利拉许多钱财，收买她与参孙相好，并套出他为何力大无穷的秘密。参孙在达利拉的三次诱惑下以编造的故事将其蒙混，但是最后参孙还是没能顶住达利拉无休止的盘问，将自己的秘密告诉了达利拉。一日，达利拉趁参孙熟睡于自己的膝上时，让人将参孙的头发剪掉了。参孙醒来，发现自己的头发被剪，神力也一并消失了。可怜的参孙在爱情的迷惑下，违背了与神定下的誓约，从一个英勇的大力士变成了一个任人欺辱的瞎子。

2.3 Hallelujah一词的故事

首先，关于"Hallelujah"这个词，《Webster's Encyclopedic Unabridged Dictionary of the English Language》上是如此解释的：① praise ye the Lord；② an exclamation of "hallelujah!"；③ a shout of joy，praise，or gratitude；④ a musical composition wholly or principally based upon the word "hallelujah."

其次，"hallelujah"在歌曲中虽循环往复、重叠出现，但在每个段落、每一句中的每一个hallelujah都可以有不同层次的理解和不同的诠释方式。每段副歌部分的第一个hallelujah，可以取其基本义，即上述韦氏字典中的第一个义项，是希伯来语，意为“赞美我主”“感谢神”，是基督信徒嘴里告白时经常使用的一个词。在第二段歌词中，“她击碎了你的宝座，并剪掉了你的头发”后面紧接的歌词是“and from your lips she drew the hallelujah”（从你的口中，她套取了最为关键的机密，逼你说出了hallelujah）。此处的hallelujah，像极了力士参孙在吐露秘密后的那一声无奈的叹息！在情爱面前，哪怕再英勇无畏的男子也会犯下致命的错误！歌词的最后一段，“maybe there's a god above/ and all I've ever learned from love/ was how to shoot someone who outdrew you/ it's not a cry you hear at night/ it's not somebody who's seen the light/ it's a cold and it's a broken hallelujah”（也许天庭间的确有上帝，但我从爱中却学会要先发制人。爱并非是在黑夜里的伤心哭泣，也并非是在晦暗的生命中得到的启示，而是让人无助又心碎的祈求你宽恕的哈利路亚）。此处的cold和broken都修饰hallelujah，既是冰冷的，又是破碎的，让人不免联想到大卫王在受到神的惩罚时，奉迎地弹唱忏悔曲的样子，可怜而无助。小结一下：这首歌由翻唱者Jeff Buckley的一声轻叹开始，伴随大卫抚琴出场，其基调就已确定下来：关于爱和情。当“the baffled king”受到神的惩罚而弹琴奉迎时，他念“hallelujah”；当他的魂魄被美人与爱情俘虏时，在他心灵极度陶醉、幸福、痴狂与深陷的那一刻，他喊出“hallelujah”。“hallelujah”可以是神圣的、动人的，或者破碎的。

再次，早在1985年1月，原唱Lenard Cohen在接受《Actuel》杂志采访时，关于“Hallelujah”一词，曾经说过这样一段话：“I intended to say ‘Hallelujah’. There is a religious Hallelujah，but there are many other ones. When one looks at the world and his proper life，there's only one thing to say，it's Hallelujah. That's the way it is...”从中可以看出，除了宗教意味颇浓的hallelujah之外，作者也赋予了这个词非宗教的其他含义。正如他所说：“当一个人回望这个世界和他的生命旅程时，只能用一个词来概括，那就是哈利路亚。”

最后，这首歌现在经常被用作背景音乐，来表达当噩耗传来，并且人们无力抗拒时的心绪；一种“活着足以赞美”的含义已成为大众对此歌的普遍理解。

3 结语

弄清楚其中的文学典故，可以更好地理解一首歌曲。而一首好歌曲，可以抒情，可以励志，可以讲述故事，可以教人向善，也可以教人学好英语。有志于学好英语的学习者们，可以尝试着深挖一下歌词的含义，以及歌词背后的故事。这样，除了能学习语言本身，还能更多地了解相关文化、文学知识，也能更多地了解人性。

On Hamlet's Delay

杨文彦

Abstract: Why does Hamlet delay so long to kill Claudius? Hamlet's indecision and irresolution have confused many readers in the past a hundred years. Why can't he just "shuffle off the mortal coil" and kill his uncle straightway? Is it only a theatrical device? By analyzing Hamlet's characters, we draw a conclusion that Hamlet hesitates to take immediate action is not because of his inability to act decisively but because of his extreme sensibility.

Key words: Hamlet; delay; melancholy; timidity; characters; sensibility

1 Introduction

The issue of Hamlet's delay has aroused so many critics' interests that they have presented various interpretations concerning this matter. Some critics attribute his procrastination to mere contrivance on Shakespeare's part; some ascribe this issue to Hamlet's timidity; and others impute the delay to his Oedipus Complex. My interpretation of his delay mainly seconds the Romantic critics', which assert that Hamlet's nature renders Hamlet unable to act.

作者简介:杨文彦,女,北京工商大学副教授,主要研究方向为语言学、英美文学、英语教学。

2 Is It only a Theatrical Device?

George Stubbesattributes Hamlet's much-discussed procrastination to Shakespeare's contrivance. "Had Hamlet gone naturally to work, there would have been an end of our play." Similar to this idea, Elmer Edgar Stoll argues that Hamlet falls within the tradition of the Elizabethan revenge tragedy. In this content, the delay is not a critical problem, but a theatrical device.

This aesthetic approach is rather valid. Suppose Hamlet followed the Ghost's instructions immediately to kill Claudius without wavering and meditation, the play would only be a one-act play. Furthermore, in the prayer scene, Hamlet's hesitation arouses a sense of suspense. Thus, the delay does complicate the tragedy and enrich an otherwise simple and direct revenge plot.

Though this interpretation is plausible, it is not the exclusive one. This approach only explains a minor cause leading to the procrastination, and its essence is ignored and not touched upon. The delay is a result from Hamlet's inner flaw. But what's Hamlet's inner flaw? Is it timidity as suggested by some critics his inner fault, which brings his inaction?

3 Arguments Against Hamlet's Timidity

Hamlet himself is the obstacle towards action. His nature hinders him advancing forward at once. Some critics think that Hamlet's delay lies in his cowardice. For instance, Thomas Sheridan portrays Hamlet as " a young man of a good heart and fine feeling who had led a studious contemplative life and so become delicate and irresolute." Following this notion, Gothe presents an often-quoted phrase concerning Hamlet's traits- "an oak-tree planted in a costly vase."

This group of critics, with Gothe at the head, analyze Hamlet as such a pure, noble and tender young prince that he is unsuited for the hard task, which is set for him by his father's ghost. That is to say, Hamlet lacks courage that enables him to take immediate actions. This understanding is brilliant and thoughtful, but not entirely just. Is Hamlet too weak to carry out the vengeance? A careful reading of the play proves the falseness in this statement. The plot tells us, however, that Hamlet is far from being represented as a person too timid to take any action. Two occasions can best illustrate his resolution. First, he hesitates not to run his sword through the eavesdropper behind the arras, thus Polonius is killed. Secondly, with a quick and crafty hand, he sends the two courtiers–Rosencrantz and Guildenstern to the death that had been planned for himself. So Hamlet lacks no courage and bravery to take actions and cowardice cannot be attributed to Hamlet.

4 Arguments Against Hamlet's Melancholy

Another plausible interpretation comes from A. C. Bradley, a major Shakespearean critic and widely studied by later ones, who asserts it is the melancholy brought about by his mother's hasty remarriage that prevents Hamlet from revenge. His approach initiates the later pattern that Hamlet is always associated with melancholy.

The young prince suffers from the corrupted world, as exemplified in the world of Denmark. What's more, he is suddenly placed in an unexpected and unimaginable situation: father is murdered and mother hastily remarries to the murderer. No wonder Hamlet behaves melancholy frequently. Anybody in Hamlet's situation would behave similarly.

Beneath Hamlet's melancholy, some sanguine elements often break out. "The specific sanguine characteristics are those we associate with social adjustment: wit, affability and 'gracious faculty' of speech, tolerance, level-headedness, 'constant loving affection', congeniality, loyalty to friend and country, bravery of spirit and action–those characteristics we might sum up generally in Shakespeare's words generous and noble". These qualities are applicable to Hamlet in all essential details. It is only through excessive grief that Hamlet has become "melancholy."

What is it, then, that inhibits Hamlet in fulfilling the task set him by the Ghost? A through study of Hamlet's character is necessary for the attempt to solve this problem.

5 Hamlet's Characters

With the reference to the above-argued criticisms, the complicated nature of Hamlet is revealed to the readers. Some consider him delicate and irresolute, while some think him "noble", which contains the meanings of courageous and brave; some judges him melancholy, while some regards him sanguine. These seemingly contradictory elements combine together, creating a controversial character in Shakespearean cannon. However, in discussing one's character, its basis is the most crucial for the understanding.

5.1 The Essence in Hamlet's Character

"The basis of Hamlet's character seems to be an extreme sensibility of mind, apt to be strongly impressed by its situation, and over-powered by the feelings which that situation excites." In addition, this sensibility also endows Hamlet with a fundamental quality in perceiving the world around him. That is to say, this excessive sensibility not only allows Hamlet to comprehend the uniqueness in a situation, which is usually ignored by others, but also drowns himself in his own world of meditations concerning the situation. This quality can be observed immediately in Hamlet's first substantial speech in the play.

"Seems, madam? Nay, it is. I know not 'seems',
'Tis not alone my inky cloak, good mother,
Nor customary suits of solemn black,
Nor windy suspiration of forced breath,
No, nor the fruitful river in the eye,
Nor the dejected havior of the visage,
Together with all form.s, moods, shapes of grief,
That can denote me truly. These indeed seem,
For they are actions that a man might play;
But I have that within which passeth show-
These but the trappings and the suits of woe."

When questioned by the Queen why he is particularly sad about his father's death, which is a "common truth" -everybody dies, instead of answering his mother directly to the point, Hamlet speaks for all the melancholy men rather than clarifying his own grief. This indicates that Hamlet suffers greatly from his father's death (Here, truth is still nor revealed and his father's death is considered as a natural one) and can't release himself from his bitter thoughts. So when questioned, he instantly utters his meditation, which deals with all men involved in the same situation. Certainly, after the fact is exposed-his father's death is not a natural one but a murder, he plunges even more deeply into his reflection world than before. During his second meeting with the Ghost, chiding his delay, he claims he has "lapsed in time and passion."

Another example illustrating the point can be detected in Hamlet's often-quoted statement- "Frailty, thy name is woman." Gertrude's speedy remarriage irritates Hamlet so deeply that his first soliloquy expresses his utter despair in his inner world.

"O that this too too solid flesh would melt,
Thaw, and resolve itself into a dew!
Or that the Everlasting had not fixed
His cannon gainst self-slaughter! O God! God!
How weary, stale, flat, and unprofitable
Seem to me all the uses of this world!
Fie on't! ah, fie! 'Tis an unweeded garden
That grows to seed; things rank and gross in nature
Possess it merely. That it should come to this."

His mother's remarriage prompts Hamlet to ponder the world around him. In his inner world, he inquires the meaning of life and begins his disappointment with the world. He also begins to mistrust in all women. That's why he urges Ophelia to "Get thee to a nunnery."

Therefore, Hamlet's sensibility plays a significant part in his comprehension of the world. Confronting a situation, his sensibility drowns himself in his inner world.

"And thus the native hue of resolution/ Issicklied o'er with the pale cast of thought." In another words, his extreme sensibility leads him to a world of reflection.

5.2 Hamlet's Attempt to Achieve Justice

Burdened with his introspection, Hamlet attempts to be just, to provide a convincing judgment towards his action. That's why he keeps suspecting the identity of the Ghost. Before he sees the Ghost himself, he "doubt some foul play" . Right before their first meeting, Hamlet once again questions his identity- "Be thou a spirit of health or goblin damned." Even after he accepts the summon for vengeance, he wavers because he continues his doubt that "it is a damned ghost" until the mouse trap, which is designed by Hamlet to test the Ghost's words. After he obtains the evidence to prove the murder, in the prayer scene Hamlet lets the opportunity slip again. The reason is quite obvious. It is not because Hamlet unable to act but if he killed Claudius during his prayer, "Why, this is hire and salary, not revenge!" The reader should bear in mind that the Ghost prompts Hamlet to revenge is that the Ghost was sent into the other world without having had time to repent of his sins. Hamlet of course remembers his father's misery in the purgatory. This conscience prevents him to take immediate action but waiting for a fit chance, for instance, "When he is drunk asleep, or in his rage; / Or in the incestuous pleasure of his bed; /At gaming, swearing, or about some act/ That has no relish of salvation in't." This also can explain why Hamlet kills Polonius without wavering in the closet scene. Hamlet mistakes Polonius, who hides himself behind the arras as an eavesdropper, for Claudius. He thinks "Is it the King?" before he thrusts his sword and utters "I took thee for thy better (Claudius)" after Hamlet realizes his mistake. So the error makes Hamlet think the proper moment for the vengeance comes and hesitates not to kill Polonius.

Therefore, Hamlet's over sensibility leads to his struggle for judgment and justice. During the process of his judgment, he misses the chance to kill Claudius. He declares "And praised be rashness for it/ Our indiscretion sometimes serve us we/ When our deep plots do pall." The tragedy of Hamlet is indeed a tragedy of his

excessive sensibility.

6 Conclusion

Some critics understand Hamlet's delay as a theatrical device to complicate the direct revenge plot, but it is a rather minor function of the issue. The key cause of his procrastination is Hamlet's inner fault, not the inner fault as suggested by Sheridan, or by A. C. Bradley. Hamlet hesitates to take immediate action is not because of his inability to act decisively but because of his extreme sensibility. It's because of his sensibility that Hamlet can penetrate into the world around him. It's because of his sensibility that Hamlet is controlled by passion and meditation resulting from the situation. It's because of Hamlet's sensibility that he attempts to be just and tries to discern the situation. Hence, whatever happened, Hamlet will meditate before act. He prefers meditation to action, which leads to his delay.

Bibliography

[1] BRADLEY A C. Shakespearean tragedy. Lectures on Hamlet, Othello, King Lear, Macbeth [M]. 2nd Ed. New York: Macmillan, 1905.

[2] GOTHE J W. Wilhelm Meister's Apprenticeship[M]. London: Bell and Daldy, 1873.

[3] HARRIS L L. Shakespeare criticism[M]. Detroit: Gale, 1984.

[4] MACKENZIE H. Shakespeare: the critical heritage: 1753–1765[M]. London: Routledge & Kegan Paul, 1976.

[5] SHAKESPEARE W. Hamlet[M]. Beijing: Commercial Press, 1995.

[6] SHERIDAN T. Boswell's London Journal: 1762–1763[M]. New York: McGraw–Hill Book Co., 1950.

[7] STATES B O. The melancholy dane in Hamlet and the concept of character[M]. Baltimore and London: The Johns Hopkins UP, 1992.

[8] STOOL E E. Art and artifice in Shakespeare: a study in dramatic contrast and illusion[M]. Cambridge: Cambridge UP, 1933.

多面体的莎士比亚

全凤霞

摘 要：莎士比亚通过其戏剧展示了丰富的人文主义思想和哲学家的深刻。他赞颂母爱、仁慈、同情等人性之美，批判神性和神权统治，提倡对真挚爱情的向往和追求。莎士比亚是诗人加工厂，在他的作品中，诗性无处不在。

关键词：哲学家的深刻；诗人加工厂

莎士比亚在其辉煌的作品中，充分显示了他人道主义的崇高。他赞颂母爱、仁慈、同情等人性之美，批判神性和神权统治，提倡对真挚爱情的向往和追求。他建构的是丰富、复杂和深刻的人性，让人们在认识自己的同时，理解他人、理解社会、理解时代。歌德高度赞扬莎士比亚："莎士比亚多么无限丰富和伟大呀！他把人类生活中的一切动机都画出来和说出来了！而且显得多么容易，多么自由！"莎士比亚热爱人类："人类是一件多么了不得的杰作！多么高贵的理性！多么伟大的力量！多么优美的仪表！多么文雅的举动！在行为上多么像一个天使！在智慧上多么像一个天神！宇宙的精华！万物的灵长！"让我们从中获得了多少鼓励和做人的尊严；同时他爱憎分明，对社会的种种罪恶深恶痛绝："谁愿意忍受人世的鞭挞和讥嘲、压迫者的凌辱、傲慢者的冷眼、被轻蔑的爱情的惨痛、法律的迁延、官吏的横暴和费尽辛勤所换来的小人的鄙视……"（《哈姆莱特》第3幕第1场）。莎士比亚还教给我们为人处事的技巧，他说，"一件功劳要是默默无闻，可以消沉了以

作者简介：全凤霞，女，土家族，湖南省张家界市人，英美文学硕士研究生，北京工商大学外国语学院讲师，研究方向为莎士比亚戏剧。

后再做一千件的兴致，褒奖便是我们的酬报。一回的鞭策还不曾使马儿走过一亩地，温柔的一吻早已使它驰过百里。”（《冬天的故事》第1幕第2场）从中让我们铭记以柔克钢的哲学。莎士比亚还了解最毒妇人心：“来！注视着人类恶念的魔鬼们！解除我的女性的柔弱，用最凶恶的残忍自顶至踵贯注在我的全身；凝结我的血液，不要让怜悯钻进我的心头……来！阴沉的黑夜，用最黑暗的地狱中的浓烟罩住你自己，让我的锐利的刀瞧不见它自己切开的伤口。”（《麦克白》第1幕第1场）最重要的是，莎士比亚教我们怎样热爱和欣赏大自然，怎样热爱生活和发现生活中的美。他说“我要在这里访寻几滴露水，给每朵花挂上珍珠的耳坠。”（《仲夏夜之梦》第2幕第1场）原来，生活中处处充满情趣，每滴小小的露水都是美丽的珍珠，生活中的美就在这小小的点滴里。莎士比亚真的离我们很近，在大自然清新鲜亮的气息里，我们仿佛看见莎士比亚站在青青的草地、清清的河边，召唤着：“快来吧！这儿是大自然，你们的家！”

莎士比亚在他的剧作里还昭示了他哲学家的深刻。当代人奉为至上的生活哲学“平平淡淡才是真”，也在400多年前荡涤着莎士比亚的心灵：“狂暴的快乐将会产生狂暴的结局，正像火和火药的亲吻，就在最得意的一刹那烟消云散，最甜的蜜糖可以使味觉麻木；不太热烈的爱情才会维持久远；太快和太慢，结果都不会圆满。”（《罗密欧与朱丽叶》第2幕第6场》）莎士比亚也是最会把握分寸的人。比如当亲人故去时，他会教你用情的度：“适当的悲哀可以表示感情的深切，过度的伤心却可以证明智慧的欠缺。”（《罗密欧与朱丽叶》第3幕第5场）400年前莎士比亚关于保持理智与情欲之间的平衡的忠告对现在的我们更具现实意义：“要是我们的生命之中，理智和情欲不能保持平衡，我们血肉的邪心就会引导我们到一个荒唐的结局；可是我们有的是理智，可以冲淡我们汹涌的热情，肉体的刺激和奔放的淫欲。”（《奥瑟罗》第1幕第3场）莎士比亚还教我们慧眼看世界，他说“发光的不都是金子”（《威尼斯商人》第2幕第7场）；“虽然权势是一头固执的熊，可是金子可以拉着它的鼻子走”（《冬天的故事》第4幕第3场）。

莎士比亚是个全才。他懂园林艺术的嫁接术：“我们常把一枝善种的嫩枝接在野树上，使低劣的植物和优良的交配而感孕。这是一种改良天然的艺术。”（《冬天的故事》第4幕第3场）莎士比亚是一个重视睡眠的人：“那清白的睡眠，把忧虑的乱丝编织起来的睡眠，那日常的死亡，疲劳者的沐浴，受伤的心灵的油膏，大自然的最丰盛的菜肴，生命的盛筵上主要的营养。”（《麦克白》第2幕第2场）

莎士比亚是诗人加工厂。在他的笔下，产生过多少伟大的诗人啊，有多思的哈姆莱特，多情的罗密欧与朱丽叶，激情的麦克白夫妇，雄壮的查理二世，雄辩的勃鲁托斯和安东尼……这是一个没有结尾的名单，就连朱丽叶的父亲凯普莱特也是一位相当有才情的诗人。如：当朱丽叶为罗密欧的放逐和表哥的离世悲痛得泪如雨下时，他父亲 “诗兴大发”：“咦！还在哭吗？雨到现在还没有停吗？你这小小的身体里面，也有船，也有海，也有风；因为你的眼睛就是海，永远有泪潮在那儿涨退；你的身体是一艘船，在这泪海上面航行；你的叹息是海上的狂风；你的身体经不起风浪的吹打，会在这汹涌的怒海中覆没的。”（《罗密欧与朱丽叶》第3幕第5场）当朱丽叶喝了劳伦斯神父给她的药剂“佯”死时，朱丽叶的父亲用诗一样的语言沉痛感叹：“死像一阵未秋先降的寒霜，摧残了这一朵最鲜嫩的娇花”，“死神是我的新婿，是我的后嗣，他已经娶走了我的女儿”。（《罗密欧与朱丽叶》第4幕第5场）莎剧的诗意是无处不在的，生活中最普通的场景经过莎翁神笔的稍加点染也能变得妙趣多姿。

阅读莎士比亚的作品，有时就像是一次心灵之旅。《哈姆莱特》就是我们的心灵向导之一。有时又像是视觉旅行，《麦克白》就是一个恐怖的画廊。莎士比亚通过他独特的语言让读者通过自己的感官想象力编织出了一个个风格多变的图像世界。人们阅读着《哈姆莱特》，欣赏着《仲夏夜之梦》，或感叹于剧中人物的命运多舛，或沉醉于绿色原野的魔幻神奇。读者情不自禁地赞叹着莎士比亚，崇拜着他，内心亲近着他。莎士比亚是真正说不尽的。

参考文献

[1] 莎士比亚. 莎士比亚全集[M]. 朱生豪,译. 北京:人民文学出版社,2010.

[2] 莎士比亚. 仲夏夜之梦[M]. 朱生豪,译. 北京:中国国际广播出版社,2001.

[3] 莎士比亚. 罗密欧与朱丽叶[M]. 朱生豪,译. 北京:中国国际广播出版社,2001.

[4] 莎士比亚. 奥瑟罗[M]. 朱生豪,译. 北京:中国国际广播出版社,2001.

[5] 莎士比亚. 麦克白[M]. 朱生豪,译. 北京:中国国际广播出版社,2001.

[6] 莎士比亚. 威尼斯商人[M]. 朱生豪,译. 北京:中国国际广播出版社,2001.

A Brief Analysis on Chinese Cultural Elements in Animated Movie *Kung Fu Panda*

张洪萍

Abstract: DreamWorks Animation Studio released globally an animated blockbuster *Kung Fu Panda* in 2008, choosing one of the most popular and renowned Chinese traditional elements, martial arts as the core element of the film. The film instantly won high reputation and caused a sensation in the entire movies, especially among the Chinese audiencesbecause of thedistinctive fragrance of Chinese culture factors, Chinese national treasure—panda, the quintessence of Chinese culture—martial arts, the Chinese style philosophy—Confucianism, Taoism, Chinese architecture, etc. Superficially the moviereflects Chinese culture and Chinese elements, but by its very nature, it's the reflection of the trend of cultural globalization.

Key words: *Kung Fu Panda*; American values; Chinese elements; cultural globalization

1 Brief Introduction to the Big Film, *Kung Fu Panda*

In June, 2008, DreamWorks Animation Studio released globally an animated blockbuster *Kung Fu Panda*, with the most popular and renowned Chinese tra-

作者简介:张洪萍,天津人,北京工商大学外国语学院副教授。

ditional elements, martial arts as its core element.

The story of *Kung Fu Panda* is like this: a fat and clumsy panda named Po lives with his foster father—Mr. Ping, a duck, in Peace Valley. Po is fascinated with kung fu while his father wants him to be a cook and take over the restaurant. Apparently, Po looks just like another portly panda, but what hidden beneath his furbears the mark of the chosen one. During the day, Po works very hard in his family's noodle shop, but by night, he dreams of becoming a true master of the martial artsto protect the villagers from the villains. When an ancient prophecy has come to pass, Po realizes that he is the only one who can save his people from certain destruction. In the end, with the help of the legendary Furious Five, Tigress, Crane, Mantis, Viper, Monkey and their wise mentor, Master Shifu, the noble Pomasters the martial arts and transforms his greatest weakness into his greatest strengths. It is these incredible strengths that beat the malevolent snow leopard Tai Lung. He fulfills his dream as the hero who saves his people during their darkest hour.

Kung Fu Panda is a good example of proper using of Chinese cultural factors while perfectly merging Chinese factors and Western factors. It is a product of the integration of Chinese culture and American values.It's a story of how a person of no importancegrew to be a great man with a great dream at the end.

2 Some Major Chinese Factors in the Film *Kung Fu Panda*

2.1 Panda

Panda is Chinese national treasure. In recent decades the Giant Panda has served as an emblem for the country and it becomes the spirit of China.The panda Po who is a leading character in the film Kungfu Panda catches the eyes of the audiences. Chinese panda is black-eyed and has a gentle demeanor. But in the film Kung Fu Panda, the American panda Po has a pair of green eyes which resemble the Caucasian. Instead of docile that everyone loves, he become chatty, obese, slothful, and edacious, and interpersonal relationship are not going well. No doubt , the film aims to tell a typical "American Dream" story of how an extremely ordinary character manages to succeed in achieving a great accomplishment. The audience are always being reminded that this is an American made animated film. No matter how much Chineseness the producers have attached in the film and how many Chinese elements are used, it is impossible to get rid of American spirit.

2.2 Chinese Architecture

At the very beginning of the movie, the Chinese white and black painting catches the audience's eyes. Lots of buildings with green bricks and white tiles as well as golden and red palaces erect on the mountain circled with smoky clouds. These characteristic Chinese architecture and architectural groups are also highlights in this filmimpressed the audiences. In China, there is a saying that: The right saddle must be put on the right horse." This means that all things have to be reasonable allocated to produce the best result. From the film we can see that either the noodle restaurant or the temple, the street or the alley, make audience clear- cut Chinese feelings. Poe's noodle restaurant, scarlet lantern high overhang, pots and pans, daily necessities ornaments, are also obvious delicate and elegant Chinese- style design. Audience may also find the flying petals, tortuous paths, distant pavilion and terrace are as picturesque as the scenery that is depicted both in many Chinese paintings and ancient Chinese poetry.

2.3 Chinese Kung Fu-Martial Arts

The major theme and clue of the film *Kung Fu Panda* is Chinese martial arts. The highest state of the Chinese martial arts is the harmony of the body and the mind. The functions of the martial arts in fighting are: defending oneself against the opponent, checking the attacks and winning the fight. On the level of philosophy, the martial arts focus on "unification of man and nature", i. e., the unification of existence and nonexistence, acting and stopping, Yin and Yang. On the social level, the martial arts stress cultivation of mind and personality, awareness of the natural law and complacency. They thus break all prejudices with regard to winning and losing and to success and failures, and take a calm attitude.

In *Kung Fu Panda*, the undefeatable secret of martial arts lie in the dragon warrior scroll. However, when Po unfolds the scroll, to his great amazement, there is nothing written on it. Not even a single word. This "assume formlessness" method is the supreme pursuit of martial arts to a certain extent, and the tactic does not rigidly adhere to a style. Instead of blindly imitating the movements and techniques, the producers of *Kung Fu Panda* grasped the marrow of the Chinese martial arts.

2.4 Chinese Philosophy

In the film, Po has been caught in perilous situations. Po has to defeat Tai Lung who is very strong and whose power is obviously several times greater than him. Although the hope of winning seems to be distant and dim, he never gives up on himself. His positive attitude can find its origin in Chinese Confucian philosophy.

The situation that Po is facing in the films is very much like what sage Confucius and his disciple Yan Hui were going through hundreds of years ago. How could Po find delight and joy from critical time and harsh living conditions? There are two key possibilities. Firstly, Po wasnever depressed or in despair. He was optimist. Second, Po was capable of self-reliance and tolerance, not in the sense of being content with what he was and what he had, but of being acceptance of whatever destiny might bring him.

Po is even more unlikely to become a historic savior. Even if Master Oogway sticks to the idea that Po is the chosen one and the only dragon warrior who has formidable strength underneath, Master Shifustill thinks thatit's impossible and regards it as a joke. After a series of frustration, Master Shifu happened to know Po's biggest hobby—food. He thus decides to take full advantage of it to give Po who is seemingly incorrigible a training. As expected, Po somehow transforms his biggest weakness into biggest strength and becomes a martial-arts master in reality as well as in name.

Master Shifu's strategy seems to be superficial but on looking deeper, another more subtle truth emerges. His strategy makes the best use of Po's weakness according to the specific situation. It turns out, fortunately, very effective. This dialectical speculation which had been prevailing in ancient China indicates that everything has two aspects that are in a state of continuous opposition and mutual transformation.

There is another very impressive scene in *Kung Fu Panda* where Master Oogway is bidding farewell to Master Shifu. With the pink petals dancing about in the wind, Oogway is more like vanishing into the other world rather than "pass away," as we usually call it.

This scene represents another Chinese philosophical thought in two aspects. Firstly, many Chinese philosophers believe that the circle of life is just like the blooming and withering of a flower. Oogway's disappearing with the withered petals implies the end of his life. Secondly, the beautiful and romantic scene seems to be telling the audience that Oogway is not "dead" literally but is integrating into the entire universe. His flesh and blood may no longer exist but his soul has raise to a more higher level thus can remain immortal. This is very much similar to one of the most ideal concepts which are promoted by Taoism—Heaven-Man Oneness, in which the famous Taoist Zhuang Zi pictured the paramount level of human life that Chinese people have been always pursue.

3 Conclusion

By studying of the film of *Kung Fu Panda*, we can find that the whole film is full of Chinese cultural factors like the Chinese images, Chinese architecture, theory of Taoism, theory of Confucianism, and theory of Buddhism. All of these Chinese cultural factors are the real charming and innovation of the film of *Kung Fu Panda* and also one of the reasons why it is popular around the globe. What was worth mentioning is that the Chinese and Western cultural factors kept their harmony co-exist in the film.It is not always beneficial if we keep our extraordinary traditional cultures to ourselves. Only by sharing them with the world can our cultures be known and loved by people all over the world.

Bibliography

[1] 解兰,秦岁明. 以中国文化融入现代理念的民族动画创作——解读美国动画片《功夫熊猫》[J]. 电影评介,2008(22).

[2] 李玲梅. 内外兼修才是真功夫——浅谈《功夫熊猫》给中国动画的启示[J]. 中国电视,2008(11).

[3] 刘喜梅,崔红娟,朱卫红.《功夫熊猫》:天真浪漫的中国式武侠[J]. 电影文学,2010(12).

[4] 王魏.从《花木兰》到《功夫熊猫》——试析中西文化的碰撞与融合[J]. 电影评介,2008(19).

[5] 左亚男,高昂.《功夫熊猫》:中国元素的戏仿与美国精神的建构[J]. 电影文学,2010(3).

[6] 贾玉新. 跨文化交际学[M]. 上海:上海外语教育出版社,1997.

[7] 阎云飞.《功夫熊猫》是写给中国的情书[J]. 新闻晨报,2008(5).

[8] 高莉. 试析《木兰辞》与美国电影《Mulan》中的中美文化差异[J]. 怀化学院学报,2006(3).

[9] 周琳玉. 从影片《木兰》看迪斯尼配方对"他者"文化的身份改写[J]. 四川外语学院学报,2006(9).

大学英语学习与中国文化传播

梁桂霞　李晓蕊

摘　要：本文从实际教学中遇到的问题和现状出发，讨论了在大学英语学习过程中将中国文化传播结合于其中的必要性，着重提出了英语教学的目的之一是更好地进行跨文化交流。根据现有研究成果，分析了目前英语教学中存在的“中国文化失语”现象，并从理念和实际出发，提出了可行的将中国文化传播融入大学英语学习中的一些策略。

关键词：大学英语；文化传播；中国文化失语；跨文化交际

1 引言

2007年，教育部组织有关专家制定的《大学英语课程教学要求》指出，“大学英语是以外语教学理论为主导，以英语语言知识与运用技能、跨文化交际和学习策略为主要内容，并集多种教学模式和教学手段为一体的教学体系”，并明确指出了英语对于加强国际交流的重要性。2013年8月14日，全国大学英语四、六级考试委员会发布公告对四、六级试卷结构进行改革，原单句汉译英调整为段落汉译英。翻译内容涉及中国的历史、文化、经济、社会发展等。在2012年改革后的第一次四、六级考试中，翻译题大打中国文化牌。四级有三种考卷，翻译主题分别是关于中国结、中国食品、茶与咖啡

项目/基金：本论文是北京工商大学2015年大学生科研与创业行动项目(编号SJ201502046)的成果之一。

作者简介：梁桂霞，北京工商大学外国语学院副教授，研究方向为跨文化及翻译。李晓蕊，北京工商大学经济学院2012级在读学生。

等，而六级翻译是关于中秋节与丝绸之路。多数考生反映内容很熟悉，但翻译难。这一现象表明，培养学生在对中国文化深刻理解的基础上用准确的英语翻译中国文化知识的能力，并最终提高大学生群体跨文化交际的能力，应该成为大学英语改革的重点。加之中国申办2022年冬奥会成功，继2008北京奥运会后，中国又将掀起一场全民学习英语的热潮。大学生作为英语学习的主力军，同样也要肩负起传播中国文化的重任。因此，在大学生英语学习过程中加强对中国文化的融入是很有必要的。

2 在大学英语学习过程中导入中国文化的必要性

语言与文化存在着密不可分的联系。文化是一种社会现象，是人们长期创造形成的产物，同时又是一种历史现象，是社会历史的积淀物。确切地说，文化是凝结在物质之中又游离于物质之外的，能够被传承的国家或民族的历史、地理、风土人情、传统习俗、生活方式、文学艺术、行为规范、思维方式、价值观念等，是人类之间进行交流的普遍认可的一种能够传承的意识形态。语言是人类文化的载体和重要组成部分。每种语言都能表达出使用者所在民族的世界观、思维方式、社会特性以及文化、历史等，都是人类珍贵的无形遗产。语言肩负着文化交流的重要使命。所以外语教学不仅仅是语言教学，还应该包括文化教学。

外语教学不仅仅是介绍与引进外国的文化、知识、技术、科学，同时也担负着传播本国文化的使命，为政治、经济、贸易、往来等服务。这就说明了跨文化交际在语言学习方面的重要性。教育部高等教育司张尧学司长对大学英语水平的定位是综合应用能力，要能够听懂中国国际广播电台的英文广播，要能读懂《China Daily》和专业综述文章，要能表述中国国情和文化。将中国文化融入大学英语教学，对于提高大学生跨文化交际能力以及综合文化素质等方面具有不可替代的作用。

所以，在当前英语学习中必须加强对中国文化的传播，继承和发扬中华民族优秀传统文化，树立对本民族传统文化的认同感和自豪感，从而在跨文化交际中不妄自菲薄，始终保持自尊、自强，把中国的优秀文化展现在世界人民面前。因此，大学英语学习中对于中国文化的导入是十分必要的。

3 大学英语学习中的“中国文化失语”现象

纵观历史长河，中华文化在很长的一段时间里都起到了滋养人类文明的作用。但是随着中国加速推进现代化和世界化的同时，中国人，尤其是年轻一代，逐渐忽视了对自己民族文化的关注。而英语，作为世界通用语，随着“地球村”的深化，对我们的生活有着越来越深的影响。英语的全球化，像是一把双刃剑，一方面促进我国与世界的文化交流和沟通，另一方面，又对我国的文化造成一定的冲击。面对这一形势，我们应当认识到，英语学习的目的是在交流、吸收外来文化的同时，更好地传播自己民族的文化。

从丛在《光明日报》上发表的一篇题为《“中国文化失语”：我国英语教学的缺陷》中提到，“许多中国青年学者虽然具有相当高程度的英语水平，但在与西方人交往的过程中，始终显现不出来自古文化大国的学者所应具有的深厚文化素养和独立的文化人格，有些博士生有较高的基础英语水平，也有较高的中国文化修养，但是一旦进入英语交流语境，便会立即呈现出中国文化失语症”。当西方同行怀着敬意探询*Confucianism/Taoism*（儒/道）的真谛时，我们的学者却心有余而力不足，只能顾左右而言他。他发表的这篇文章引起了人们对外语教学中中国文化教育的关注。

清华大学的张为民教授等对126名该校非英语专业的本科生进行了使用英语转述中国特色文化话题的能力测试，内容包括中国食物、民俗以及历史名胜古迹。结果表明，大多数受试者不能很好地用英语表达自己民族的文化，在可以接受的表述中还有较大部分为解释性意译。在此之后，相继有很多英语教学方面的相关调查，调查结果均显示，现阶段，大学生运用英语表述中国文化的能力存在着一定的欠缺，“中国文化失语”现象是客观存在的。除此之外，英语教师作为英语知识的传播者，其文化素养、教育理念在一定程度上直接影响着所教授学生的中国文化素养。邓文英、敖凡对四川省内10所高校的50名英语专业教师进行问卷调查。结果显示，英语教师在中国文化的英语表达方面也存在一定的缺陷，这会影响他们教授学生用英文表达中华文化的能力。由此观之，外语教师需要首先提高自身的中国文化英语表达能力，才能有效的提高大学生的中国文化英语表达能力。

4 将中国文化融入大学英语学习的策略分析

4.1 从母语层面深入了解中国传统文化，掌握其精髓

要想实现跨文化交流，作为中国文化传播的主体，我们首先要对中国传统文化有足够的了解，在我们庞杂的知识体系中明确什么才是中国文化的精髓。要想掌握其精髓，最好的方法莫过于直接的去接触，而作为中国人，对于中文的掌握是我们最有利的优势。了解一国的文化，只有通过其特有的语言文字。中华文化源远流长，其特有的道家、儒家思想是在历史长河中由特定的历史背景和文化酝酿而生的，掌握其精髓还需对中国历史有所了解。结合中国的发展情况，不断地思考、学习，才会把握中华文化的命脉。所以，了解中国传统文化，掌握其精髓不是一蹴而就的事，需要国家、社会、教育者和受教育者提升自身文化素养，加强对本民族文化的了解。只有足够了解本民族文化，才能做到更好的跨文化交流，为传播中国文化打下坚实的文化基础。

4.2 树立平等的文化交流意识

现阶段，我国对英语实行了平民化教学，一般幼儿园都已实现了双语教学，在学生生涯中中考、高考、大学四、六级更是强调了英语学习的重要性。由此可见，从个人到国家都十分重视英语的学习。与此形成鲜明对比的是，很多学生不明白自己为什么要学习英语，有的认为只是为了更好的去了解西方文化。由此观之，强调英语学习的跨文化交流的重要性迫在眉睫。学习外语，最主要是为了交流沟通，交流与沟通又必然是双向的，当沟通只重视一方时，文化交流必然出现偏颇，造成不平等。树立平等的文化交流意识，就可以在外语学习之初建立合理的学习目标，有效地加强对本民族文化的外语表达的重视。

4.3 寻找中西方文化相通点，达到中国文化传播的目的

由于语言的产生有其特定的历史背景和文化氛围，所以要想将一门语言准确完整的翻译成另一门语言有一定的困难。这就需要我们在英语学习的过程中，主动去发现中西方文化的共同之处，并且具体落实到词汇的学习上。在英语教学中的文化教学应遵循“求同存异”的原则，即在文化教学中应以

寻求目的语文化和母语文化的相通点为主要目的，从而让学生在母语文化环境中流利而地道地用目的语表达母语文化。

4.4 加强翻译教学中的文化传播

无论是从母语层面掌握中华传统文化精髓，树立平等的文化交流意识还是挖掘中西方文化的相通点，以上三点均是从理念方面加强对中国传统文化的传播。在实际学习中要加强对于中国文化的传播，就需要在大学英语教学中强调对学生汉译英技巧的传授和训练。尤其是在翻译题材的选择上，侧重一些具有优秀中国文化特色的内容。通过训练，使大学生掌握一些描述中国传统文化及中国当今社会现状的表达方法，进而能够使用英语介绍与传播中国的传统文化。

5 结语

中国文化的导入是大学英语教学与学习的重要组成部分，同样也是提高学生英语实际运用水平，增强其跨文化交流的重要保障。中国是拥有悠悠五千年历史文化的文明古国，如果在学习外语的过程中，摒弃了自己的文化或者无法将自己的文化用所学语言进行传播，无疑是人才培养和外语教学的一大败笔。了解并掌握自己国家的文化，运用所学将其传播出去，有助于在全球化的进程中加强自身的竞争力，更有助于中国传统文化的有效传播。

参考文献

[1] 高莉君. 大学英语教学中的中国文化认同教育[D]. 重庆:西南大学,2009.

[2] 万琼. 从课堂观察看大学生英语教学中的中国文化渗透[J]. 湖北师范学院学报:哲学社会科学版,2011(4):140-142.

[3] 马慧. 大学英语教学中的中国文化导入[J]. 南昌师范学院学报,2014(1):81-83.

[4] 张焕成. 大学英语教学中中国文化导入探析[J],中国民航飞行学院学报,2009(3):61-63.

[5] 张为民,朱红梅. 大学英语教学中的中国文化[J],清华大学教育研究,2002(增1):34-40.

[6] 曹迪. 大学英语教学中融入中国文化的思考[J]. 教育探索,2013(12):26-27.

«l'écriture plate» dans *La place* d'Annie Ernaux

吉　山

Résumé: Annie Ernaux, femme écrivain contemporaine en France, est issue d'une classe pauvre. Pour qu'Annie puisse sortir de la classe inférieure, ses parents font tout ce qu'ils puissent faire. La barrière infranchissable surgit entre eux au moment où Annie a réalisé l'ascension sociale. Donc, elle s'impose à écrire pour sauver tout ce qu'elle a vécu. En 1984, *La place* a récompensé par le prix Renaudot. Cette œuvre est caratérisée par «l'écriture plate» qu'Annie a utilisé pour la premier fois dans son écriture. Ce mémoire consiste à analyser les raisons et la mise en œuvre de la technique-«l'écriture plate»-dans *La place*.

Mots-clés: Annie Ernaux; «l'écriture plate»

1 Introduction

Annie Ernaux, née en 1940 à Lillebonne, est une femme écrivain française. Avec *La Place*, elle a obtenu le prix Renaudot en 1984, puis le prix Marguerite Duras 2008, le prix François Mauriac 2008, le prix de langue française 2008 et le prix des lecteurs du Télégramme 2009 pour *Les Années*.

Elle a passé son enfance et sa jeunesse à Yvetot. Ses parents y sont tenus une petite café-épicerie. Sa mère a voulu qu'Annie ait pu monter dans la classe bour-

作者简介:吉山,女,北京工商大学助教,主要研究方向为法国文化、法语教学。

geoise. Cependant, en montant dans le monde dominé, elle devenait une ennemie envers la classe de ses parents. Elle se considère comme une transfuge de sa classe. Chaque œuvre d'Annie nous représente son vécu et sa mémoire. Le lecteur peut retrouver sa propre vie par les œuvres d'Annie Ernaux.

Comme elle cite une phrase de Jean Genet en épigraphe dans *La place* «Je hasarde une explication : écrire c'est le dernier recours quand on a trahi». Dans *La place*, elle utilise «l'écriture plate» la première fois qu'elle n'abandonne plus. «l'écriture plate» est une marque de son création en quelques sortes. Nous traiterons notamment trois problèmes dans ce mémoire :

(a) Qu'est-ce que «l'écriture plate» pour Annie Ernaux?

(b) Pouquoi Annie Ernaux choisit «l'écriture plate»?

(c) La mise en application de «l'écriture plate» dans *La place*.

2 «l'écriture plate» dans *La place* d'Annie Ernaux

La place raconte la vie de son père en base de ses souvenirs d'une façon documentaire. Pour elle, «écrire est profondément lié à ma situation sociale en tant qu'individu.»Annie annonce qu'elle a une posture d'écrire. Dans *l'écriture comme un couteau*, elle s'explique le terme : «Tout ce que je sais, c'est que ce livre a inauguré comme je l'ai dit une posture d'écrire, que j'ai toujours, exploration de la réalité extérieure ou intérieure, de l'intime et du social dans le mouvement, en dehors de la fiction.» La posture d'écriture incarne en deux côtés : la forme littéraire et le style d'écriture. Elle qualifie *La place* de l'autobiographie. Sous cette forme littéraire, elle applique «l'écriture plate» dans ce récit. (elle préfère le récit à l'œuvre)

2.1 Qu'est-ce que «l'écriture plate» pour Annie Ernaux?

Roland Barthes a émis l'écriture blanche la première fois dans *Le degré zéro de l'écriture*. Une écriture blanche, c'est une écriture neutre, au plus près du réel. Frédéric-Yves Jeannet la caractérise l'écriture clinique. Annie Ernaux l'appelle «l'écriture plate» : «C'est ce que j'ai appelé dans *La place* «l'écriture plate, celle-là même que j'utilisais en écrivant autrefois à mes parents pour leur dire les nouvelles essentielles.» Ces lettres aux quelles je fais allusion étaient toujours concises, à la limite du dépouillement, sans effets de style, sans humour, toutes choses que auraient été perçues par eux comme des *manières*, des *embarras.*»

Le lecteur voit les choses, les corps et les actes par cette écriture sans fard et sans affect et se rappelle sa propre vie. C'est aussi l'intention d'écrir pour Annie: Écrire pour sauver, sauver la mémoire collective, sauver quelque chose du temps où l'on ne sera plus. Avec cette écriture, elle réalise à représenter réellement les choses par les mots justes.

2.2 Pouquoi Annie Ernaux choisit «l'écriture plate»?

Annie choisit une écriture dépassionnée, clinique, humble au cours de son chemin littéraire. Grâce à ces phrases sans afféteries, ces mots simples et crus, elle peut représenter ses souvenirs au plus juste, au plus précis et au plus réel.

Comme elle a écrit dès les premières pages de *La place*: «Pour rendre compte d'une vie soumise à la nécessité, je n'ai pas le droit de prendre d'abord le parti de l'art, ni de chercher à faire quelque chose de «passionnant», ou d'«émouvant». Je rassemblerai les paroles, les gestes, les goûts de mon père, les faits marquants de sa vie, tous les signes objectifs d'une existence que j'ai aussi partagée. Aucune poésie du souvenir, pas de dérision jubilante. «l'écriture plate» me vient naturellment, celle-là même que j'utilisais en écrivant autrefois à mes parents pour leur dire les nouvelles essentielles.»

Annie Ernaux veut « rester dans la ligne des faits historiques, du document.» Donc, «l'écriture plate» lui vient naturellement. C'est un style objectif «qui ne valorise ni ne dévalorise les faits racontés» avec une écriture «sans jugement, sans métaphore, sans comparaison romanesque». On peut dire un style ernausien avec les mots du peuple.

Annie veut faire un livre juste de son père. Elle s'explique « il faudra que j'explique tout cela». Je voulais dire, écrire au sujet de mon père, sa vie, et cette distance venue à l'adolescence entre lui et moi. Une distance de classe, mais particulière, qui n'a pas de nom. Comme de l'amour séparé.»

Il faut trouver les mots les plus justes pour la plus just représentation de la vie de son père. Elle détaille le sens de « juste »: « La seule écriture que je sentais *juste* était celle d'une distance objectivante, sans affects exprimés, sans aucune complicité avec le lecteur cultivé. C'est ce que j'ai appelé dans *La place «l'écriture plate»*, celle-là même que j'utilisais en écrivant autre fois à mes parents pour leur dire les nouvelles essentielles. Ces lettres auxquelles je fais allusion étaient toujours concises, à la limite du dépouillement, sans effets de style, sans humour, toutes choses qui auraient été perçues par eux comme des *manières*, des *embarras.*»

Il y a une douleur insérée profondémment dans son cœur : «Pourquoi mon père ne lit-il pas, pourquoi a-t-il des *manières frustes*... l'autre douleur, celle que j'ai eue de le perdre brutalement, au moment où je venais passer une semaine chez mes parents après avoir réalisé, au fond, son rêve, pour moi d'ascension sociale... Il fallait que j'écrive sur mon père, sur sa trajectoire de paysan devenu petit commerçant, sa façon de vivre, mais faire un livre juste, correspondant au souvenir vivant de cette douleur.»

«l'écriture plate» peut faire exister les choses, *voir* en oubliant les mots et représenter la vérité. Mais certains critiquent que la vérité dans les livres d' Annie Ernaux est grâce au «je» autobiographique. Ce n'est pas simplement le «je» qui peut désigner seulement. Annie réitère en plusieurs occasions: «*Journal du dehors* et *La vie extérieure* où le *je* est très souvent absent, il n'y a pas moins de *vérité* et de *réalité* que dans les autres textes: c'est l'écriture, globalement, qui détermine le degré de vérité et de réalité, pas seulement l' emploi du *je* fictionnel ou autobiographique. Il y a pas mal de récits autobiographiques qui donnent une insupportable impression de manquer la vérité. Et Des textes dits romans qui l' atteignent....Pour moi, la vérité est simplement le nom donné à ce qu'on cherche et qui se dérobe sans cesse.»

De plus, «l'écriture plate» lui fait trouver un accès de l'émotion paradoxale envers ses parents. Autrement dit, elle se libère de «l'écriture plate»: « Je suis venue au monde pour cela, pour dire ce qui m'est arrivé [...]. C'est difficile, c'est lourd, mais c'est un devoir. Mon devoir. Pour que d'autres puissent s'avouer peut-être [...] : vous me donnez envie de parler de moi. C'est ça, le rôle de l'écriture, quand elle mérite de s'appeler littérature. Un rôle de purification: de catharsis», explique-t-elle.

2.3 «l'écriture plate» dans *La place*

Le livre commence par la mort du père, évoque ses gestes, ses paroles, et ses habitudes... dont elle peut se souvenir de son père. Pour décrire la vie de son père le plus froidement possible, Annie applique les phrases extrêmement dépouillées.

La perte du père est sans doute le souvenir très douloureux, mais nous ne voyons aucun sentiment sous sa plume. «Mon père est mort deux mois après, un jour pour jour. Il avait soixante-sept ans et tenait avec ma mère un café-alimentation [...]»

En suite, elle relate le deuil d'une vision exceptionnellement objective. Avec des mots pauvres et des structures syntaxiques simples, le lecteur oublie même que c'est la mort d'écrivain et fait attention aux coutumes de l'enterrement.

«c'est un dimanche, au début de l'après-midi[...]Je crois avoir demandé à ma mère de lui fermer les yeux. Autour du lit, il y avait aussi la sœur de ma mère et son mari [...]On a commencé de prévoir l'inhumation, la classe des pompes funèbres, la messe, les faire-part, les habits de deuil [...]Les pompes funèbres sont venues le lundi [...]La veille de l'inhumation, on fait cuire une pièce de veau pour le repas qui suivrait la cérémonie [...]Il y a eu le serrement des mains. Par une erreur du sacrisation digigeant l'opération à moins qu'il n'ait imaginé ce moyen d'un tour supplémentaire pour grossir le nombre des assistants-les mêmes gens qui nous avaient serré la main sont repassés. Une ronde cette fois rapide et sans condoléances.»

Pour montrer l'existence réelle de son père, Annie utilise la langue poplaire, ou quelque fois crue: «Soudain, ma robe s'accroche par la poche à la poignée du vélo, se déchire. Le drame, les cris, la journée est finie. Cette gosse ne compte rien! »

«Sous l'insulte, sortant de son calme habituel: CARNE ! J'aurais mieux fait de te laisser où tu étais. Echange hebdomadaire: Zéro! Cinglée! »

Le fançais est une langue marquée du temps. Le temps reste très important dans l'écriture. Dans *La place*, Annie choisit le passé composé au lieu du passé simple: «j'écris au passé composé parce qu'on parle au passé composé.»

Annie élucide : «Le passé simple me rappelle mes rédactions d'élève, l'artifice par lequel je donnais de la noblesse aux actions ordinaires [...], il me rappelle une écriture qui n' avait aucune réalité, qui avait pour avantage principal d être bien notée.»

«l'écriture plate» refuse le pathos. Cependant, elle ne signifie pas une écriture sans métaphore. C'est une rhétorique spécifique qui défie l'esthétique traditionnelle. Nous pouvons trouver certaines métaphores dans ses textes ni blanches ni plates.

«Il disait toujours ton école et il pronoçait le pen-sion-nat, la chère Sœu-œur (nom de la directrice), en détachant, du bout des lèvres, dans une déférence affectée, comme si la prononciation normale de ces mots supposait, avec le lieu fermé qu'ils évoquent, une familiarité qu'il ne se sentait pas en droit de revendiquer.»

Comme Jean Pierrot a dit lors du colloque: «cette écriture plate ne reproduit pas la platitude de la parole courante, mais se caractérise par une rhétorique spécifique.»

3 Conclusion

La syntaxe simple, l'expressions courante, la distance objective, le sentiment calme, Annie applique la langue accessible à ses parents et au peuple. Elle reste tout à fait fidèle au monde origine avec «l'écriture plate». Cette écriture est contre certaines modalités de la littérature. *La place* entame son parcours du style particulier, «Il est vrai, souligne-t-elle, que l'écriture de *La place* marque un moment important pour moi : avec ce livre, j'ai trouvé ma trajectoire d'écriture. Depuis, il n'y a pas eu de changement majeur, j'ai creusé le même trou.»

La place marque bien la mise au point d'une nouvelle écriture contre le ton de dérision des premières œuvres, qui entretenait une connivence avec la vision et l'esthétique bourgeoises, et contre la fiction. Le choix ethnographique est lié au retour à une écriture naturelle.

Un adjectif n'est pas suiffisament à définir le style d'Annie Ernaux. Donc, je mets le style destiné. Écrire est pour elle une obligation de faire la culture dominée surgir dans la langue dominante. Annie ne se considère pas écrivain, «juste comme quelqu'un qui écrit, qui doit écrire.» Annie annonce son intention d'écrire: Écrire pour sauver, sauver la mémoire collective, sauver quelque chose du temps où l'on ne sera plus. Le mot *destiné* lie profondément ses deux classes hostiles, deux langues différentes et deux cultures séparées. Pour rester fidèle, Annie trouve une façon de transcrire, nommée «l'écriture plate». Grâce à cette écriture, elle trouve une façon de sauver sa propre existence et laisse assez d'espace au lecteur pour se réfléchir.

Bibliographi

[1] ERNAUX A. La place[M]. Paris:Gallimard,1983.

[2] DUGAST-PORTES.Francine,Annie Ernaux:Étude de l'œuvre[M]. Paris:Gallimard,1994.

[3] ERNAUX A. La honte[M]. Paris:Gallimard,1997.

[4] ERNAUX A. L'Écriture comme un couteau ,entretien avec Frédéric-Yves Jeannet[M]. Paris:Stock,2003.

大学英语教学中的文化平衡

王劲松

摘　要：在大学英语教学实践中，随着人们对语言与文化关系的认识越来越深入，英语国家文化的导入已得到了足够的重视。但随之出现的问题是对中国文化导入的忽略，从而导致学生难以用英语准确流畅地介绍中国文化。本文分析了产生这一现象的原因和维持大学英语教学中文化平衡的重要性，并提出了保持这一平衡的方法。

关键词：大学英语教学；西方文化；中国文化；文化平衡

1 引语

2013年4月，在教育部高等学校大学外语教学指导委员会第一次全体会议上，教育部高等教育司副司长刘贵芹的主旨发言分析了大学外语教学面临的四个新形势。其中之一是，"高等学校职能的新拓展给大学英语教学传承什么样的文化，怎样传承文化成为又一个重大课题。大学英语兼具工具性和人文性的特点，因此应探索如何在发挥好大学英语工具性的同时更加充分发挥大学英语在文化传承方面的重要功能，引导大学生既能吸收借鉴国外优秀文化成果，提高跨文化交流能力，又能传承中华优秀文化传统，树立文化自觉和文化自信，增强对中华文化和社会主义文化的认同。"

在现阶段大学英语教学中，教师已不再只关注语言知识的讲解和输入，

项目/基金：本文得到2015年北京工商大学教育教学改革研究项目的资助，项目编号为JG155102。

作者简介：王劲松，北京工商大学讲师，主要研究领域为语言学、教学法。

而是在讲解语言知识的同时介绍相关的文化背景知识，因为语言是文化的载体，是无法脱离文化而独立存在的。美国学者克拉姆契（Kramsch）说过：“语言是人们进行社会生活的主要手段。当它被用于交际场景中的时候，它便以多样而又复杂的形式与文化发生着联系。”为了掌握一种语言，了解相关的文化背景知识是非常必要的。但随之出现的问题是过于重视英美文化的输入。在跨文化交际中，对目的语文化的了解只是交际的一部分，而另一重要部分应该是把母语文化的优秀成果介绍出去。现在大学英语教学对后者的关注明显不足，因而导致了大学英语教学中文化失衡。

2 导致大学英语教学中文化失衡的原因

2.1 教材中有关中国文化的内容较少

教材是学生学习时的重要资源，也是教师实现教学目标的主要媒介。但现在广泛采用的大学英语教材中，涉及中国文化的文章少之又少。现在教材的选材很重视内容涵盖广泛，语言地道实用，但绝大多数文章涉及的是西方国家的政治、经济、历史、文化、科技等内容。有些教材设计的初衷是“在教材中融入世界各国的文化传统、风俗习惯和价值观念，引导学生探讨和鉴别中西文化差异……潜移默化地传授文化知识，培养文化意识、提升学生对不同文化的理解以及在跨文化交际情境中使用恰当、得体、地道英语的能力”。但由于现在很多学生对中国传统文化缺乏足够的了解，所以很难自发地进行中西文化对比，而只是接收大量的有关西方文化的信息。长此以往，难免会对本土文化的认同产生障碍。在这种情况下，如果教师不能有意识地在教学中进行中国文化的导入和中西文化对比，那么文化失衡将不可避免。

2.2 教师对教学目标的片面理解

在教育部颁布的《大学英语课程教学要求（教学大纲）》中对教学目标是这样描述的：“大学英语的教学目标是培养学生的英语综合应用能力，特别是听说能力，使他们在今后工作和社会交往中能用英语有效地进行口头和书面的信息交流，同时增强其自主学习能力，提高综合文化素养，以适应我国社会发展和国际交流的需要。”

教学大纲对大学英语教学目标的描述是比较全面的，其中特别提到了“提高综合文化素养”这一点。近年来，人们逐步认识到语言与文化的不可分割性及文化因素在跨文化交际中的重要性，从而越来越重视外语教育中的文化教学。但随之出现的问题是只注重对英语国家文化的导入而不重视中国文化。

人们往往认为，凭借英语这一工具，人们可以更好地了解西方的文化与发展和最前沿的科技动态，也可以了解西方的风俗习惯以避免在国际交往中造成误解而带来不良后果。这确实是大学英语教育所要承担的重要任务，但应该只是任务之一而非全部任务。英语的另一重要任务是把中国的优秀文化传播出去，让世界更好地了解中国。这个任务是被长期忽视的。无论是在教材的选材上，还是教学内容的安排上，这个问题都是比较突出的。

3 保持大学英语教学中文化平衡

在全球经济一体化的今天，文化全球化成为世界文化发展的新趋势。在这种新形势下，中国文化与其他文化之间的碰撞不可避免。要提升中国文化的国际地位，获得“中国文化的话语权”，就必须加快文化建设的步伐，使其与经济发展的速度相适应；必须在有选择地吸收西方文化的同时，高度重视中国优秀文化的继承和发扬。大学英语教学也应该在这一进程中发挥重要作用。

在本科阶段的课程设置中，大学英语均为必修课，所占课时、学分比例都是比较高的。客观要求和一些学生的主观需要，比如出国读研或求职等，使学生比较重视英语课的学习。这为利用大学英语教学进行适当的中国文化导入提供了有利条件。但目前中国文化导入的不足导致了“中国文化失语症”的出现。清华大学的张为民等对该校126名非英语专业本科生进行了用英语谈论中国特色文化话题的测试，内容涉及中国的食物、民俗及名胜古迹。结果显示，大多数受试者很难用英语将相关内容比较准确地表达出来。这如何能实现完整的跨文化交流呢？跨文化交流应该是双向的，平等的。但在大学英语教学中只重视英语国家文化导入的做法无法培养学生用英语介绍和传播中国优秀文化的能力，甚至会逐渐减弱学生对本土文化的认同感。

即使就英语学习本身而言，对中国文化的充分了解是可以有效促进英语学习的。早在1991年，胡文仲、高一虹就对来自全国的26名"最佳外语学习者"做过一项调查。调查结果显示："调查对象在学习外语和外国文化的过程中逐渐培养了自己突出的扬弃能力。这种能力不仅有助于他们的语言和交际能力，而且对于整体人格的完善也有着积极的作用。对待母语、母语文化的态度与对待外语、外国文化的态度是互动的；对于母语、母语文化和对于外语、外语文化的掌握是相互促进、相得益彰的。"

那么如何保持大学英语教学中的文化平衡呢？首先，教学大纲中应该对中国文化的适当导入提出更明确的要求。作为大学英语教学的指导性文件，这一要求的提出必然影响教材的编纂和选择以及教学目标的确定。其次，作为学生学习的重要资源的教材应适当增加中国文化元素。以每册书十个单元，每个单元三篇文章的教材为例，可以在每个单元中包含一篇介绍中国文化的文章，潜移默化地引导学生关注中国文化。如何有效地执行教学大纲和使用教材则是教师要发挥的重要作用了。教师首先需要转变观念，不要只把介绍目的语文化看作英语教学的任务，而要意识到大学英语教学在传承中国文化方面的重要作用，有意识地把对中国文化的介绍和中西文化对比引入到自己的教学中来，培养学生对中西文化的鉴别能力。

4 结语

在大学英语教学中导入中国文化要避免走入另一个极端，要保持好中国文化与英语国家文化导入的比例，让学生能够充分接触和了解多种文化，在认同本土文化的前提下接纳不同文化。

参考文献

[1] 胡文仲，高一虹. 外语教学与文化[M]. 长沙：湖南教育出版社，1997.
[2] 教育部高等教育司. 大学英语课程教学要求（教学大纲）[M]. 北京：外语教育与研究出版社，2004.

[3] 刘艳. 文化定势在帕尔默文化语言学中的意象图式的诠释[J]. 赤峰学院学报:汉文哲学社会科学版,2009(3).
[4] 张为民,朱红梅. 大学英语教学中的中国文化[J]. 清华大学教育研究,2002(S1).
[5] KRAMSCH C. Context and culture in language teaching[M]. 上海:上海外语教育出版社,2004.

海明威：同情女人的男人

赵 双

摘 要：本文从文本入手，剖析海明威作品中的主要女性角色，指出海明威是一个具有双性视角、强烈女性意识的男性作家；说明了海明威是一位具有深刻的洞察力和同情心的极为敏锐的作家。

关键词：女性；同情心；敏锐

20世纪美国文学中，海明威是贡献最大、影响最深远的作家之一。有关其本人及其作品的评论不仅浩如烟海，同时也立论分歧。评论家们争论的焦点之一是他小说中塑造的女人形象。很多评论家对海明威塑造的女性形象颇多微词。自从Leslie Fiedler在他的一篇颇有影响的论文《没有女人的男人》中指出：海明威笔下的女性存在着很大的局限性，被简单地两极分化成对男人的主体位置起破坏作用的魔女，和对男人百依百顺的、符合传统道德规范的女性。这两类特定的范畴随之被众多的评论家重新引用。一些女权主义者甚至认为海明威笔下的女性都是粗俗的。

然而，并不是所有的评论家都怀有敌意。如Wendy Martin和Mona Rosenman曾经强调，应该站在历史的背景下，而不应用现代人的道德观念和期望去看待这些生活在不同时代的女性。显然越来越多的评论家对指责海明威对妇女抱有敌意或漠不关心的这一看法已越来越不以为然。在这里通过对海明威小说中塑造的女性形象的细致分析，阐释并说明海明威对女性内在感受表现出了极度的敏感。他对女性生活的沮丧和感情受挫的敏感出色地表现在很

作者简介：赵双，硕士，天津大学讲师，主要研究方向英美文学。

多故事中。海明威笔下的女主人公都有其独特之处，她们完全超越了西方评论家对其女性形象的两极界定范畴。

1 两极范畴的重新阐释

海明威笔下的许多女性都超越了狭隘的范畴。如：《某件事情的结局》和《三天的打击》中是什么原因使得Nick非要抛弃Marjorie？许多评论家的解释都对Marjorie不利，认为她是一位自我意识强、对男人的主体位置起破坏作用的女性。事实上，真正的原因是由于Marjorie处处表现得和Nick一样内行。她能与Nick的技能、经验和强壮较量，她的能干使Nick感到了威胁，因为传统观念上只有男人才具有这些品质。对于Nick的离去，Marjorie表现得很有尊严，一点也不像依赖男人的女子，令人钦佩；反而Nick在分手之后倍感失落。整个故事中Nick的幼稚和优柔寡断与Marjorie的坚定和果断形成了鲜明对比。《艾略特夫妇》中不应由于Hubert的性冷淡而去责备Cornelia Elliot。《白象似的群山》中Jig面对的是一个设法迫使她去流产，而不顾她个人感情的丈夫。这些女性只是想得到生活的满足和称心如意，却由于丈夫的视而不见和无知而无法得到。海明威把女性对生活的沮丧和感情的受挫敏锐出色地表现在这些故事中，寄予了他对女性深深的同情。

海明威对女性的同情还表现在他对有过错的女性的描写之中。如《短暂的幸福生活》中的Margot尽管淫荡轻浮，却被描写成一个非常聪明、有抱负的女子。她陷入追求时尚的婚姻困境中，成为其阶级和美貌的牺牲品。海明威作品中的女性形象中最典型的魔女就是《乞力马扎罗的雪》中的Helen和《太阳照样升起》中的Brett。可怜的Helen曾经饱受生活的折磨，Harry给她带来了重新生活的勇气和信心。面对死亡，Harry最终承认，他对Helen的无情和冷酷，他把艺术上的失败归罪于妻子是错误的。Brett身上有许多可怕的品质，然而，Brett进退两难的处境正是20世纪20年代的妇女所要面对的，最终离开Romero使她超越了邪恶的破坏者的形象。

在海明威女性形象的两极界定范畴中，对男人百依百顺的、符合传统道德规范的典型女性如：《密执安河上》情犊初开的少女Liz，对一个感情麻木、自我为中心的小伙子的迷恋和多情。通过Liz，海明威表达了对女性的理解和同情：是男人的自私限制了妇女对性和自由的渴望。《永别了，武器》中Catherine的顺从是为了逃避战争给她带来的精神创伤，女性特有的直觉和理解力也使她超越了传统女性的“顺从的、没有头脑的”固定形象。另一个相似的战争受害者是《丧钟为谁而鸣》中的Maria，由于心灵的创伤把Robert Jordan当作爱人和保护者。

海明威的许多故事都表明，他不应被认为是一个具有很强的厌女情结、好战的、对女性抱有敌意的人或被称为大男子主义者。海明威对女性内在感受表现出了极度的敏感，他对女性生活的沮丧和感情受挫的敏锐出色的反映在很多故事中。海明威笔下的女性不是作为陪衬或对立面而存在，她们都是与众不同的，她们完全超越了西方评论家对其女性形象的两极界定范畴。

2 海明威的双性视角

维吉尼亚·沃尔夫在《一间自己的房子》中写到：“纯粹男性的大脑，就如同纯粹女性的大脑一样不能创作……创作行为完成之前要在大脑中进行某种男女间的合作。”在书的结尾，沃尔夫又强调，“伟大的头脑是雌雄同体的”。海明威能超越自身的性别身份，从女性视角去观察事物，去揭示女性对事物的反应以及内在感受，因此他笔下的女性富有个性的光芒。海明威这种采纳异性身份、把女性情感结合起来的能力是一种敏锐的双性视角，它能使作家客观的观察和表现事物并把女性描写成拥有个体意识和独立行为的人。

在他的故事中，海明威提出了这样的问题：如果男人和女人可以摆脱社会的性别禁忌，如同居住在瑞士阿尔卑斯山的Catherine和Frederic，或生活在性解放城市巴黎的Jake和Brett，或生活在偏远地方的David和Catherine一样，将会怎样？如果社会没有限制男人和女人的性别角色，将会怎样？如果男女之间性的关系更加开放，将会怎样？事实上，海明威在他的故事中通过尝试雌雄共体来表达他男女性别平等的主张。Brett、Jake、Frederic、Catherine及其他很多角色都在尝试击倒性别限制的壁垒，一种性别不再永远占主导地位，另一种也不再总是服从。

海明威的双性视角在他的一些短篇小说中，尤其是他关于婚姻和已婚夫妇的故事中得到了很好的体现。《雨中的猫》中作家塑造了一个被丈夫排除在其生活之外的年轻妻子。作者从女性视角展开叙述，通过夫妻之间的对话充分展现了两人感情的隔阂以及女性在夫妻关系中得不到重视的忧郁和悲哀，像雨中的猫一样，无奈而又迷茫。《伊甸园》女主人公Catherine是一位大胆反判的"新女性"，为激发丈夫的创作想象，Catherine与David进行了"性别交换"的尝试：Catherine将自己白皙的皮肤晒得黝黑，怂恿David把头发剪成和她一样短并染成同一种亮色。她对David宣称："我是个女孩，也是个男孩。我可以做他们能做的一切事情。"在塑造Catherine这位"新女性"的同时，海明威也向我们展示了他的双性视角。作家站在异性的立场上，融入女性所熟悉的感情、行为和价值观，通过Catherine展示了那些被歧视，被压抑、被排挤的女性试图步入男性世界以及对理想的人格形象——"双性共体"的追求。实际上海明威在这里正是以男女性别界定的模糊性来象征和暗指千百年的传统观念的根本动摇，海明威是在努力寻求打破不合理的的传统性别模式，并且力图构建一种理想的两性模式。

这些故事充分说明，海明威能够超越自己的性别身份，把女性成分纳入自己的意识之中。海明威在其小说中体现的双性视角，是对父权制度和性别角色的陈规模式不合理性的揭露，以及对女性受男性歧视和排挤遭遇的同情。

海明威能超越男性作家的狭隘视角去洞察和同情女性的苦难。在海明威的故事中，女性都扮演着传统角色：情人、妻子和母亲，但她们都通过自身的独特之处超越了那些特定的性格特征和行为。海明威的理想女性既非魔女也非天使，她们有血有肉，真实可信，她们同时又寄托着作家两性间融洽共存的理想。另外，在小说中，海明威通过尝试雌雄共体来探究两性在社会和家庭中的适当角色和地位，也表达了他两性平等的观念。

参考文献

[1] 戴桂玉. 双性视角作家海明威[J]. 外国文学,2003(6):77-82.

[2] 戴桂玉. 海明威:“有女人的男人”[J]. 外国文学评论,2001(4):71-77.

[3] 欧内斯特·海明威. 海明威短篇小说全集 [N]. 陈良廷,译. 上海:上海译文出版社,1981.

[4] 沃吉尼亚. 伍尔芙:一间自己的房间[M]. 贾辉丰,译. 北京:人民文学出版社,2003.

[5] 赵迎. 从小说《伊甸园》看海明威的双性视角[J]. 东岳论丛,2012(5):31-34.

Tocqueville's View on the Sovereignty of the People in America

李 洁

Abstract: Based on the first four chapters of Tocqueville's *Democracy in America*, this paper presents some of Tocqueville's views on the sovereignty of the people, provides a brief analysis of its origin, its relation to social democracy, its application in the 1830s America and its potential dangers. As a matter of fact, Tocqueville maintained, "The principle of the sovereignty of the people governs the whole political system of the Anglo-Americans. Every page of this book (Democracy in America) will afford new applications of the same doctrine."

Key Words: Tocqueville; the Sovereignty of the People in America

The United States in the first half of the nineteenth century attracted the attention of quite a number of foreigners, who made the "Grand Tour of America" in those years. Alexis de Tocqueville was one of them. When this French nobleman arrived in the United States in 1831, he was more interested in democracy than he was in America—or rather he was interested in America as a precedent of the "great democratic revolution". His deep insight into American institutions and American character during his nine-month stay in America has been embodied in his famous work *Democracy in America*. According to Tocqueville, democracy and

---

作者简介:李洁,北京工商大学外国语学院讲师,研究方向为英语语言文学。

the absolute sovereignty of the people were the most striking characteristics in America. This paper will focus on Tocqueville's view on the sovereignty of the people in the United States based on the first four chapters of his book.

1 The Origin of the Principle of the Sovereignty of the People

By the sovereignty of the people, Tocqueville means that every citizen was "put in the possession of his rights." Put it simply, it refers to the people's administration of government. To understand his idea on the sovereign of the people, a brief analysis should be offered on the origin and the social causes of this principal. Tocqueville states, "in America, the principle of the sovereignty of the people is recognized by the customs and proclaimed by the laws...from their origin, the sovereign of the people was the fundamental principle of most of the British colonies in America." The origin of the principle should be traced back to the township of the New England in the colonial America, which was the place where the people most directly exercised power to rule.

England established three types of colonies in America: royal colonies administrated by the English government, proprietary colonies belonging to proprietors and self-governing colonies largely independent of English control. The last mode of colonies, which was favorable to liberty, was adopted only in New England where a different form of local government called the town meeting came into being. On town meeting days most citizens gathered in the town halls to discuss town problems, levy taxes on themselves and elect town officers. And in the discussion, all citizens had the right to express their thought and ideas. Just as Tocqueville described, "the affairs of the community were discussed, as at Athens, in the marketplace, by a general assembly of the citizens." Through this form of self-government, the people of New England "continually exercised the rights of sovereignty; they named their magistrates, concluded peace or declared war, made police regulations, and enacted laws." The principal town officers were the "selectmen", whose duties were to administer the laws that the voters adopted in the town meeting. Although the right to vote was limited by religious and property qualifications, the New England town meetings provided larger opportunities to participate in government than citizens enjoyed in other colonies. The local governments dealt with everyday problems of immediate concern to the people and most citizens received their first lessons in self-government at the local level.

The primitive form of the sovereignty of the people in the English colonies enabled them to "have always enjoyed more internal freedom and more political independence than the colonies of other nations; and this principle of liberty was nowhere more extensively applied than in the States of New England..." Moreover, the general principles were all recognized and established not only by customs but also by law. What should not be forgotten is that the laws in New England were not imposed by authority, but were freely voted by all the persons interested in them, thus the participation of the people in public affairs, the voting of taxes, the responsibilities of administrative powers, personal liberty were established in the laws of New England. The experiences of self-government in the colonies enabled the Americans to understand the rules of governing themselves, fostering and maintaining the principle of the sovereignty of the people.

2 Social Democracy and Its Relation to the Sovereignty of the People

According to Tocqueville, the sovereignty of the people in America was one of the political consequences of social democracy. By social democracy, he meant a society in which equality was widely accepted as a primary social value.

In the Jackson's time, equalitarianism became the major theme of American life, which impressed Tocqueville so deeply that he concluded the democratic societies like America were "ardent, insatiable, incessant and invincible" in their passion for equality. Degler also commented on this new democratic spirit of the 1830s: "in the years between 1820 and 1860, Americans made it clear that theirs was to be an equalitarian and open society. Earlier expressions of this sentiment had been sporadic and moderate; in the Age of Jackson it was blatantly and continuously proclaimed."

Tocqueville claimed the eradication of primogeniture was the final step of equality. Inheritance law in America required equal sharing of property among the children, thus the land would be continually broken up and great landed fortunes would be nearly impossible to sustain. This law, according to Tocquville, exercised the great influence on the social state of a people. It not only shattered an aristocracy and divided and distributed both property and power again, but also affected the minds of the people. "The law of partition has reduced all to one level." Wealth, rather than family or tradition in Europe, would be the primary determinant of social stratification. The availability of land and the possibility of a good life resulting from individual ownership of land made the rapidity of social advancement possible. All these changes and opportunities cultivated the egalitarian sentiments in a society in which the majority possessed property and almost all of them could read and write. "Men are there seen on a greater equality in point of fortune and intellect." Thus the idea of equality was increasingly growing.

In America, the passion for equality incited men to wish all to be "powerful and honored." With such a social condition and the sentiment for equality, equality would eventually find its way into the political world. Tocqueville asserted there were two ways of establishing equality in the political world: either granting every citizen or no citizen rights. Instead of falling into absolute power, America was the first nation to establish and maintain the sovereignty of the people, "allowed by their circumstances, their origin, their intelligence and their morals."

3 The Application of the Sovereignty of the People in the 1830s

According to Todd, in the early years of America's history, political democracy was limited. When the Constitution was adopted, the right to vote and to hold public office was restricted in varying degrees in different states. However, the second quarter of the nineteenth century witnessed an unprecedented expansion of popular participation in politics. Jackson's presidency symbolized the era and stimulated the growing democratic spirit. In the 1830s, American political thought and institutions were undergoing the most profound transformation as political control was shifted from an older aristocracy of education, position and wealth to the "common man," the average America. Political power was more evenly divided between well-to-do people and the average Americans.

Tocqueville made his observation in this historical context and concluded that the principle of the sovereignty of the people had acquired "all the practical development which the imagination can conceive" in the United States in the 1830s. The application of this principle was first demonstrated by altering the elective qualification and expanding the suffrage, which Tocqueville thought introduced the most democratic forms into the government. According to Degler, even during the eighteenth century, more people could vote in the United States than in England and other European countries. In the years after 1815, the suffrage was expanded. The following decades witnessed the flood tide of the suffrage movement. A new principle was established that manhood, not property, was the most just basis for political rights. Americans could rest their government upon the consent of all the white males.

The suffrage was by no means the only one of the alterations showing the growing democratic spirit. "Sometimes the laws are made by the people in a body, as at Athens;" Tocqueville wrote, "and sometimes its representatives, chosen by universal suffrage, transact business in its name, and under its immediate supervision." During Jackson's presidency, governors were elected instead of being chosen by the legislature. And a large number of other offices were made elective on the state or local level. Besides, property holding as a qualification to hold office was also abandoned. Elections were usually held every year for local and state offices. Those who had the right to vote did so and in large numbers. "The people reign over the American political world as Deity does in the universe," wrote Tocqueville. There is a vivid statement on this principle of sovereignty of the people given by Michel Chevalier, the French minister of the interior dispatched to the United States in 1834: "The farmer and the mechanic are the lords of the New World; public opinion is their opinion; the public will is their will; the President is their choice, their agent, their servant...American society is essentially and radically a democracy, not in name merely but in deed." Besides, the rotation of public office also facilitated the democratization of administration on both the federal and state levels. Americans made sure that their government, like the society at large, reflected their firm belief in the equality of men.

Tocqueville's observation and generalizations concerning the sovereignty of the people were shrewd and perceptive against the historical background of the 1830s. However, the sovereignty of the people only included the white males and Tocqueville failed to comment on the political rights of the Negroes, women and American Indians.

4 Potential Dangers of Equality and the Principle of the Sovereignty of the People

Tocqueville concerned himself with the potential dangers that equality and the principle of the sovereignty of the people might bring about in the democratic America. He argued that the passion for equality often overrode the desire for freedom; consequently people often surrendered freedom for the sake of equality. Furthermore, in a society made up of equal citizens, each person was individually weak and not strong enough "to engage in the struggle alone with advantage." They had to increasingly subordinate their concern for individual liberty and freedom to their new respect for the majority. To Tocqueville, a majority of equals, just like a single all-powerful ruler, could abuse its power. In a democracy, Tocqueville argued, this abuse becomes the "tyranny of the majority."

Tocqueville did not claim that the tyranny of the majority as yet existed to any great degree in America. Still, he saw evidence of it developing. For example, de Tocqueville found that in the North, free black males who had the right to vote often were discouraged from voting by the white majority.

Bibliography

[1] BREEN T H. The power of words: documents in American history [M]. New York: Harper Collins College Publishers, 1996.

[2] DEGLER C N. Out of our past: the forces that shaped modern America [M]. 3rd ed. New York: Harper & Row Publishers, Inc., 1984.

[3] HEFFNER R D. Democracy in America by Alexis de Tocqueville [M]. New York: the Penguin Group, 1984.

[4] TODD L P, MERLE C. Rise of the American nation [M]. New York: Harcourt Brace Jovanovich, Inc., 1977.

从意识形态角度看林纾译本《黑奴吁天录》对原作的改写及对今天的启示

高瑾玉

摘　要：本篇论文对林纾的译本《黑奴吁天录》进行个案研究，探讨决定译者翻译策略的社会文化因素。论文将林纾译本与原文进行对照，找到两者的不同之处，也即译者在翻译时对原文的改动。论文重点对目的语的意识形态因素进行分析，证明翻译并非在真空中进行，而是受目的语文化的制约；翻译过程不仅仅是一个语言转换的过程，而且是一个源语文化与译语文化间的协商对话过程。林译本的成功也给我们实行文化走出去战略提供了有益的启示。

关键词：意识形态因素；翻译策略；文化

1 Lefevere有关文学翻译改写的理论

几千年来，翻译一直被看作语言符号之间的转换，而忠实也被毫无争议地作为检验翻译作品的唯一标准。随着Evan-Zohar的多元系统理论的引入，翻译理论家走出语言的范畴，而将重心放在翻译与文化之间的相互作用，文化因素对翻译的制约，以及语境、历史、传统等更大的问题上。Lawrence Venuti也指出："翻译过程中的每一步——从译本的选择，到翻译策略的运用，再到对译文的编辑、评论和阅读——都受到在目的语中流行，有着特定

作者简介：高瑾玉，硕士，北京工商大学外国语学院讲师，研究方向为翻译理论、文学。

主次级别的多种文化价值观的干涉。”

Lefevere在他的《翻译、改写及对文学名声的操纵》中具体研究了影响文学译本接受的因素，指出翻译受到以下三个因素的影响：① 文学体系中的专职人员，其中包括评论家，其评论影响一部作品的接受；决定是否对一本书进行研究的教师；译者本人，译者决定译本采用何种诗学策略，有时还要决定采用何种意识形态立场。② 文学体系以外的赞助人。赞助人也许是某个特定历史时期具有权威或影响力的个人，团体（如出版商、媒体、政治阶层或政党），决定文学及文学观念传播的全国性研究机构、学术杂志以及教育机构等。赞助人因素包括意识形态因素、经济因素及地位问题。其中意识形态因素决定了主题的选择以及推出的形式。在Lefevere的定义中，意识形态因素不仅限于政治，同时还指决定我们行为的形式、传统及信仰。③ 诗学因素。他指出意识形态因素决定了译者将采取何种策略，解决有关原著中的语域，即原作者所熟悉世界中的物件、概念、风俗，以及原作所使用的语言问题。他还进一步指出，在翻译过程的每一个层次中，如果语言因素的考虑与意识形态和诗学因素的考虑发生冲突时，后者总会占上风。

本文试从意识形态角度，对林纾译本《黑奴吁天录》(《Uncle Tom's Cabin》)中所进行的改写及所使用的翻译策略背后的因素进行分析。

2 林译本对《黑奴吁天录》的意识形态改写及背后的原因

2.1 一本宗教小说

《黑奴吁天录》的作者斯托夫人（Harriet Beecher Stow）生长在一个清教家庭，新教在她一生中扮演着重要角色，她的丈夫也是牧师和讲经的教师，她的这本反奴隶制小说浸润着强烈的宗教色彩。奴隶制与基督教观念的互不相容是小说的主题，作者在书中不遗余力地阐明奴隶制与基督教的道德教条是相违的。小说中，基督教代表了宇宙大爱、宽恕和自我牺牲，如果将这些信条付诸实践，是不可能允许一部分人压迫和奴役另一部分人的。在作者看来，基督教与奴隶制不仅互不相容，而且前者可以用来反抗后者。作者通过书中的场景，向她的大多数信教的北方读者大声疾呼，奴隶制是邪恶的、反基督的，在一个公民社会是不可容忍的。

作者在书中着力塑造了汤姆这个角色。他诚实、宽厚、富于爱心及自我牺牲精神，是作者刻意塑造的“黑皮肤的耶稣”。通过汤姆这一形象，作者意欲说明，黑人也和白人一样，是道德而良善且充满智慧与正义感的，都是上帝的儿女，而拯救他们就是拯救自己的兄弟姐妹。与汤姆对应的白人角色夜娃，是作者塑造的另一个基督式人物，她善良而充满同情心，从不因汤姆的黑奴身份而歧视他，相反，因为共同的信仰而与汤姆亲近。通过夜娃这一形象，作者给白人树立了可以效仿的榜样。书中几乎所有正面角色都是基督教的信仰者或同情者，而恶人都是不信教的。书中70多处引用《圣经》，也从另一方面证明了小说浓烈的宗教意味。

小说在汤姆之死中达到了高潮。在这个场景的描写中，作者刻意隐喻了耶稣之死。像耶稣一样，汤姆也是为了拯救别人而甘愿牺牲自己，汤姆所经历的肉体痛苦正像耶稣在十字架上忍受的痛苦，他也曾有短暂的对信仰的动摇，就像耶稣在极度痛苦中喊出的：“我的神，我的神，为什么要遗弃我!”但最终他克服了自己的软弱，恢复了对上帝的信仰。汤姆在死前对加害他的恶人说：“我真心原谅你们!”也隐喻着耶稣在最后一刻的话：“父啊，原谅他们吧，因为他们不知道他们做的是什么。”

总之，对上帝的信仰代表着作者在书中对奴隶制问题开出的药方，对黑人，是安慰、希望和忍受命运的力量源泉；而对白人，则是一种激励，使他们听从上帝的召唤，像爱手足一般去爱奴隶，基督教的信仰成为统领全书的最重要的主题。

2.2 译本对原作的意识形态改写

(1) 对汤姆形象的改动。

在我们检视林译本时，我们发现，全书中有关宗教的部分，有着大段的删节，主人公及书中其他人物作为虔诚基督徒的形象变得面目全非，通过宗教实施拯救的主题荡然无存。

在书中开篇的章节，有一段汤姆叔叔的话，共172个词，描绘出了汤姆作为一个虔诚的基督徒和一个牧师的形象。这是有关汤姆性格的重要段落，而译者将其全部删去。第7章，汤姆与克鲁大嫂讨论奴隶贩子的态度时的对话，成功描绘了汤姆作为基督徒的形象，并为最后汤姆基督式的死亡埋下了伏笔，是刻画汤姆的重要章节，而译本中已将其尽数删去。有时有关宗教的章节虽未全部删除，却大大简化了，从而缺少了原著中浓郁的宗教色彩。

在圣·克雷（St. Clare）因为失去女儿夜娃（Eva）而陷入悲痛之中时，汤姆用圣经中的话语安慰他，克雷在悲痛中怀疑上帝与天国的存在，而汤姆坚定的信仰使其加深了对基督教的同情。他“觉得自己被汤姆那信仰与感情的浪潮漂浮起来，仿佛看到了天国……”汤姆的讲道对圣·克雷最终下定决心解放奴隶起到了至关重要的作用，加强了宗教主题。而汤姆有关信仰及上帝的长篇大论，在译本中只剩下寥寥数语：“汤姆欲前慰解，而不期先哭。主仆相向呜咽，至于无声。”夜娃死后，圣·克雷与汤姆读圣经，在读到《最后审判》一章时，省悟“有些人不能进天国”不是因为“他们犯了弥天大罪”，而是因为他们“没有多做善事”。在跟亚菲力（Ophelia）讨论奴隶制问题时，他再次从《圣经》中得到启示，认为“一个人，如果不竭尽全力，来反对这个成为我们整个社会基础的可怕的不公正制度，必要时甚至不惜牺牲生命的话，那他就不是一贯笃信基督徒。”

而在译文中，这些长篇讨论圣经的谈话都悉数略去，仅剩这些文字“圣格来读既，若置身亡母之前，凄恋万状，以手自支其颐，谓亚妃立曰：‘吾之生趣尽矣。今唯发宏愿，尽释吾家之奴。若更有力，则尽举南美之奴而释之，而后始满吾愿力。’”

这段文字给人的印象是，圣·克雷之所以决定解放奴隶，不是基于他对基督教的严肃思考，而是因为在失去母亲，进而又失去夜娃以后，他找不到人生的意义，世俗的爱代替了宗教的主题，成为他作出此重大决心的动因。

在全书的高潮汤姆之死的描述中，原文有大段大段的文字，激情描绘在恢复对上帝的信仰后，汤姆感到的狂喜与力量，但这些充满感情和宗教热情的文字在译本中仅剩“汤姆此时，畏葸之状，一扫而空。天甫辨色，即闻吹号之声，逼令赴工。汤姆昂然上道。畏葸之情即除，冤抑之念亦息。觉人世欣慕之事，既等云烟，苦恼之情，亦同安乐，似己之躯壳，与己之灵魂，判然不相附丽。”译文还将原文中的God（上帝）除很少的几处译为“主”以外，均译为充满儒道意味的“天”“天意”“正道”“道”等，将“sit down with me on my throne”（在我宝座上与我同坐）的宗教式奖赏，译为儒家此世的“有为”。所有这些删改，使得汤姆最后所说：“我从心底里宽恕你！”显得突兀而失去了凭依，也令作者为刻画汤姆基督式形象，而将汤姆之死与耶稣之死所做的隐喻，这一浓墨重彩的一笔，意义尽失。至此，读者在译本中看到的汤姆再也不是原作中为作者竭力歌颂的英雄，那个凭借对上帝的坚定信念，有着坚强性格、独立意志的人，而成为一个抽掉了灵魂的人，一个好心肠、助人为乐却只知一味隐忍的被动、软弱形象。

(2) 哲尔治路线。

在探讨奴隶制解决之道时，作者还提供了另一条道路——哲尔治（George）路线，亦即反抗的路线。书中的哲尔治是一个睿智的奴隶，他逃出了奴隶庄园，逃亡到了加拿大。他并不反对暴力，虽然他也尊重妻子信奉的宗教。他相信自己与白人有着一样的力量与智慧，因此应得到与白人同等的权利。在失散已久的姐姐资助下，他在法国学习四年，最终决定举家搬迁到非洲，意欲建立一个非洲人自己的共和国。

虽然哲尔治在书中是一个远没有汤姆重要的角色，但译者将与其有关的章节全部保留。在这种改动下，他的形象凸显出来，与汤姆弱化的形象相比，哲尔治在译本中成为一个远较原著重要、几乎与汤姆并置的角色。

3 在改写的背后

我们可以从林纾写作的时代背景及译者个人的政治倾向上，找到在这些改写背后的意识形态因素。

3.1 时代背景

中国在鸦片战争中的失败唤醒了国人，他们意识到中国并非“世界中央的国度”，而将西方列强的船坚炮利视为失败的原因，由此展开了洋务运动。而1895年甲午战争的失利，使国人进一步认识到，若要强国，只有坚船利炮是不够的。康有为、梁启超发起的改良运动，将希望寄托在政治改革上。在政治改革同样遭到失败后，他们将注意力转向普通民众，意欲唤起国人。梁启超在将欧洲政治改革中小说所起的作用奉为样板。在他著名的《论小说与群治的关系》一文中，梁启超力陈小说在教化民众方面所起的作用：“欲新一国之民，不可不先新一国之小说。故欲新道德，必新小说；欲新宗教，必新小说；欲新政治，必新小说；欲新风俗，必新小说；欲新学艺，必新小说；乃至欲新人心，欲新人格，必新小说。何以故？小说有不可思议之力支配人道故。”将小说的地位提高到前所未有的高度。凭借他巨大的影响力及国人对亡国危机的意识，晚清时期的小说创作及翻译，数量上达到空前的水平。由此可以看出，这一时期的小说翻译，主要是作为社会政治改革的工具，艺术美学方面的考虑已在其次。

3.2 国人对基督教的态度

鸦片战争后，传教士随着战舰来到中国，他们享有在中国全境传教的权利，同时还能租赁及购买土地建筑教堂，总体来说在当时的全国各阶层，基督教都是不受欢迎的。士绅阶层将其看作帝国主义的代表和民族耻辱的象征，同时也将其视为对儒教及中国传统文化的挑战与威胁。普通民众对基督教则是既恨又怕。加入教会的中国人多是吃不饱饭的穷人，他们加入的目的大多为混饭吃，所谓“吃教”。另外，迷信也增加了排外情绪。比如在山东，就有算命先生及道士宣传外国人破坏了当地的风水，甚至有谣传说传教士在教堂挖出孩子的心脏和眼睛。总体来说，民间将教会看作魔邪的异类而加以排斥。此外还有传教士滥用租赁权，为了赢得更多会众而干涉当地官员政务。虽然也有传教士通过传播科学知识及对政治改革提出建议来帮助中国人，但无法改变当时国人头脑中对基督教及基督徒总体的负面印象。

3.3 林纾其人及翻译此书的目的

林纾是一个有着强烈爱国思想的知识分子。1894年鸦片战争失败后曾上书清政府，反对割让辽宁南部、台湾及澎湖列岛。戊戌变法后他经常与当时著名的改良派林旭等议论国事。1898年他再一次上书清政府，反对割让胶州湾给德国，遭到清政府的拒绝。

林纾赞同梁启超将小说作为教化民众工具的主张，“吾谓欲开民智，必立学堂；学堂功缓，不如立会演说；演说又不易举，终之唯有译书。”林纾翻译此书时正值八国联军入侵北京，林纾悲愤难抑：“呜呼！今日神京不守……即尽译西人之书，岂足为补？虽然，大河垂枯，而泉眼未涸，吾不敢不导之；燎原垂灭，而星火犹熠，吾不能不然之！”面对山河破碎的局面，救国情切的林纾仍将译书以挽狂澜于即倒，看作自己无法推却的职责。

在译本的跋中，林纾更是直陈自己翻译此书的目的并非“巧于叙悲以博阅者无端之眼泪，特为奴之势逼及吾种，不能不为大众一号。”“今当变政之始，而吾书适成，人人既蠲弃故纸，勤求新学，则吾书虽俚浅，亦足为振作志气，爱国保种之一助”。说明他译书的目的意在唤起民众，为救亡图存尽自己的一份力量。

4 结语

综上所述，基督教虽然在几百年前传入中国，但大规模的传教士入境及教堂的修建还是始自晚清，无论是基督教义，还是耶稣，普通百姓或未有所闻，或知之甚少，对于基督式以牺牲为拯救的理念无法理解。因为深受孔教及佛教浸染，是非分明、奖善惩恶、善恶有报成为国人不争的信条。在中国的文学戏剧中有杀身成仁的英雄，或是柔弱无辜的殉难者。前者大义凛然，舍生取义，以牺牲自己而成全社会人伦，他们气概非凡，尽显英雄的悲壮之美。而另一类悲剧主人公，则只是被凌辱欺压的对象，无辜受难，被动等待别人的拯救，或另一世的补偿或奖赏。基督式的既是受难又为解救的英雄对中国文学来说，是一个空白。如果没有意识形态的干扰，单纯以文化交流为目的，那么这种文化空白正是译者最应注意引入的。但是正如Lefevere所说，意识形态的因素在翻译的改写中起着举足轻重的作用。译者所处的时代、整体的时代氛围及译者本人的政治文化倾向，都决定了他不可能将汤姆作为一个基督徒的形象完全接受，更无法和不愿将原作者的解救理念照单全收。对于一个将翻译看作救亡图存宣传工具的译者，基督教代表着侵略者及其所代表的文化，那么无论从爱国保种的实际层面出发，还是作为一个儒教的真诚信仰者和奉行者，他对基督教的抵御是不言而喻的。而译者竭力推崇的抵抗路线，在哲尔治身上得到了体现，那么作者将有关他的章节全数保留，并通过淡化汤姆形象，使其跃升为几乎与汤姆有着同样重要性的角色，也就不足为怪了。

长期以来，晚清的翻译一直在翻译界受到诟病，被视为不规范翻译的标本，但文化翻译学派理论的引入，让我们得以在更大的范围内理解翻译及翻译作品，当我们用Lefevere的理论去观照林纾及林纾们的译作时，我们看到，所有的删改甚至曲解，都是两个文化碰撞时必有的一步。翻译确实不会在真空中进行，目的语文化对翻译作品的选择，翻译内容的取舍及翻译策略的选择都起着决定性的作用。而文化的理解是不可能一蹴而就的，必须经过像探戈舞似的进进退退，相互协商，才会达到最终的理解。如果说林纾在《黑奴吁天录》中让我们隐约瞥见了基督教悲剧模糊的身影的话（毕竟，译本还是写到了汤姆的教徒身份，而他的所做作为至少给中国读者留下了文学中的基督徒的正面印象），那么曹禺的《日出》及《雷雨》，冰心有关基督式博爱的篇章，已经让国人真正领略了基督教理念的真意。我们难道不能说林译《黑奴吁天录》在这个由误解到理解，由排斥到接受过程中正是最先迈出的一步？而林纾译本在目的语文化中的成功移植，在我们实行文化走出去战略的今天，也带给我们有益的启示。既然文化的相互理解是如此漫长的过程，文化的接受那么深地受到目的语文化的制约，那么我们的文化推广就应细致耐心，在没有大的负面影响的情况下，对各种译本抱着包容的心态，允许误解的存在。另外，要深入研究目的语文化的需求，找好切入点，选择目的语文化最有准备的地方。我们要记住的只是，只要走出去，每一个译本都是迈向文化理解的新的一步。

参考文献

[1] BASSNETT S, LEFEVERE A. Constructing cultures: essays on literary translation[M]. Clevedon, Philadephia: Mutilingual Matters, 1998.

[2] GOSSETT T F. Uncle Tom's cabin and American culture[M]. Dallas: Southern Methodist University Press, 1985.

[3] LEFEVERE A. Translation rewriting and manipulation of literary fame[M]. London and New York: Routledge, 1992.

[4] NORD C. Translating as a purposeful activity-functional approaches explained[M]. Manchester: St. Jerome Publishing, 1997.

[5] STOWE H B. Uncle Tom's cabin[M]. London: J.M.Dent and Sons, 1968.

[6] TOURY G. Descriptive translation studies and beyond[M]. Amsterdam and Philadelphia:

John Benjamins,1995.

[7] VENUTI L. The translator's invisibility: a history of translation[M]. London and New York: Routledge,1995.

[8] 陈福康. 中国译学理论史稿[M]. 上海:上海外语教育出版社,2000.

[9] 陈平原,夏晓虹. 二十世纪中国小说理论资料[M]. 北京:北京大学出版社,1989.

[10] 陈平原,等. 历史传承与文化创新[M]. 北京:北京大学出版社,2001.

[11] 郭延礼. 中国近代翻译文学概论[M]. 武汉:湖北教育出版社,2001.

[12] 孔慧怡. 翻译·文学·文化[M]. 北京:北京大学出版社,1999.

[13] 李保均. 明清小说比较研究[M]. 成都:四川大学出版社,1996.

[14] 李凯. 儒家元典与中国诗学[M]. 北京:中国社会科学出版社,2002.

[15] 林纾. 黑奴吁天录[M]. 魏易,译. 北京:商务印书馆,1981.

[16] 梁漱溟. 中国文化要义[M]. 上海:学林出版社,1978.

[17] 鲁迅. 中国小说史略[M]. 天津:百花文艺出版社,2001.

[18] 聂振彬. 王国维美学思想[M]. 沈阳:辽宁大学出版社,1997.

[19] 王宏志. 翻译与创作:中国近代翻译小说论[M]. 北京:北京大学出版社,2000.

[20] 王列耀. 基督教文化与中国戏剧的悲剧意识[M]. 上海:上海三联书店,2002.

[21] 谢天振. 译介学[M]. 上海:上海外语教育出版社,1999.

[22] 张法. 中国文化与悲剧意识[M]. 北京:中国人民大学出版社,1989.

[23] 张俊才. 林纾评传[M]. 天津:南开大学出版社,1992.

浅谈日本演歌

侯丽颖

摘　要：演歌是深受日本大众喜爱的歌曲形式，是一种独特的日本文化。本文介绍了其产生发展历程、艺术特征、演唱方式、表达主题、美学理念以及和日本人生活的关联。随着时代的变迁和发展，如今演歌已失去了往日的辉煌，正面临着窘境。它的未来如何，我们只能拭目以待。

关键词：演歌；历史；文化

“演歌”是广受日本人所喜爱的一种歌曲形式，它的叫法很多，诸如“宴歌”“缘歌”“颜歌”，亦称之为“怨歌”。它的音阶独特，歌词富有韵律、寓意深刻、意境悠远，唱腔充满感情。演唱者在演唱的过程中为淋漓尽致地演绎歌词所表达的内容，在演唱技巧上多使用装饰音。演歌所表达的独特内涵能扣击日本人的灵魂，是我们了解日本文化的一个窗口。

1 演歌的发展历史

演歌，最初称为“演说歌”，它的产生来源于“自由民权运动”。19世纪末，日本政府对国内空前高涨的自由民权运动实施了严厉的镇压，政治家们失去了话语权，于是便走上街巷，借助歌曲的形式用歌声来表达对藩阀政治的见解和主张、嘲讽当时的政治体制，以此来传播先进的政治理念和主张。

项目/基金：本文得到2015年北京工商大学教育教学改革研究项目的资助，项目编号为JG155220。

作者简介：侯丽颖，女，满族，辽宁北镇人，北京工商大学外国语学院教师，主要从事日语教学与日本文学研究。

“演说歌”在这种特殊的历史背景下应运而生。当时，尽管也出现了流行歌曲，但不是主流，大多数的演说歌是用来讽刺抨击政治的一种手段。后来，“演说歌”被简称为“演歌”得以确立下来。明治后期，出现了“演歌师”，他们借以歌咏心情来嘲讽社会。随着自由民权运动的远去和时代的变迁，演歌的题材逐渐扩展到人们的日常生活，其用途也发生了转变：不再是乱世时借以呼喊自由的工具，而是保留了原有的曲式，经过不断的改良，成为表达日本人独特情感的大众娱乐歌谣，真正走入了音乐领域。演歌师在大正时期使用西洋音乐的手法来进行创作，如鸟取春阳的《鸟笼》在当时家喻户晓。进入昭和时代，唱片业兴起，外资唱片公司进入日本，西洋音乐的演奏家逐渐成为主流，代替了民众歌曲的演歌艺术家。流行歌曲成为主流，演歌渐行渐远，流行歌曲在这一时期得到了迅速发展的同时，也给演歌注入了新鲜的元素和歌唱技巧 。演歌最初的形成是作为宣传政治主张的一种工具，而后与民众的日常生活、情感相结合，成为日本传统的演唱形式，获得了强大的生命力。

2 演歌的特色

演歌是独具特色的一门音乐艺术，但它并不是纯粹地道的，是将西洋音乐元素和本土的音乐元素完美地融合在一起才形成的，即将西洋曲式中的七音阶模式加以变化，去掉第四个和第七个音节，只使用五个音，而它的曲式是很典型的和风曲式。日本文化的形成是一个“扬弃”的过程，兼容并蓄地对待异文化，然后形成自己的文化特色。这点在演歌的形成上亦不例外。

演歌的演唱风格大致有两种：一种是借鉴西洋声乐的发声技巧，打开口腔，主要靠喉咙发声，这样的演歌演唱方式发音清晰，风格大方。另一种是运用花腔的技巧和独特的曲调，从民谣和浪花节传承下来的演唱技巧，即把喉部收紧，注重鼻腔、口腔、咽腔、胸腔之间的共鸣，这样演唱出来的演歌带有如泣如诉般的悲鸣和历史沧桑感。日本人很喜欢后者的演唱方法，我们熟知的美空云雀、北岛三郎、森进一都是采用的这种演唱方法。聆听那婉转哀伤的曲调，完美的唱腔，听者会情不自禁地被带到演歌的世界。

3 演歌的主题

演歌所表达的主题具有宽泛性，贴近大众生活，多表现男女苦恋之爱、思乡感怀之情，呈现出来的是“悲伤”“怨恨”等的情绪。由“恋情”“眼泪”“别离”“命运”构成的情感世界，容易引起大家的共鸣。北岛三郎说：“演歌里面有生活的味道、颜色、人们的情感，浓缩着日本人的全部生活。”日本演歌是日本人性格特征的真实写照：细腻、多愁善感、重情重义、对自然界敏感。“冷风入骨心底寒”“男人的世界重道义薄人情”……承载着他们的人生态度。日本人的精神世界离不开演歌，它早已成为日本人生活中不可或缺的一部分。

4 演歌的美学理念

“物之哀”是日本的美学理念。从演歌的歌词、旋律中我们不难发现这一传统的美学特点。演歌中表达幸福洋溢的数量很少，多是表达日式的略带失意的哀愁，从对自然万物的感伤中深刻思索人生的。演歌是日本人真性情的流露，从中我们可以品味日本文化的特质。

演歌真实地记录着日本人的情感，流淌着思愁别绪，感慨着人生的境遇。演歌是人们情感交流的工具，在共鸣中体味人生，抒发感怀。特别是演唱者那细腻悠长的感情，加上哀婉的曲调，再细耳聆听那些寓意深刻的歌词无不使人触及到自己心灵深入的暗礁而哀叹、共鸣。演歌散发着浓浓的乡土气息和地域特色，以羁旅为主题也是它的一大特色。思乡唱起家乡的演歌，对远离家乡的日本人有着别样的慰籍作用。《长崎今天是雨天》《知床旅情》等带有地域特色的演歌安抚了漂泊在外的孤旅的心。

5 演歌的文化特质

日本演歌是能够反映“很日本”的东西，流动着日本文化气质和内涵，蕴涵着日本的传统、文化与历史，是日本文化的代表，是我们研究了解日本文化的一个载体。演歌并不是纯粹的日本货，它把西洋的音乐元素和本土的音乐元素完美地融合在一起。从中我们可以看到日本人对异文化的接受方式的包容。演歌曾让日本人骄傲、自豪。随着全球化进程的迈进，日本演歌也正逐步走向国际。在2007年巴西圣保罗举办的庆祝日本人移民100周年的活动中，演歌受到了好评，演歌走出了日本国门。现在在海外只要提起日本歌曲，人们自然便会想到演歌。演歌已经走过百年，就像世上万物都在发生变化一样，随着时代的变迁，人们的审美情趣也呈现出多元化特征，演歌的受众人群现在多是中老年人。但是不管怎么说，演歌是日本音乐文化的重要组成部分，是日本人独特的思想感情的流露，不仅是音乐的一部分，其浓厚的文学色彩更是日本文化的一个缩影。

参考文献

[1] 胡澎. 演歌中的爱情、酒与乡愁[N]. 中国社会科学报,2009-08-27(2).

[2] 日東書院. 演歌ヒット曲集[M]. 日本:日東書院,1984.

[3] 徐元勇. 日本演歌——一种特殊的歌曲艺术形式[J]. 日语知识,2006(1).

由欧美爱情喜剧类电影探讨其社会文化

刘天奇　刘明宇

摘　要：爱情喜剧类影片作为一种典型的类型片，是不同价值观念的产物。本文选取了四部欧美典型爱情喜剧类影片并对其进行分析，探讨了其中蕴含的社会文化。

关键词：欧美爱情与喜剧电影；社会意识；文化底蕴

电影作为一门相对而言更为接近现实生活的艺术门类，不同类型片都不同程度地反映了社会文化，其中尤以爱情喜剧类最为典型。本文分三类对四部欧美典型爱情喜剧电影进行分析，并结合欧美历史与时代潮流，探讨爱情喜剧类电影背后蕴含的社会文化。

1 美式疯狂：《宿醉》(《The Hangover》)

《宿醉》是一部于2009年发行的R级（限制级）喜剧电影，并分别在2011年和2013年推出了两部续集，是近年来比较难得的成功的喜剧系列电影。

《宿醉》将故事的发生地设定在了拉斯维加斯（Las Vegas）。年轻的道格在结婚前两天决定和他的三个好友去那里进行最后一场属于他们的单身派对，结果却发生了一连串令人哭笑不得的荒谬事。由于影片结合了大量流行元素深得年轻人的喜爱。从文化意义的层面来说，这部电影的成功之处有

项目/基金：本论文为2015年北京市级大学生科研与创业行动计划项目的成果，项目编号为SJ201502072。
作者简介：刘天奇，男，北京工商大学外国语学院2013级学生。刘明宇，男，北京工商大学外国语学院讲师。

两点。

第一，本片的故事发生地为拉斯维加斯。这座位于美国西部的城市依靠博彩业扬名世界，并且娱乐服务业极为发达，具有满足年轻一代娱乐需求的物质因素。此外，拉斯维加斯在2014年成为最多新婚夫妇选择的蜜月旅行目的地，由此可见这种开放、年轻的城市文化帮助了影片在更多年轻人中取得口碑，而同时它也是美国年轻人追逐潮流、具有冒险精神的反映。

第二，作为一个移民国家，多民族构成的特性使得种族问题始终在美国社会比较敏感。2015年年初的奥斯卡颁奖礼甚至因为白色人种过多而受到一些媒体的抨击，而《宿醉》则很好地平衡了这个问题。影片中不仅有亚裔、墨西哥裔美国人的参演以及传统印第安文明的元素，还邀请到了黑人拳击手泰森加盟。它体现的不仅是美国社会多民族特点，更是一种多元文化下开放包容的生活方式。

2 欧式浪漫:《两小无猜》(《Jeux d’enfants》),《爱》(《Amour》)

相比美国的开放与自由，欧美地区的影视作品大多呈现出较高的艺术性，这种艺术性体现到爱情中就是浪漫。这种浪漫除了源自于情感本身外，受益于自文艺复兴起来弥漫在欧洲大陆上的艺术气质，更平添了一些唯美与深度。

作为电影的故乡，法国影片在欧洲有很强的代表性。之所以选择这两部法国影片，是因为它们分别呈现出了两种不同的艺术特质，也就是关于爱情两种不同的浪漫形式。《两小无猜》是2003年上映的一部影片，法文片名《Jeux d’nfants》直译为《小孩儿的游戏》，英文名《Love Me If You Dare》则是这个游戏的名字，即爱我你敢不敢。游戏的规则很简单，那就是只能说“敢”。电影中的男女主角因为这个游戏而在幼时彼此熟悉，并且每一次游戏之后双方都要付出一定的代价，随着时间的流逝这种代价逐渐增大，在最后他们互相拥吻着被封入建筑工地的混凝土地基，选择了与爱同眠。

如果说《两小无猜》的极致浪漫是一种自我毁灭，2012年的《爱》则是一种冷峻。电影讲述一对同为音乐老师的夫妻，年过八旬却仍然相爱，直到妻子遭遇一场疾病，两个人的爱情也开始面临最大的考验，这种考验不仅来自于生命的衰亡，更是来自于记忆的失去。妻子的身体虽然仍在丈夫身边却不能与他一同生活，不能分享他的兴趣、观点和回忆，“爱”该如何在这个失衡的二人世界中延续、坚持与重生，是整部影片的核心命题，同时也使得影片没有陷入悲情主义的泥沼，以一种严肃的表现方式将浪漫呈现出来。由此我们可以发现，浪漫除了作为一种情感氛围之外，更重要的是作为一种思考方式存在于欧洲社会。

3 中西碰撞：《喜宴》(《The Wedding Banquet》)

从影史角度而言，1993年的《喜宴》并不能算是一部欧美影片，它由台湾导演李安执导并且几位主演皆为华人，但由于其故事的发生环境是美国，并且对中西文化碰撞有独特的定位和精准的呈现，因此我们也将它作为入选影片。

定居美国的高国伟是一个同性恋者，他和男友Simon住在纽约的曼哈顿，但高国伟在台湾的父母并不知道此事，并且急切地想抱孙子。于是Simon出了个主意：与国伟同公寓里另一位来自大陆的非法女移民顾玮玮结婚，这样既可以安抚国伟的父母，又能使玮玮拿到美国绿卡，同时还能保持Simon和国伟之间的同居关系。而国伟的父母闻知喜讯后欣然来到纽约，为儿子操办喜事，于是这个看上去的万全之策却引来了更复杂的事端。

影片精准又不失幽默地表现了中西方不同的婚姻和家庭观念，为了瞒过父母，国伟和玮玮的第一次假结婚是在教堂，国伟的父亲却因“不热闹，没有喜气”而十分气愤，于是之后又在唐人街的一家餐厅举办了一次“中式婚礼”。由于婚礼之后的“闹洞房”国伟和玮玮被迫同居并使玮玮有了身孕。在父母高兴的同时，国伟和Simon却为此大吵并在无意中让其父亲知道了他们的关系。影片的结尾，玮玮在老人的劝阻之下接纳了传统的家庭意识，决定把孩子生下来，两位老人也接受了儿子与Simon的关系返回台湾，中西不同的文化传统在这种妥协中达到了一个相对的平衡。

同性题材是解读这部电影的另一切入点，《喜宴》把同性写入中西文化矛盾的故事之中，实则是把它放在一个侧面的位置。自20世纪60年代受一些革命性团体尤其是女性主义和黑人解放运动的启发，同性恋解放运动在欧美国家便一直存在，同性题材的电影在早期产生阶段表面可能与友情相关，底层却是同性情色的文本，如1969年的《午夜牛郎》（《Midnight Cowboy》）。20世纪90年代以来，一些直面同性题材的影片也开始得到大众认可，如1993年的《费城故事》（《Philadelphia》）、2005年的《断背山》（《Brokeback Mountain》）和2013年的《阿黛尔的生活》（《La Vie d' dele》）等。2015年6月27日，美国最高法院宣布裁定同性婚姻在全美合法，使得这一少数群体在社会中进一步得到包容与尊重。

4 结语

抛开当下流行于世界各地的好莱坞大片而言，得益于较好的人才储备和完善的发行体系，欧美的爱情喜剧类电影是在世界范围内受众最广的类型片。近年来随着多媒体技术的发展以及互联网的进一步普及，国内的观众可以更易看到一些相对小众的欧美爱情喜剧类影片，从而领会到欧美的社会文化，而且这也不失为一种简单有效的方法。

此外，以“爱”和“喜”这两种人类基本情感为基础的此类影片，可以在最大程度上超越语言的障碍，得到更多人的共鸣。并且通过对上述四部影片的分析可以看出，欧美爱情喜剧类影片不仅可以影射其历史文化底蕴，更可以彰显其时代潮流。因此，在全球经济文化交流日益频繁的当下，这种隐藏在影片背后的社会文化更值得我们去思考和关注。

翻译研究

语言学与教学研究

外国文学与文化研究

教育、教学探讨与实验教学研究 ☜

析英语教学中的悖论现象

杨怀恩

摘　要：学生花在英语学习上的时间与效果不成正比，主要原因是现行的英语教学以应对考试为主，违背了语言学习的基本规律。英语教学中出现的种种悖论极大地妨碍了学生创造性思维的培养，行政主管部门、教师、学生该深刻反省，回归语言教学的正常渠道。

关键词：英语教学；悖论；应试教育

英语学习热已经持续了三十多年，无论是政府部门还是普通百姓都十分重视英语学习。英语在各种升学、晋职以及公派学习选派中占有重要地位。然而，英语教学中出现了许多不可思议的现象，这些现象对正常的英语教与学都产生了不少的副作用。

悖论现象一：PETS考试低龄化。

PETS是全国英语等级考试（Public English Test System）的简称，设计的初衷是针对国家公派出国人员的一种测试体系。尽管对考生无年龄、职业的限制，但考生却从最初主要是已经工作的成年人逐渐转变为以小学生为主。为什么这么多的小学生热衷于参加PETS考试，其真实目的是为小学升初中做准备，如果有一个理想的PETS成绩学生可以挑选重点中学。

悖论现象二：以交际为主的教学不受欢迎。

一位澳大利亚志愿者来贵州一所小学教授英语。他给孩子们讲故事、和

项目/基金：本文是北京工商大学大学生科研与创业行动计划的研究成果，项目编号为SJ201502063。

作者简介：杨怀恩，男，山西人，北京工商大学外国语学院教授。

他们做游戏、画卡通画帮助孩子们认识各种动物、植物等，使学生对英语发生了浓厚的兴趣，学生的口语有明显的提高，深受孩子们的喜爱。但两个月后家长从最初的赞赏和感激变为不满，强烈要求校长更换老师，他们认为这样的教学，虽然生动活泼，却对提高英语笔试成绩没有帮助。最后，这位澳大利亚志愿者只能遗憾地离开了中国。

悖论现象三：澳大利亚中学交流生英语考试成绩不及中国学生。

2001年秋季，理工大学附中来了10位澳大利亚初中交流生，英语测验的前10名没有一个是澳大利亚学生。任课老师分析了试卷后，发现这些澳大利亚学生的听力水平明显高于中国学生，然而阅读理解和完型填空不如中国学生。中国学生从小学起就接受了严格的应试教育，每周一次的英语测验后，老师会重点解释考点以及答题技巧。

悖论现象四：高考考什么？中学英语教什么？

2009年来自四川的大一新生英语听力水平明显落后于其他地区学生，原因是2008年四川汶川大地震后当地高考不考英语听力。随之，中学英语课上也不再进行听力练习，而将主要精力放在应付英语笔试上。

悖论现象五：大学英语学习以通过四、六级为首要任务。

大学英语教学中，凡是学生认为对四、六级考试不重要的教学内容，他们就不认真学习，有时甚至抵制，讲解考试方式和答题技巧的内容他们才感兴趣。

悖论现象六：批判型教学受冷遇。

2011年我校聘任一位在北京外国语大学任教的美国教授为英语专业上课。该教授是国际问题专家，学识渊博，极富学者风范，然而该教授在我校并未受到学生欢迎，一个学期后该教授拒绝继续为我校学生授课。一个在重点大学深受欢迎的知名教授为什么对我们的学生没有那么大的吸引力，问题的根源在于他用美国大学里常用的讨论式、启发式方法授课，而我们的学生关注的是如何通过专业英语四、八级考试，对讨论问题不感兴趣。

悖论现象七：学生花在英语学习上的时间最长，效果却不尽如人意。

英语是高考、考研中最重要的科目之一，学生花费大量时间做模拟测验，老师予以讲解。考生判断一个好老师的标准是看其能否把考题讲得透彻，是否能把考试规律总结出来。可以说，英语考试是各种应试考试中受害最深的。

上面提到了在小学、中学、大学公外和英语专业学生的教与学中存在的一些问题。同样的问题也出现在我校的研究生英语教学中。2011年我校聘请了美籍华人梁博士。梁博士先后在清华大学、中国政法大学等国内知名大学讲授英语和法学，为我校研究生公共英语授课时常用批判式思维的方式讲授课程。应该说，研究生阶段学生有必要了解掌握批判式思维，培养思辨能力，为将来从事科研工作做必要的准备。遗憾的是，部分学生反对这种教学方式，理由同样是对他们通过北京市研究生统一测试没有直接的帮助。

上面提到的种种悖论现象看似不符合英语学习的目的，然而从小学到大学教育又普遍存在，应试教育影响之广之深触目惊心。

具体来说，儿童学习英语是通过参与各种生动有趣的活动，如说、唱、玩、演等实物情景和图画情景从而对英语产生兴趣，让他们在一个比较自然的环境中习得英语。悖论现象二中澳大利亚外教的教学方法是符合儿童学习语言的规律的。师生之间的互动和融洽，极大地促进了学生在没有压力的情况下掌握基本词汇，并能逐步习惯用英语交流，然后再慢慢学习语言知识点和知识技能。这也符合教育部《英语课程标准》提出的英语教学需要以“学生的综合语言运用能力发展为出发点”的要求。

所有的中学生都面临着高考，中学英语教学不得不全力应对高考，课堂教学围绕高考模式、高考题型进行训练无可厚非。但若所有的课程都只考虑考试因素，学生就只能被训练成考试工具。这种急功近利的英语学习理念，甚至在大学生中也很流行，因此也就出现了悖论现象六中提到的现象，部分大学生对那些在课堂上企图以一种完全不同的思维模式来教授英语的西方知名教授排斥，也就不足为奇了。

语言说到底只是一种交流工具。英国著名的应用语言学教授Widdowson指出，“语言学习的最终目的是获得交际能力”。美国加利福利亚大学洛杉矶分校教授Schumann指出：“Second language acquisition is just one aspect of acculturation and the degree to which a learner acculturates to the target language will control the degree to which he acquires the second language.”

Critical thinking翻译为“批判性思维”“审辩式思维”“思辨能力”，在美国被普遍确立为高等教育的重要目标，对培养大学生创新能力有非常大的价值。从大的方面说，大学生的创新能力决定一个国家在未来全球化激烈的竞争中的成败；从小的方面说，大学生只有具备critical thinking才能在未来的竞争中脱颖而出。悖论现象六中提到的部分大学生要求美国教授重点讲授英语四、六级考试语言点，说明相当多的学生已经沦落为应试教育的受害者。行政主管部门、教师、学生需要深刻反省，回归语言教学的正常渠道。

参考文献

[1] 李祥坤,陈家刚. 当前外语交际能力培养中的误区及其应对[J]. 外语教学,1999(3).

[2] 武宏志. 批判性思维:语义辨析与概念网络[J]. 延安大学学报:社会科学版,2010(1).

[3] SCHUMANN J. The acculturation model for second language acquisition[M]. Arlington, VA: Center for Applied Linguistics, 1978.

[4] WIDDOWSON H G. Teaching language as communication[M]. Oxford: Oxford University Press, 1978.

利用大学英语四、六级考试的正面反拨作用积极促进大学英语教学

汤惠敏

摘　要：语言测试是语言学习中很重要的一个方面，对语言学习起着重要的作用。语言测试是检验语言教学的手段，也是语言教学中非常重要的一个环节。语言测试有其效度、信度和反拨作用，语言测试的反拨作用是指测试对教学和学习的影响。大学英语四、六级考试是大学英语教学中一项重大且重要的考试，对大学英语教学既有良好的反拨作用，也有一些不良的反拨作用。大学英语四、六级考试实行了多年，有较高的信度和效度，对教学也到了一定的正面促进作用，当然也带来了一些负面的影响。我们要将测试与教学有机结合起来，不能完全以应试来指导教学，要将测试服务于教学，促进大学英语教学的改革，进一步提高大学英语的教与学。

关键词：语言测试；信度；效度；反拨作用；大学英语四、六级考试；大学英语教学

1 引言

语言测试是语言学习中很重要的一个方面，对语言学习起着重要的作用。语言测试也是当前外语教学改革中的一项重要任务。语言测试和语言教学是密不可分的，语言教学是语言测试的基础，语言测试是检验语言教学的

作者简介：汤惠敏，北京工商大学外国语学院讲师，主要研究方向为外国语言学及应用语言学。

手段，也是语言教学中非常重要的一个环节。

刘润清和韩宝成的研究提到，语言测试是语言测量的一种方式，语言测试的目的有多种，或是用于诊断及反馈，或是用于筛选和选拔，或是用于编班，或是用于科研或调查等。此外，研究中还提到语言测试的多种形式，按学习阶段来分，有期中测试、期末测试、随堂测试、编班测试等；按用途来分，有成绩测试、水平测试、潜能测试及诊断测试；按考试方式来分，有综合性测试和分离式测试；按对考试分数的解释来分，有标准参照式考试和常模参照式考试；按照评阅方式，又可分为主观性测试和客观性测试，等等。语言测试的类别有很多种，要根据目的来确定使用哪种形式的语言测试。

2 测试的效度、信度及反拨作用

2.1 测试的效度和信度

在谈到测试的时候，就不可避免地会谈到其效度和信度。因此，测试的信度和效度有必要也很有意义来进行讨论。

测试的效度，也指测试的有效性，是指测试在多大程度上考察了它想考察的内容。测试的信度是测试中很重要的一个指标。效度有面子效度、内容效度、结构效度、共时效度等。对语言教学来说，主要是内容效度和结构效度。

测试的信度跟分数的持久性和稳定性有关，信度测量分数的准确性、一致性、可靠性和公正性。一般说来，测试的信度越高，测试就越可靠。

2.2 测试的反拨作用

测试的反拨作用是指测试对教学和学习的影响。测试可以影响教学，不管其影响是积极的还是消极的，这种现象就称为反拨作用。一方面，通过测试，教师可以发现教学中的问题，掌握学生的学习进度，学生也可以通过考试督促学习。测试有积极的反拨作用。另一方面，测试也有副作用，测试什么学生就学什么，学生只关注测试的内容，学生以测试为目标，而不是以学习内容为目标，学生有应试的倾向，这些就是测试的消极反拨作用。

3 大学英语四、六级考试及其对大学英语教学的正面反拨和反面反拨

当前，在国内高校里，大学英语主要采用大学英语四、六级考试来衡量大学生的英语学习水平。大学英语四、六级考试是大学英语教学中一项重大且重要的考试，是全国范围内的标准化考试，是大规模的考试，在我国已有二十多年的历史，时常成为人们关注的焦点，高校、教师和大学生等都非常重视四、六级考试及其成绩。大学英语四、六级考试与大学英语教学大纲的要求一致，旨在公平而又准确地测量中国大学生学习英语的能力，同时给老师提供反馈信息来使老师更好地改进教学。大学英语四、六级考试也是标准参照式考试。

大学英语四、六级考试对大学英语教学既有良好的反拨作用，也有一些不良的反拨作用。大学英语四、六级考试在一定程度上促进了大学英语教与学。在准备四、六级考试中，学生努力地学习单词、语法等内容，加强听、读、写、译等方面的能力和训练，为后续的英语学习打下了基础。随着大学英语四、六级考试改革的进一步推行，其考试题型越来越注重交际和运用，学生并不是单一地训练语言技能，更注重听、说、读、写等各个方面的综合能力，这样有利于提高学生的英语综合素养及其运用英语的能力。考试题型中，写作、听力、阅读等题型都跟现实生活紧密联系，主观题占的分值比较大，客观题也并不是全部都是单一的四选一题型，都注重考察测试学生的实际运用英语能力和交际能力。

在一些高校里，因为大学英语四、六级通过率与教学成果挂钩及学位挂钩，教师和学生都关注四、六级通过率，注重应试的一面，忽略了语言的全面性，测试什么教师就在课堂讲什么，影响了正常教学的进行。重视通过率的教学模式也会导致学生越来越多地关注应试的技巧和策略，这与以测试促教学的目的也是相背离的。尽管很多学生通过了考试，但部分学生并不能很好地运用英语来进行交流，实际运用英语的能力并不是考试分数反映的那样，通过了并不能表示他们很好地掌握了英语。

4 结语

语言测试和语言教学是密不可分的，两者相互影响。语言测试随着语言教学的不断深入，其形式也在不断完善和发展。一般说来，信度、效度高的语言测试会对语言教学起着正面的反拨作用，会促进语言教学的发展；反之，信度不高效度也不高的语言测试会对语言教学起着消极的反拨作用，会在一定程度上阻碍语言教学的发展。

大学英语四、六级考试实行了多年，有较高的信度和效度，对教学起到了一定的正面促进作用，当然也带来了一些负面的影响。我们要进一步推进大学英语改革，推动大学英语四、六级考试的改革，注重英语基础能力及实际运用英语的能力，更好地促进大学英语的教与学。

由于测试跟教学紧密相连，测试的结果对个人及教学都有影响，因此，教师在教学中要将测试与教学有机结合起来，不能完全以应试来进行教学，要将测试服务于教学，促进大学英语教学的改革。

现在我校正在进行大学英语教学改革，一方面大力推进课堂英语教学，另一方面也非常重视大学英语四、六级的考试。作为大学英语教师，我们一方面要不断提高自己，大力提高课堂教学的水平；另一方面也要重视大学英语四、六级考试，尤其是其给教学带来的正面反拨作用，利用其正面的影响，发现教与学中的问题，进一步提高大学英语的教与学。

参考文献

[1] BROWN H D. Principles of language learning and teaching[M]. Englewood Cliffs, New Jersey: Prentice Hall Regents, 1993.

[2] HUGHES A. Testing for language teachers[M]. Beijing: Foreign Language Teaching and Research Press, 2000.

[3] JOHNSON K, JOHNSON H. Encyclopedia dictionary of applied linguistics: a handbook for language teaching[M]. Beijing: Foreign Language Teaching and Research Press & Blackwell Publishers Ltd., 2001.

[4] RICHARDS J C, et al. Longman dictionary of language teaching and applied linguistics[M]. Beijing: Foreign Language Teaching and Research Press, 2000.

[5] 刘润清,韩宝成. 语言测试和它的方法(修订版)[M]. 北京:外语教学与研究出版社, 1991.

[6] 杨惠中. 语言测试与语言教学[J]. 外语界, 1999(1):16-25.

大数据时代大学英语教学面临的挑战与机遇

关 涛

摘　要： 互联网的高速发展和信息的急剧膨胀将人类社会带入了一个崭新时代——大数据时代。海量的数据规模、多样的数据类型、快速的数据分析和巨大的数据价值等特点给教育领域带来了颠覆性的变革。大数据时代的到来使大学英语教学面临前所未有的挑战和机遇，师生双方都要与时俱进，勇敢接受挑战，把握机遇，共同努力使大学英语教学再上新台阶。

关键词： 大数据；大学英语教学；挑战；机遇

1 引言

互联网技术革新和数据大爆炸将人类生活引入了一个大数据时代。大数据这一概念最早由全球知名咨询公司麦肯锡提出，指一般软件工具难以捕捉、管理和分析的大容量数据。国际数据公司（IDC）总结了大数据的四个特征：即海量的数据规模（Volume）、快速的数据流转和动态的数据体系（Velocity）、多样的数据类型（Variety）、巨大的数据价值（Value）。维克托·尔耶·舍恩伯格在《大数据时代：生活、工作与思维的大变革》中前瞻性地指出，大数据带来的信息风暴正在变革我们的生活、工作和思维，大数据开启了一次重大的时代转型。如今，大数据概念已渗透进各个领域，从方方面面影响着人类生活，让人越来越意识到“大数据”之“大”，并不仅仅

项目/基金：本文得到2015年北京工商大学教育教学改革研究项目的资助，项目编号为JG155102。

作者简介：关涛，文学博士，北京工商大学外国语学院副教授，主要从事英美文学和英语教学研究。

在于容量之大，更在于：通过对海量数据的交换、整合和分析，去发现新的知识，创造新的价值，从而带来“大知识”“大科技”“大利润”和大发展。若要在大数据时代立于不败之地，必须掌握在海量数据中获取有用信息的能力，去发现规律和预测未来。

大数据在社会诸多领域催生了巨大变革，如工业、产业、商业等，教育领域也正因为大数据时代的到来发生着翻天覆地的变化。因为其国际通用语言和高校必修课的特殊性，大学英语教学首当其冲受到全方位的挑战，但挑战同时也创造机遇。如何应对挑战和把握机遇是让大学英语课程不被淘汰的关键，值得所有从事大学英语教学的专家和教师思考。

2 大数据时代给大学英语教学带来的挑战

2.1 对传统教学理念和教学模式的挑战

大数据时代给教育领域带来的最大冲击就是教学资源的最大化，知识变得无处不在。除了课堂之外，大学生还可以利用微课、慕课和网校等在线学习平台来获取知识，使英语学习可以随时随地、便捷高效地进行，同时还可以实现互动的效果，学生可以结合自己的实际需求来选择学习时间和学习内容，从而真正实现教学个性化和多元化的理想境界。这无疑对传统的大学英语教学理念和教学模式形成了巨大挑战。

大学英语教师不能再满足于简单的课上面授和课下批改作业的方式，而是一方面要提高信息技术水平，如熟悉常用软件、网络通讯、网络教学平台的使用和微课、慕课的制作等，另一方面还要学习和掌握利用电脑软件和网络平台搜集的学习数据来进行分析，从而深入了解学生的水平及需求，及时调整教学方案，合理安排教学活动，来创造英语学习环境，以便激发学生的学习热情和兴趣。

2.2 对传统教学角色的挑战

在最早的大学英语课堂上，教师以教材为中心，重点讲解单词、难句和课文理解；当多媒体普及大学课堂时，大学英语教学从课本搬上了幻灯片，教师把纸质教案变成了PPT，另外再加上一些音频和视频文件，看似已经丰富了教学方式，但依然是教师充当主要角色，学生始终处于被动的次要角色，要学什么想学什么仍然是教师说了算。而大数据时代的大学英语教学中，这种传统的角色关系注定要发生巨大的转变。

大数据时代信息无所不在，英语学习资源极大丰富，学生可以轻而易举地获取各自需要的学习内容，传统的大学英语教学显然已无法满足学生的需求，这无疑使教师拥有资源的权威性受到了挑战。许多世界知名大学在互联网上发布了经典的视频课，不仅让学生们学习了英语，更重要的是帮助他们了解世界文化和专业知识。这些视频课显然比枯燥的传统的大学英语课更具有吸引力，大有取代教师课堂讲授的趋势。未来大部分的英语教师将不再是知识的讲授者和课堂的主宰了，而是成为课堂的组织者和学生的引导者，根据学生的个性化需求来整合学习资源，并加以分析和处理，通过多媒体和网络学习平台发布给学生，引导学生在课下自主学习，课上则进行练习和答疑，鼓励学生开展合作式、探究式的讨论，培养他们理解、分析和解决实际问题的能力。

2.3 对传统大学英语教学评价的挑战

教学评价分为两个层面。一是教师对于学生学习的评价，二是学生、同事和教学督导对于教师授课的评价。

大学英语教师对于学生学习的评价基本上停留在终极评价的层面，也就是期末考试的成绩占据绝大比例，平时的作业和测验只占微不足道的比例，这是大学英语课学生多班级大的特点造成的。教师不可能有足够的时间和精力去评判每一次作业，而大数据时代的大学英语课将打破这种僵局，真正实现形成性评价。教师可以通过网络学习平台整合听、说、读、写、译各方面的测试内容，提供多元的评价形式，详细记录学生每一次的学习时间、过程和效果，并记入总成绩。总结性评价也将实现机考和网考形式，随机产生试卷，从而杜绝作弊，使学习评价更公平公正。

以往对教师的评价多采取召开师生座谈会和学生填写评价卡的形式，难以搜集到最有说服力的数据。大数据时代，对教师的评价方式也发生了转变。学生、同事和督导在听课后在线填写对该教师的评价，既有标准化的打分，也有开放性的评价，网络在后台整理分析对该教师的评价数据，总结归纳出优缺点和意见建议。教师若想在教学中始终获得好评，就必须认真研究评价数据，据此调整和改进自己的教学内容和方式，来吸引学生的兴趣。

3 大数据时代给大学英语教学带来的机遇

维克托指出，大数据时代最大的转变就是放弃对因果关系的渴求，而关注相关关系。也就是说只要知道“是什么”，而不需要知道“为什么”。这颠覆了千百年来人类的思维惯例，对人类的认知和与世界交流的方式提出了全新的挑战。大数据时代带给大学英语教学的机遇也基于此。

3.1 给教师职业发展带来的机遇

大数据时代，网络给大学英语教师提供了海量的教学资源，教师可以先通过大数据分析学生的共性与差异，再去有针对性地选择教学所需要的视频、音频、文字等信息，充实教学内容，激发学习兴趣。大数据使得教师对学生的学习评价变得简便可靠，大大减少了教师的工作量，使他们有更多的时间去参加技术培训，更新知识结构，提升业务水平，从而实现教学相长。大数据时代也为教师提供了更为丰富的科研资源，众多的搜索引擎和文献数据库可供使用，大数据可以随时随地分析教师各自的学术关注点，把最有用的相关信息整合出来，使科研工作变得更为便捷高效。

3.2 给学生个人发展带来的机遇

《国家中长期教育改革和发展规划纲要（2010—2020年）》明确提出：“关注学生不同特点和个性差异，发展每一个学生的优势潜能。”大数据时代使这个目标成为可能。大学英语教学将一改往日枯燥乏味的局面，教师必须关注师生关系，了解学生个体需求，为学生提供理想的英语学习环境和合理的学习任务，从而提高学生英语应用能力和解决实际问题的能力。

学生在课余还可以根据自己的学习需求，选择微课、慕课和网校学习，构建国际视野，提高语言水平，享有更多自由的学习、承担更大的责任，使学习变成自我主导的过程。

4 结语

大数据时代，在线教育即将普及，网络课程大有代替大学英语课堂教学的趋势。面对如此重大的挑战，师生双方都应当与时俱进、不断提升，放弃残缺的守旧思想，大胆应对改革。

基于互联网技术而发展起来的大数据应用，将会对教育领域产生颠覆性影响，数据的挖掘和分析只是整个变革过程中的一个技术手段，而远非变革的全部。大数据的本质是基于互联网基础上的信息化应用，其真正的“魔力”在于信息化与教育的融合，使教育质量得到大规模提升。

参考文献

[1] 陈金平. 大数据时代大学英语教师的职业发展[J]. 当代外语研究,2014(4).

[2] 王凡. 大数据时代的大学英语写作教学改革[J]. 读与写教育教学刊,2014(11).

[3] 王卫林. 浅谈高校教师如何适应大数据背景下的英语教学[J]. 赤子,2015(7).

[4] 徐子沛. 大数据[M]. 桂林:广西师范大学出版社,2014.

[5] 颜健生. 大数据时代高校英语数字化教学的转型思考[J]. 鸡西大学学报,2015(3).

外语教学法动态研究初探

彭 淳

摘 要：本文通过综述吴本虎的课堂互动动态模型和姬建国的动态外语教学法模式总结了外语教学方法研究领域的动态研究趋势，也提出了这些动态研究成果要对中国外语教学有指导意义，还需要针对中国外语教学的一些具体情况做进一步的改进。

关键词：外语教学法，动态模型，大学英语教学

1 外语教学法研究的趋势

外语教学法从最早的拉丁语教学模式，19世纪40年代到20世纪40年代的语法翻译法（grammar-translation method），系列法（series method），自然主义教学法（natural methods），直接法（the direct method），到后来多种教学模式并举，如美国的听说法（audio-lingual method）和英国的情景法（situational，language teaching）；20世纪60年代的交际教学法（communicative approach）；20世纪70到80年代的涌现的大量外语模式方法如静默法（the silent way），群体学习法（community language learning），暗示法（suggestopedia），行动反应法（total physical response）以及强调理解的自然法（the natural approach）。外语教学方法研究的钟摆一直不停摇摆，车轮一直不断向前。进入21世纪后，外语教学研究领域出现了新的动向：重视外语课堂教学的互动性和多变性，在研究上引入动态模型并在实践中注重根据学生的具

作者简介：彭淳，北京工商大学外国语学院讲师，主讲课程为大学英语，研究方向为应用语言学和外语教学。

体需求和反应来使用以某种方法为主的多种方法组合并不断做出调整。浙江师范大学的吴本虎教授提出的课堂互动过程动态模型和美国纽约市立大学的姬建国博士提出的“动态外语教学法”的内部结构都是很好的例子。

2 吴本虎的课堂互动过程动态模型

吴本虎建立了一个课堂互动过程动态模型以期为课堂互动提供一个更佳途径。这个动态模型比较全面地考虑了课堂互动中的诸方面因素，把教师学生话语交流作为信息加工和传递的动态过程来看待。吴本虎认为，课堂互动的过程对于学生的语言习得进步和教师对语言环境的建造和重建两方面都有累积递进的影响。

图1显示出：在课堂互动的环境里，师生双方的内部信息处理和外部语言交流是持续不断和同时发生发展的。当老师通过发出声音信号输出信息时，学生几乎是同时把这些信号代表的信息输入大脑。信息传输中的干扰可能会造成学生方面的信息输入与教师方面的信息输出有所差异。输出信息的制造和输入信息的接收都需要记忆和思考的参与。在课堂互动过程中，信息输入的完成很少会导致语言信息处理过程的终止。相反，它通常会引发信息输入的产生而进入下一阶段的互动过程。学生接收到教师的语言信号后会进一步制造信号输出，这会使他/她的语言信号传送到教师方，并引起教师方面接收信号后开始信息加工和输入。同样，教师方面的信息输入也会导致进一步的信息输出，并开始又一轮的信息流动和处理。在新一轮的语言交流中，无论教师还是学生的信息处理、信息产生还是信息接收，都与前一轮的交流有着紧密的联系而不是彼此孤立的。因为之前输入和输出的信息都或多或少地存储于互动者的记忆中并对后续的信息处理和信息传输施加影响。

吴本虎的这个动态模型不同于以往对外语教学的静态描述，把外语教学课堂互动当作一个多方参与、发展变化中的信息交流过程，把教师和学生、信息输入和输出都融入到一个不断发展变化的系统中。但是，语言教学的研究除了课堂互动的复杂和可变性还应该考虑课堂以外的许多因素，如教学目标、教材使用、学习者的动机和风格、教师的条件和风格等。

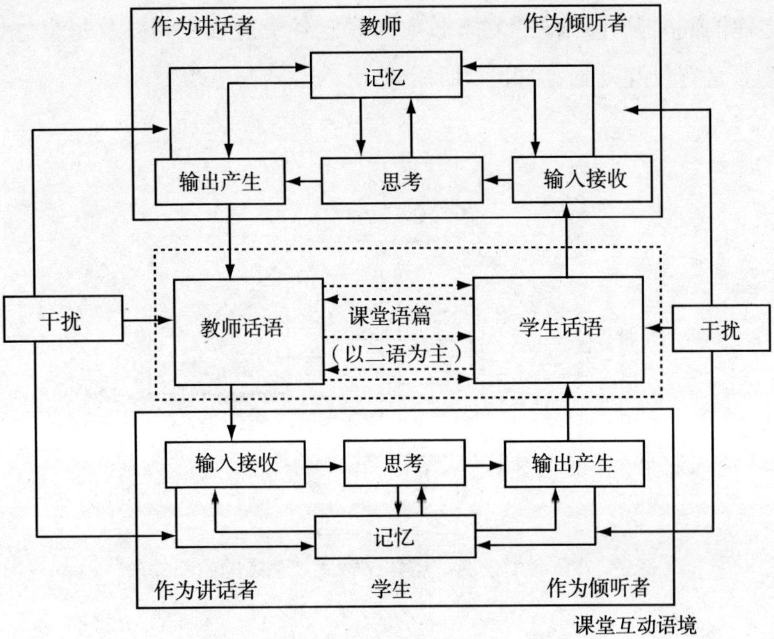

图1　吴文虎的外语课堂互动动态模型

3 姬建国的动态外语教学法的内部结构

姬建国的动态外语教学法模式从更宏观的角度解析外语教学的复杂和流动性。他把外语教学看成四个动态过程构成的整体。这四个过程分别是：分析学生需求、确定教学方法、调整教学方法、运用教学方法，如图2所示。

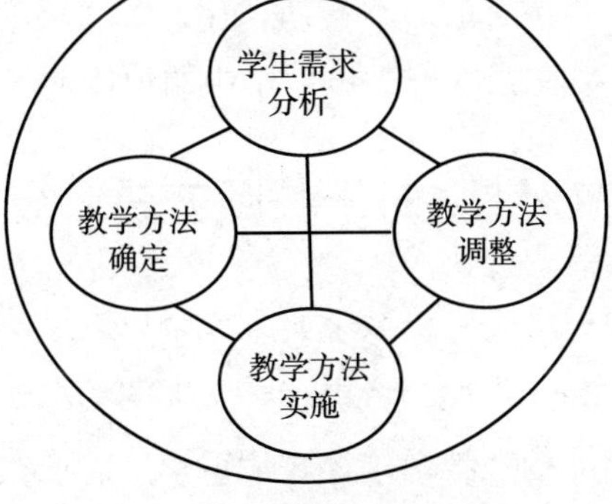

图2　动态外语教学法内部结构

姬建国同时阐述了他的动态教学法模式各个过程之间以及每个过程内的相互关系是有机互动的，如图3所示。

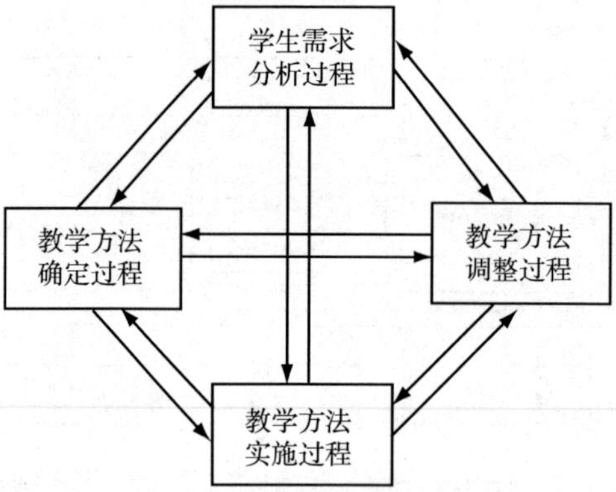

图3 外语教学法有机整体结构之“动态的内部关系”

姬建国还分析了动态教学法机制与课堂教学过程之间的关系。课堂教学过程中教师与学生、学生与学生、学生与教材之间的交流将学生的需求回馈到教学法运作系统。当教师捕捉到这些回馈信号并决定做出反应时，就会启动学生需求分析程序，逐次进入确定、调整和运用教学方法的过程。

姬式模式认为，教学方法的设计与实施总体上保持着互动性和共时性。教学法内部的各种机制和课堂教学过程的互动应保持协调一致。教学法和教学过程之间的互动性和共时性也使得外语教学法内部的各种机制保持动态。这个模式把外语教学当作一个动态的变化过程，包括了教材、教法、教师和学生多方变量，并且以学生的需求和回馈作为牵动整个系统运转和调整的动机，充分重视了学生实际情况在外语教学中的地位。

4 外语教学动态研究中对于教师变量考虑的不足

从以上综述的两种动态外语教学研究成果可以反映出近年来研究领域对于外语教学的复杂性和变化性的考虑。吴文虎的动态模型强调课堂教学中互动的持续性，姬建国的动态教学法模式注重学生需求在教学法确定、实施和调整中的发动作用。这样的动态研究对于外语教师在实践中灵活把握教法并用于实践有着很积极的指导作用，有助于外语教学研究摆脱纸上谈兵、机械片面的情况。外语教师可以结合课堂上的实际情况，通过理论学习，借鉴不同教法之所长，制定最切合实际的教法并不断调整以达到最佳教学效果。

但是，笔者认为，在诸多外语教学动态研究中对于教师这一变量考虑不够充分。在教学互动中，学生的年龄、学习动机、学习风格、情感因素固然是非常重要的因素，但是教师本身的条件，如语言素质、授课风格、工作环境等对于外语教学的实际效果也同样有着不容忽视的影响。比如在中国这样的外语环境较差的国家，除了外语学习者接触外语的机会与在英语广泛使用的国家的外语学习者的语言环境不同，教师的语言条件也大为不同。固然外语教师应该具备较高的外语素质，但是以中文为母语的外语教师和英语为母语的外籍教师在教学法的选择和使用上是否应该各有侧重来扬长避短？虽然外语教师责无旁贷地要充分调动课堂、激励学生参与、缓解学生的紧张情绪、对学生的回馈足够敏锐并及时做出反应，但是作为真实个体存在的教师由于年龄、性别、性格甚至身体条件的差异，在授课风格上也有天然的差异。某一种授课风格是否就是最佳风格？教师是否可以根据学生需求变化出不同的形象，做个面面俱到的课堂组织者和语言示范者？从外语教师的角度看，根据自身特点在外语教法的掌握和使用上摸索出自己的路子，扬长避短，才能做到事半功倍。而外语教学研究在这个领域如果能给第一线的教师提供更多的理论支持，对于实际教学的效果提高也会起很大促进作用。

除此以外，课堂互动是否如吴氏模型中设想的那么充分？互动的程度显然会受教学环境如班级人数、教室的布局、课时的多少等的限制。而在注重学生需求的姬氏动态教法模型中，教师有多大的自由度针对学生情况对考试内容、课堂节奏及内容选择做出调整也是需要具体情况具体分析的。在中国这样竞争激烈的国家里，统一的考试是必然的选择。统一的考试意味着统一的教材、统一的大纲、统一的课程设置和对客观量化考试成绩的极致追求。这一国情对于外语教学法研究领域里的诸多成果在中国这片土壤上的具体实践有着怎样的影响？要切实提高外语教学的质量、改善教学效果，在笔者所列举的一系列问题上，在教法研究成果本土化的道路上还有待我们进一步的努力。

参考文献

[1] BROWN H D. Principles of language learning and teaching [M]. 5th ed. White Plains, NY: Pearson Education, 1987.

[2] JI J. Classroom process and a new model of FLT methodology [J]. Inquirer, 2007, 14: 25-29.

[3] JI J. Assessing foreign language teaching methodology: from static mode to dynamic process [J]. Language Association Journal, 2007, 58: 3-11.

[4] WU B. Towards an understanding of the dynamic process of L2 classroom interaction [J]. System, 1998, 26: 525-540.

大学生英语演讲备赛策略

刘 婧 汪辰菲 王诵夏 朱 玥

摘 要：大学生参加英语演讲比赛对自身各项素质的提高具有非常重要的意义。本文从英语演讲技巧、比赛赛制以及其他影响英语演讲的因素多方面综合探讨适合大学生的英语演讲备赛策略。

关键词：英语演讲；备赛策略

1 引言

近年来由中央电视台、外研社、北京市教委等单位面向全国及北京市举办的各种英语演讲比赛，吸引了众多大学生积极参与。然而多数参赛大学生欠缺英语演讲比赛的相关知识，也缺乏系统性的训练与备赛指导，一定程度上影响了自身水平的发挥。因此，本文试从大学生的角度探索有效的英语演讲比赛备赛策略。

2 英语演讲技巧

优秀的英语口语水平是英语演讲的基础，但只有同时掌握一定的英语演讲技巧才能够成为合格的英语演讲者。英语演讲技巧涉及方方面面，以下主

项目/基金：本论文为2015年北京市级大学生科研与创业行动计划项目的成果，项目编号为SJ201502067。
作者简介：刘婧，女，汉族，湖南人，北京工商大学外国语学院副教授，研究方向：翻译理论与实践，英语演讲教学。汪辰菲，女，汉族，北京人，北京工商大学外国语学院商务英语专业学生。王诵夏，女，汉族，江苏南京人，北京工商大学经济学院金融学专业学生。朱玥，女，汉族，北京人，北京工商大学外国语学院商务英语专业学生。

要从四个方面展开。

2.1 语言技巧

（1）多用实词，多用短句，少用结构复杂的长句。在英语演讲中，and、but、so、then等虚词要尽量少用，that、which等词引导的定语从句也只会使句子结构变得复杂，这样使听众难以跟上演讲者的思路，从而影响演讲的效果。相反，多使用实词、短句，可使演讲的内容更清晰，气势更磅礴。

（2）注意使用各种修辞手法。英语演讲中增加感染力和气势常用的修辞手法有：渐进、对照、排比、反问等。

（3）根据听众对象，注意演讲的总体措词。演讲的总体措词是严肃一些还是活泼一些，是有较明显的说教口气还是用平等的口吻等，都要根据听众对象而定。如果场下听众是同龄的学生，那么演讲的内容风趣一些往往就能引起共鸣。另一方面，如果是上了年纪的听众，太多的笑料反而会被认为“不严肃”“不尊重”，引起反感。

（4）避免过多使用I feel、I think等主观性表达。如果通篇全是I feel、I think的内容，会给人缺乏说服力的印象。另外，perhaps、maybe这样的词语，虽然有有助于形成一种客气、谦虚的印象，但过度使用会让人觉得演讲的内容有不可靠之处。

（5）人称上少用you，多用we。用you等于把自己与听众对立起来，而用we则拉近了与听众的距离。比如：You should not smoke听上去像教训人，而Let’s not smoke听起来是一个不错的建议。

2.2 开头及结尾

（1）如何开头。

演讲的开头具有吸引听众注意、调动听众兴趣与情绪的重要作用，作为与听众的最初接触，优秀的开头应做到新颖、切题，为整篇演讲定下基调。常用的方法有：讲（自己的）故事，称赞听众，引用名人名言，使用一些不平常的数据，播放录像带或看幻灯片等。

（2）如何结尾。

演讲的结尾有着与开头同样重要的地位。优秀的结尾应起到总结全文、画龙点睛的作用。常用的方法有：重复开头，概括演讲，以趣事结尾，以号召行动结尾，以反问结尾，以一个陈述句结尾，对大家能够聚在一起表示感谢等。

此外还需注意，结尾要简洁，不要受汉语影响，说些类似“准备不足，请谅解”“请批评指正”的话。最普通的结尾就是：Thank you very much for your attention.

2.3 与听众交流

演讲是演讲者与听众双方互动的过程。因此演讲时，切忌只顾讲话而目光呆滞或低头看地，要注意时刻调动听众情绪，与听众保持眼神交流。

可以将眼睛慢慢地从一个移动到另一个人，在每一个人身上停留两到三秒钟时间；眼睛直视听众，或看着他们的鼻梁或下巴。除此之外，找到那些看起来比较友善的听众，朝他们微笑；然后目标转向那些有些怀疑的听众，也朝他们微笑。

适当的眼神交流既可以吸引听众的注意力，也可以缓解演讲者的紧张情绪，可谓一石二鸟。

2.4 演讲辅助

在有条件的情况下，在演讲中借助辅助道具也是一种不错的选择。

美国社会语言学家Albert Mehrabian在“人们是如何在演讲中获得信息”方面做了很多研究，最终发现55%的信息是通过图像获得的，通过文字获得的信息只占7%。由此可见演讲辅助的必要性。

因此，在演讲中应尽可能视觉化演讲内容，用动作、图片、图表、目录、小道具等来作为语言的补充促进听众理解，给听众留下更深刻的印象。

3 各比赛环节特点及备赛要点

纵观各大英语演讲比赛，总体赛程大都分为定题演讲、即兴演讲和回答问题三个环节。下面针对各环节，分别介绍特点及备赛要点。

3.1 定题演讲

定题演讲是指参赛选手就一个既定的题目，做好赛前准备后进行的演讲。从准备时间看，选手在赛前几个月就可以获得定题演讲题目，选手还可以在指导教师帮助下及时调整语音语调，做到充分准备。也正因定题演讲的特点，选手间的实力相差几乎不大，很难拉开档次。

由于定题演讲是给定题目的演讲，选手不能有主观选择题目的机会，因此选手在备赛时要着重训练演讲稿的撰写和演讲比赛当天的演讲技巧。一个成功的演讲者一定反复修改演讲稿。撰写演讲稿时，选手应选择适合自己的方法，比如开门见山或提出问题等。一个成功的演讲稿，就内容而言，主题应鲜明，表达要完整；就文章组织结构而言，要思维清晰，逻辑性强；就语言而言，要有感染力、形象生动，选手还可以使用相关的英语写作方法和技巧，如明喻、暗喻、夸张等修辞方法；就用词而言，用词应该精准，尽量避免使用生僻晦涩的单词或短语。除了演讲稿撰写的训练，选手还要在备赛阶段训练临场演讲技巧，熟练掌握演讲要领，训练演讲技巧和肢体语言，选手可以通过观看“希望之星”和“爱立信杯”等英语演讲的录像提前了解比赛评分标准，并按照标准进行严格的比赛模拟训练。

总之对于定题演讲来说，选手应注意演讲的“SSERD原则”：

第一，Specific是指“The topic should be specific”，主题一定要具体化；

第二，Slow是指“The rate should be slow”，语速需要放慢；

第三，Easy是指“The language should be easy”，语言要简单；

第四，Repeat是指“You should figure out a slogan to repeat”，选手需要找一个不断重复的口号；

第五，Detail是指“You should add details in your speech”，演讲中需要加入适当的细节。

3.2 即兴演讲

即兴演讲是指参赛选手就某一个题目在赛前不做准备的情况下进行的演讲。因为即兴演讲重点考查选手的临场应变能力，常被认为是最具挑战性的演讲之一。从准备时间看，因为即兴演讲不能给选手足够的时间精心准备演讲稿，选手要在赛前10~20分钟内准备好演讲，所以选手要具备较好的即兴表达技巧和临场应变能力。即兴演讲的题目灵活多样，要求选手在短暂时间内找到恰当的词语，因此选手还应具备一定的知识广度、思想深度，同时还要具备快速分析题目的能力。

即兴演讲无疑是对选手英语语言能力的考查，在高压情况下激发选手们的潜力。选手想要做到口若悬河，镇定自若，必须要做好充足的赛前准备。

美国前总统林肯曾指出："即使有实力的人，若缺乏周全的准备，也无法做到系统、有条理的演说。"选手在赛前一定要对自己的演讲稿、演讲题目做充分的准备，尽可能收集相关资料，以不变应万变。

即兴演讲不仅仅是对选手英语语言能力的考查，很大程度上是对选手们心理素质的考验，如果选手克服了自身的紧张情绪也就成功了一半，心理素质较强的选手更易在此环节脱颖而出。因此辅导教师还应该着重训练选手的心理素质，在赛前帮助演讲者克服心理压力。

第一，选手应专注于题目内容，摒弃一切干扰，舒缓紧张情绪。

第二，正确使用答题策略。遇到问题，先回答；遇到陈述，表立场；遇到难题，引用名言等。

第三，在最短时间内列出关键词或关键句。

第四，选手应合理分配时间，避免面面俱到，尽量在两三个小点内将内容解释清楚。

第五，演讲结束应适当给出总结，提纲挈领。

3.3 回答问题

演讲比赛的问答环节是赛事举办方给选手们提供的展示自己的另一个舞台。问答环节要求选手保证语音语调基本功的情况下，还要回答评委随机提出的问题，给评委留下深刻的印象。

问答环节一般分为根据定题演讲题目提出的问题和随机问题两种情况。根据定题演讲题目提出的问题，一般和选手的定题演讲题目相关，选手也比较熟悉相关内容，所以选手在备赛时可以着重准备这些方面。

第一，选手应该对演讲稿中出现的经典事例，引用故事做充分的准备工作。

第二，选手应对自己问答环节可能被问及的问题进行预测，并以书面的形式呈现出来。

第三，选手可以组成备赛小组，选手们把问题收集起来，小组成员内互相预测，开阔思路，出其不意，更可以丰富选手们的问题知识库。

针对随机提出的问题，由于这些问题和选手的定题题目无关，使得这一环节更有挑战性，对选手的能力提出了更高的要求，选手在备赛时要注意这些方面。

第一，注意英语的语言积累。选手备赛时应多朗读背诵经典阅读文章，文章题材应丰富多样，经济、政治、文化都要涉及。输入和输出的过程相辅相成，多背诵经典的文章才能在比赛时地道准确的表达，这不仅仅是自我的展示，对评委听众们来说也是一种享受。

第二，备赛时注意深入思考问题的训练。有了丰富的语言储备，选手还应该对问题有自己独到的见解和解决问题的能力看法，这正是评委老师最看重，也是打分时着重考虑的。为了训练这一点，选手应该充分利用备赛小组，小组成员集思广益，把当下热点问题搜集起来，让选手们形成思考问题处理问题的独特思路和方法，做到回答问题时能够胸有成竹。

4 非技术性问题

在实际演讲比赛中，除去英语水平和演讲技巧等技术性问题，临场心理、外在形象等要素同样关乎比赛发挥与演讲效果，因此也是不容忽视的备赛要点。

4.1 临场心理

即使赛前准备充分，临近比赛也难免遇到因紧张而出现的种种意外状况从而导致比赛失利。面对听众切勿自乱阵脚，首先要对自己抱有信心，注意适时深呼吸调整状态，以平和的心态面对比赛。

比赛中如果忘词，切勿表现慌乱或长时间停顿。应迅速稳定情绪，微微一笑，跳过忘记的部分，直接从下一部分开始。尽管也许会遗漏一些内容，但是很少有人会注意到这一点。

此外，挺拔舒展的姿势也有利于缓解紧张情绪。英语演讲比赛的选手需要适度的心理紧张。适度的焦虑和适度的唤醒水平，有助于演讲者处于一种紧而不乱、焦而不躁的状态，从而使其在演讲中发挥最佳水平。诀窍之一是张开双脚与肩同宽，挺稳整个身躯。另一个诀窍是想办法扩散并减轻施加在身体上的紧张情绪。例如将一只手稍微插入口袋中，或者手触桌边、手握麦克风等。

4.2 外在形象

参加演讲比赛需注意着装的正规与得体，比赛者的服装会带给听众各种印象。

演讲着装的首要原则是整洁、大方。通常情况下，演讲者在演讲时需要穿正装，如西装、中山装、套裙等，但轻松的场合也不妨穿着稍微花哨一点的服装来参加。

此外，发型也可塑造出各种形象来。长发和光头各自蕴含强烈的形象，而鬓角的长短也被认为是个人喜好的表征。

5 总结

英语演讲比赛是一项考验综合能力的比赛，参赛者需要在具备一定英语口语水平的基础上熟知基本的英语演讲技巧，同时还要对赛制和评判标准有基本的了解。此外，其他影响演讲的要素也同样不容忽视。要想在英语演讲比赛中取得好成绩，既要靠平日的刻苦训练，也要靠赛场上的随机应变，只有综合各项能力，才能最终取得成功。培养并提高大学生英语演讲能力、独立思考能力、应变能力，不断完善并实践大学生英语演讲比赛选手培训模式，力争在全国比赛中取得越来越好的成绩将是一个长期且极具意义的目标。

参考文献

[1] 贾爱兵，陈晓静. 英语演讲比赛选手心理紧张的原因及对策[J]. 丽水学院学报，2005(1).

[2] 金双军，杨小刚. 学习者培训对降低大学生英语演讲焦虑效果探析——一项基于英语演讲课堂教学的实证研究[J]. 外语界，2011(2).

[3] 李霞. 大学生英语演讲比赛选手培训模式的探索与实践[J]. 现代妇女(下旬)，2014(7).

Athletics and Higher Education in the U.S.

胡艺东

Abstract: Collegiate athletics is one of the most distinct characteristics of American higher education. This paper explores the origins and development of collegiate athletics in the United States. It further examinesthe impact of collegiate athletics on higher education, particularly on the academic capacity of educational institutions and student athletes. It discusses ways through which collegiate athletics has promoted academics, as well as controversies collegiate athletics has produced in recent decades, negatively affecting the academic development of college student athletes.

Key words: higher education; collegiate athletics; American culture

Collegiate athletics is one of the most distinct characteristics of American higher education. Unlike physical education typical in colleges around the world, American collegiate athletics is distinguished for its competitiveness, professionalism and nation-wide popularity. However, despite its huge popularity today, collegiate sports did not prevail until mid-19th century. Over the century, collegiate sports have become an integral part of American higher education, producing profound impact on the institution of higher education. The original purpose of developing collegiate sports and intercollegiate games was to enhance the physical and intellectual characters of college students, and ultimatelyimprove the academic ca-

作者简介:胡艺东,女,山东潍坊人,北京工商大学讲师,主要研究方向为公共英语教学、美国社会与文化。

pacity of America's higher educational institutions. However, although the development of collegiate sports has created more educational opportunities and promoted more vibrant academic cooperation and competition between schools, the conflicting goals of athletics and academics, along with improper administration by the institutions, have also given rise to academic controversies that caused college athletics to deviate from its original purposes.

1 The Origin and Development of Collegiate Sports in the U.S.

Despite its huge popularity in U.S. colleges and universities since the 20th century, sportsrarely existed on college campuses until after the antebellum years. In the beginning of the 19th century, college students were not interested in playing sports. For many students, the primary concern was to find ways to rebel against the faculty's austere control as well asthe rigorous and monotonous environment. Students engaged in rebellious activities ranging from playing coaxes to assaulting faculty and destroying campus properties. Partly as a result of the students' turmoil and partly the Enlightenment, higher educational institutions such as Harvard, Yale, Amherst, Williams and Dartmouth established the first gymnasiums in U.S. colleges and universities.Educators hoped that the promotion of sports would not only enhance the students' physical characters, but also provide an outlet for the students' excess energies and subsequently curb their rebellious activities.

The rigor and austerity of the antebellum college life led to the beginning of the institutionalization of collegiate sports, but it was not until the emergence of intercollegiate games and contests in mid-19th century that sports began toprevailon college campuses across the country. However, just like the establishment of gymnasiums, the initial purpose of hosting intercollegiate athletic contests was not to promote sports as a student activity, but to enhance the physical and intellectual wellbeing of not only the students but also the nation's people, and to consequently promote greater academic accomplishments in America's higher educationalinstitutions. The idea of using athletics to promote academics came from comparisons of American students with British students and of Americans' academic achievements with the British's. Students, educators and critics argued that American students were generally inferior to British students both physically and academically, and the academic inferiority was largely a result of the physical one. Early intercollegiate athletic contests resembled to the British convention, confined largely to competitive rowing between the most prestigious institutions. In 1852, crews from Harvard and Yale hosted the first intercollegiate contests. More games of both rowing and other sports participated by schools along the east coast followed in subsequent years.Their model was further mimicked by schoolsacross the country. This promotion of the intercollegiate athletic activities also resulted in the association between sports games and school pride, followed by greater publicity and media coverage of college athletic activities. Intercollegiate athletic events organized by east-coast schools had profound influence on higher education in the U.S. If the original purpose of promoting collegial sports was to enhance academic excellency, early intercollegiate sports among eastern schoolshad contributed significantly. Ivy League, the term that represented eight of the most prestigious universities in the world, is in fact a collegiate athletic conference comprising the eight schools, seven of which were among the oldest universities in the U.S. Today, the eight schools not only compete against each other in sports, but also compete and cooperate in teaching, research and admission.

The most important institution that organizes and regulatescollegiate athletics today is the National Collegiate Athletic Association (NCAA). Originally established in 1906 as a response to President Theodore Roosevelt's intervention in the win-at-any-cost phenomenon that plagued college football, the NCAA regulates every participants in collegiate athletics, including athletes, coaches, universities, as well as athletic organizations and conferences. Over the century, the NCAA has played a critical role in regulating and promoting American collegiate sports. Itmakes and enforces rules on games, integrity and fairness, health and safety, as well as athletes' academic performances. It also hostsnational championship games in different sports in each of its three divisions, divided based on the schools' eligibility to offer athletic scholarships. The NCAA Division I national championship gamesare the most influential collegiate games in the U.S., participated by national, even world-classathleteswho currently enrolled in Division I colleges. For instance, the winner of the 200-yard freestyle at NCAA women's swimming and diving championships in 2015 was Missy Franklin, a four-time Olympic gold medalist from the University of California, Berkley. Nick McCrory from Duke University, who wonhis fourth NCAA title in men's 10-meter platform in the 2014 NCAA championships, won the bronze medal in the 2012 London Olympic Games. The NCAA games also generate millions of revenues and attract audience of all age groups and backgrounds. For instance, the most popular college game and the largest revenue source of NCAA, the men's basketball tournamentwould attract many celebrities, including even the President of the country, to participate in bidding in the tournament's bracket each year.

2 Impacts of Collegiate Athletics on Higher Education in the U.S.

The development of collegiate athletics has exerted some positive influence on the academic capacity of American higher educational institutions, particularly through promoting competition and cooperation between institutions. When the first intercollegiate games were held among the New England colleges, people hoped that the promotion ofcompetitive sports among college students would result in their better physical and intellectual characters, such that they could match their British peers. American universities have indeed accomplished great academic achievements ever since, with the earliest participants of intercollegiate rowing games, such as Harvard and Yale, outperforming their British counterparts, Oxford and Cambridge, in many aspects. Although among all the contributing factors, the development of collegiate athletics could in no way have been the most significant one, intercollegiate athletic games have fostered greater competition and cooperation between rival schools. Competitionsbetween long-time rival schools, such as Harvard and Yale, UC Berkeley and Stanford, Duke and University of North Carolina Chapel Hill, have extended to academic performances of both the institutions and the students. Competitions thereof have also nurturedcooperation between the rival schools, with the most obvious example being the Ivy League.

The effect of collegiate athletics on individual student's academic performance has produced much more controversies. On the bright side, collegiate sports, particularly revenue-generating sports (football and basketball), havecreated many opportunities and incentives to high school athletes, especially those from lower-income families, to attend college. Schools competing in NCAA Division I offer large scholarship packages to outstanding high school football and basketball players, often covering their entire expense to attend college. As a result, children from lower-income families, many of whom are African Americans, could use their football and basketball talent as a way to win the opportunity of attaining a college education.

On the other hand, studies have shown that student athletes, particularly those of revenue-generating sports face significant academic predicament at school. According to a 1999 study, of all the male scholarship athletes in NCAA Division I schools, only 45 percent of the basketball players and 52 percent of the football players successfully graduated from college. The low graduation rates and problematic academic performance have multiple causes. First, a large proportion of college football and basketball athletes areAfrican Americans from lower-income families. Their background disadvantages make them vulnerable to academic predicament in college. Their academic performance is often further aggravated by the conflicting goals of academic achievement and athletic accomplishment. Second, since both football and basketball are professional sports offering substantial financial reward, talented student athletes often end up transferring to professional teams as soon as they achieve notable accomplishments in collegiate games. For instance, only weeks after winning the 2015 men's basketball national championship, three of the four freshmen players on Duke's basketball team quitted college, attended the NBA draft and signed up with prominent professional basketball teams. It is very common for college players to choose immediate financial rewardsin professional sports over college diplomas. This phenomenon also creates another controversy in collegiate sport—it blurs the boundary between professional and collegiate athletics. If the original purpose of creating collegiate sports in the U.S. was to use sports to promote Americans' intellectual and academic capacity, the fact that more and more student athletes only use college as anexpedient prep camp for professional athletic careersundoubtedly undermines that purpose.

Colleges have also failed, in many instances, to provide adequate institutional support to student athletes' academic endeavors. Some schools have ignored student athletes' academic need, and the effect is particularly devastating for African-American athletes. In an interview with 20 African-American former student athletes who played revenue-generatingsports in NCAA Division I schools, many of them complained of being exploited by the universities. They felt like they were "used goods" for the universities. When their intended course of study conflicted with sports training, the school often utterly ignored their academic need and made them take up a different major. In a word, because the student athletes attended colleges on athletic scholarships, their schools treated them like athletes rather than students. Other schoolshave made attempts to remedy the low graduation rate and academic performances of student athletes, but through fraudulent ways. For instance, in 2015, the alma mater of basketball superstar Michael Jordan, the University of North Carolina Chapel Hill, was found to have been conducting numerous unethical academic affairs for years. Student athletes were found to have received credit for enrollingin classes that were virtually non-existent, and passing grades were assigned to student athletes in order for them to graduate.

3 Conclusion

Collegiateathletics was established in the U.S. in order to ultimately enhance the academic and intellectual capacity of both college students and the institutionsas a whole. By improving the physical characters of young people, creating more education opportunities and promoting competition and cooperation between higher education institutions, collegiate athletics has indeed fulfilled its original purpose to at least a certain extent. However, as the popularity of intercollegiate athletic games increased over the years, the often-conflicting goals of academic achievements and athletic accomplishment, the blurring boundaries between collegiate and professional sports, and the flawed administration of collegiate athletics have all produced undesirable impact on the academic opportunities student athletes have. Until these issues are effectively addressed, collegiate athletics faces the risk of deviating from its original purpose or worse, undermining the academic development of America's higher education.

Bibliography

[1] BEAMON K K. "Used goods": former African American college student-athletes' perception of exploitation by Division I universities[J]. The Journal of Negro Education, 2008, 77(4): 352-364.

[2] HANFORD G H. Controversies in college sports[J]. Annals of the American Academy of Political and Social Sciences, 1979, 445: 66-79.

[3] LEWIS G. The beginning of organized collegiate sport[J]. American Quarterly, 1970, 22(2): 222-229.

[4] UPTHEGROVE T R, et al. Big money collegiate sports: racial concentration, contradictory pressure, and academic performances[J]. Social Science Quarterly, 1999, 80(4): 718-737.

浅谈日剧对日语学习的影响

李香春

摘　要：随着互联网的普及，越来越多的学生把观看日剧当作学习日语的一种渠道。日剧以其引人入胜的故事情节和丰富而具有特色的语言，激发学生学习日语的兴趣，提升学习效果。本文着重阐述了通过日剧学习日语的优势以及观看日剧时应注意的问题。

关键词：日剧；日语学习；优势；问题

随着互联网的普及，日剧迅速在国内传播开来，越来越受到学生们的喜爱。日剧因鲜活灵动的剧情和优越的语言环境增加和激发学生的学习兴趣和学习热情，使枯燥的学习变得轻松，从而提高学习效果。

1 通过日剧学习日语的优势

1.1 观看方便，资源丰富

现在只要有电脑和网络，就可以很方便地观看日剧。通过网络观看日剧不受时间的限制，学生可以灵活安排时间，更重要的是可以不受空间的限制，可以到中国的网站也可以到日本的NHK、TBS、富士电视台等网站观看。日剧的类型丰富多彩，题材涵盖了社会的各个领域和日常生活的方方面面，学生可以根据自己的喜好和语言能力选择适合自己的剧目。

项目/基金：本文得到2015年北京工商大学教育教学改革研究项目的资助，项目编号为JG155220。

作者简介：李香春，北京工商大学讲师，主要研究方向为日语语言文化和教学法。

1.2 突破了教材的局限性

传统的日语教学主要是以讲授教材中的词汇、语法、句型为主。虽然教材对日语学习有不可否认的积极作用，但还是存在一定的局限性。学习外语仅仅依靠教材的内容是远远不够的，学生除了合理有效地学习教材的内容之外，应积极利用各种资源，通过不同的渠道和不同的形式来加强学习。通过观看日剧学生可以身临其境的感受原汁原味的日语语言、思维及文化，学到教材上学不到的更生活化、更实用的表达方式。因此，观看日剧，很大程度上弥补了教材的局限性。

1.3 有利于掌握大量的常用词汇、正确的表达方式及良好的语音语调

良好的语言环境是学生学好日语的关键要素，但由于条件的限制，现实生活中学生很难接触到真实自然的语言环境，而日剧的广泛普及在一定程度上弥补了这一缺憾。日剧提供的是最地道、标准的发音和生活化的语言。在日剧这一真实的语言环境里，学生更容易通过画面和情节，理解日本人的思维方式，轻松地掌握大量的词汇、日常用语和正确的表达方法；能熟悉并辨析日语中的众多语音现象，掌握良好的语音语调。如：升调、降调、升降调、约音、连续、元音无声化等。而且，每一部日剧都有特定的背景、主题和内容，在不同的环境和场景中学生可以学到不同的表达方式。下面是一些在日剧中常出现的非常实用、地道的口语化的表达方式。

だから何/那又如何?

まさかそんなことはあるまい/绝不会发生那样的事情。

行かなくちゃだめ/不去不行。

冗談じゃないよ/没开玩笑。

お前に何がわかる/你懂什么?

彼女の顔を見るだけでむかつく/看到她那面孔就生气。

彼女はまだ全くの子供だ/她还是个小孩子。

これ以上我慢できない/忍无可忍。

酔っているわけないだろ/我可没喝醉。

遠慮することありゃしない/没必要客气。

相変わらず勝手な人/依然我行我素。

やれやれ、やっと/好啦，总算……

またそういうこと/又开始了。

せめてそれくらいのことは/这点小事。

何があったってほっときゃいいんだ/不管什么事，随他去就好了。

それでいいじゃないの/那不是挺好的嘛。

まさかそんなはずがない/怎么可能会那样？

結構じゃないの/无所谓吧。

1.4 有利于了解日本文化

日剧不仅为学生创造了原汁原味的语言环境，对学生了解日本文化也起着重要作用。日剧的主题涉及日本社会、政治、历史、社交礼仪、风土人情等方方面面。以日剧《冷暖人间》（渡る世間は鬼ばかり）为例，该剧讲述了发生在日本普通家庭——冈仓家中的故事，通过五个女儿和其他家庭成员的遭遇，探讨子女教育、考试、恋爱、就职、辞职、结婚、离婚、婆媳对立、老人看护等很多社会问题。该剧拍摄于20世纪90年代初，那个时候日本处于从一个创造财富的追赶者到如何守住财富的富裕国家的转型时期，也就是日本，结束连续几十年经济高增长的时期，反映了日本社会的变迁。通过观看这部剧，学生可以直观感受日本文化，更好地了解现代日本人的婚姻、工作、娱乐、衣食住行，人与人之间的关系、价值取向和生活情趣等，并对中日两种不同文化及其表现形式做出对比，思考不同。

2 观看日剧时应注意的问题

（1）遵循循序渐进的原则。日语学习是一个长久的过程，不会在短时间内得到大幅度的提高，所以通过日剧学习日语一定要耐住性子，从简单的剧目入手，脚踏实地、一步一个脚印地学下去。

（2）养成反复观看的好习惯。看日剧，只看一遍是远远不够的，尤其是对经典场景或经典台词，需要反复观看，注意发音和语音语调，理解每一个单词和句子的意思。

（3）准备好纸和笔，随时做记录。自己觉得有用的词汇、流行语、常用表达方式和一些经典台词、引发自己内心感触和共鸣的语句要记下来，等到看完之后统一整理，而且记下来的内容要及时复习。

（4）勤于模仿。观看日剧过程中，模仿是不可或缺的重要环节。只有经过模仿，才能真正地领悟真实语言环境里的很多表达方式。因此，观看过程中对剧中台词进行深度理解和学习后，一定要拿到其场景画面中对剧中人物的表情和动作进行模仿与练习，体会剧中角色的语音语调和节奏。

3 如何选择适合日语学习的日剧

日剧题材众多，短则十几集，长则几百集。在种类如此纷繁复杂的日剧中如何挑选适合日语学习的剧目，是很多通过日剧学日语的学生们面临的问题。如果选择了不适合自己的剧目，会极大地浪费宝贵的时间，花费了精力学不到东西。因此，选择日剧时要注意以下两点。第一，根据自身日语水平和爱好挑选适合自己的剧目。第二，不要选择专业术语较多，逻辑推理强，句式既长又复杂的剧目，尽量选择简单易懂、发音清晰、语速适中、贴近日常生活的偶像剧和生活剧。笔者通过近年来学生对日剧的欣赏反馈，发现很多日剧都深受学生们的喜爱，尤其是在日本收视率较高的爱情剧、偶像剧、家庭剧。下面推荐几部发音比较清晰，语言优美，适合日语学习的日剧。

（1）《东京爱情故事》。

该剧是日剧进入我国的经典之作，一度成为日剧的代名词，被称为20世纪90年代三部经典爱情剧之一。

（2）《冷暖人间》。

剧本出自日本著名编剧桥田寿贺子之手。自1990年开始在日本播出至2010年已经推出了10部，寿命长达20年。该剧秉承了桥田寿贺子一贯的写作风格，精彩而不拖沓。

（3）《恋爱补给品》。

根据冈崎真里的同名漫画作品改编。讲述了一名以工作为主爱情为辅的职业女性，在遇上不拘小节的年轻打工仔后所发生的内心变化。

（4）《公主与穷太郎》。

讲述了一个自由奔放的富家女爱丽丝，与一个带着3个孩子勉强度日，不但不悲观，还积极面对生活的穷光蛋佐藤太郎之间的爱情故事。

(5)《一公升的眼泪》。

讲述一个15岁的小女孩突然患上了不治之症，但在家人和朋友的支持下，决心努力无悔地度过每一天，不给自己的青春留下遗憾的励志剧。

总之，观看日剧对学生的日语学习确实有促进作用，日剧激发了学生学习日语的兴趣，为学生创造出轻松有趣、真实鲜活的语言环境。但实际操作过程中也应注意一些问题。只要掌握正确的方法，付出一定的时间和精力，日语水平一定能提高。

参考文献

[1] 罗红芳. 英文电影在大学英语教学中的作用与优势[J]. 电影文学,2010(14).

[2] 孙志杰. 影视剧《走遍美国》:从文化与语言解读当代美语学习[J]. 电影文学,2007(21).

[3] 黄岭. 英文影视欣赏对大学非英语专业学生英语学习的作用[J]. 河北工程大学学报:社会科学版,2014(3).

[4] 侯梦瞳. 浅析美剧对英语学习的影响及其学习策略[J]. 北方文学,2014(5).

基于Blackboard平台的Wiki模块教学与大学英语学习

李子嘉　石洪宇

摘　要：本文以大学英语学习为例，论述了Blackboard平台中Wiki模块在英语学习中的应用。在分析平台教学的各种优势的同时，作者强调，学生利用平台的Wiki工具认真完成教师布置的任务，能够将新旧知识融会贯通，扩大了知识面，提升了学习兴趣和学习效果，提高了自主学习和独立解决问题能力。

关键词：Blackboard平台；Wiki模块；英语学习

Blackboard教学管理平台（Blackboard Learning System，以下简称Blackboard平台）是美国blackboard公司研发的一套专门用于加强网络教学、辅助课堂教学并提供互动、交流的网络教学平台。该平台具有功能强大、使用方便、高稳定性等特点。它不但可以使不同课程之间相互链接，使教学在横向和纵向上得以沟通，而且“将传统学习方式的优势和e-learning（即数字化或网络化学习）的优势相结合”。

Blackboard平台虽然在我国高校运用时间不长，但是它已成为高校课程建设成就展示的一个重要平台，并因其融入了现代化教学理念，受到高校教师和学生的极大关注。有关平台建设及利用平台开展教学改革的文章涵盖很多方面，但是值得一提的是，在众多的研究中关于教师利用平台开展外语综

项目/基金：本论文为2015年北京市级大学生科研与创业行动计划项目的成果，项目编号为SJ201501035。
作者简介：李子嘉，女，山西人，北京工商大学商学院学生。石洪宇，女，天津人，北京工商大学讲师，主要研究方向为英语教学法、语言学。

合教学对学生产生影响的研究并不多见，借助平台开展怎样的活动以促进学生的学习还没有引起大家足够的关注。

Wiki模块是一种同Wiki百科一样由各种词条构成的网络协作工具，支持师生共同创作同一条目。利用Wiki模块的相关功能可以创建出词条并对想要编辑的内容进行处理，因此，本文拟就使用Blackboard平台中Wiki模块进行英语学习的相关内容展开探讨。

1 使用Wiki进行英语学习的理论基础

利用Wiki模块进行英语学习的理论基础是瑞士心理学家皮亚杰创建的建构主义理论。刘娟认为，“建构主义理论认为知识不是被动接受的，而是认知主体积极建构的：知识是学习者在一定的情景下，借助其他人的帮助，即通过人际间的协作交流，利用必要的学习资料，通过建构意义的方式而获得的。也就是说，知识的获取过程是意义的建构过程，在这个过程中学习者是认知的主体，借助自己已有的知识和经验来认知和掌握新的知识。”通过这一理论我们可以知道学生是整个学习活动的主体，而非传统意义上的完全依靠老师的“指挥”来完成学习任务，而Blackboard平台中的Wiki模块恰好给了学生一个机会，为学生的自主学习搭建了一个很好的平台。Wiki模块将学习过程发展成一个由学生主导，充分融合课上所学内容，利用网络资源，教师充当“引路人”的角色的良性循环。Blackboard平台教学以其操作简单、稳定、支持文件类型多样、易于沟通、时间具有开放性、资源丰富等优势创造出不同于传统的学习环境，为教师和学生，学生和学生之间的协作和会话提供全方位的支持，使学生对知识的理解和运用得以深化。

2 基于Wiki模块的英语课下学习

在日常的学习中，教师最容易把控的是课上的学习，而最难把控的则是学生的课下学习。学生以小组为单位利用Wiki完成一定的任务，帮助学生自我巩固课上所学内容、将各种知识融会贯通，在一定程度上可以促进学生的课下学习。在这一学期，老师为我们引入了Blackboard平台中之前很少被利用到的Wiki模块。学期伊始，老师给我们介绍了Wiki模块的具体使用方法，并对班上的同学进行分组，对本学期利用Wiki的教学计划进行了说明。班上的同学3~5个人一组，根据课上的教学进度，通过小组合作的方式完成相关Wiki页面的制作。在制作Wiki的过程中，我们首先需要熟悉掌握课上已经学过的内容，在此基础上对学过的内容进行反思，思考哪些是学习过程中的重点、难点，然后根据教材上的商务情景，利用网络资源进行扩展，充实所学的内容，将其分别做成Wiki页面，并利用Wiki模块中丰富的制作工具来完成页面的制作。想要做出来内容充实、美观的Wiki页面就需要充分利用教材、网络中的各种资源，在这个过程中就扎实地完成了课下学习。

3 利用Wiki模块学习的优势

（1）操作简单。

Blackboard平台之所以能够被广泛使用，很重要的一个原因就是其操作简单、界面友好，其中的Wiki模块更是如此。Wiki模块中的文本编辑操作中包含：编辑字体字号，插入图片、文件、链接等。因而操作者仅需了解基本的Office、电子邮件的操作方法就可以操作Wiki模块中绝大部分的工具。

（2）系统稳定、支持多人同时操作。

只要是成功上传后的文档、文件就会安全地保存在系统里，无需担心文件丢失。并且Wiki模块既可以多人同时编辑，也可以小组同学在之前同学的基础上依次编辑。Blackboard平台也可以在多种设备上操作，如在IPad上可以对Blackboard的各项功能进行操作。

（3）支持文件类型多样。

Wiki模块为了可以设计出内容充实、美观的页面，支持上传的文件类型多样，同时兼具各种功能，如可以支持在系统中直接输入数学公式、插入网络链接等。便于使用者充分地表达所思所想，不受固有格式的限制。如：在介绍某一部分的内容时，可以插入一段相关专业人士演讲的视频或是音频，增强页面的趣味性。

（4）易于沟通。

通过Blackboard平台可以实现学生与学生、教师与学生之间的沟通，没有时间空间的限制，在相关位置留言，对方一登录就会看到。传统的网络教学，缺少沟通的渠道，使得学生与学生、教师与学生之间缺乏沟通，导致小组合作不够密切，教师没有办法监督的问题。同时，小组间可以互相看到其他组做的Wiki页面，有利于交流想法、思维的碰撞。

（5）时间的开放性。

Blackboard平台是24小时开放的平台，使用者可以在没有任何时间限制的情况下充分利用平台上的资源。传统的课堂教学在很大程度上受时间和空间限制，仅仅是课堂上的时间，在教室内教学，而网络教学打破了传统的课堂教学的时间和空间限制，在教学过程中，教师与学生之间、学生与学生之间可以同步交流或是非同步交流，使得联系更加密切和灵活。Blackboard平台作为一种网络教学的途径，有力地突破了时空限制，使教师可以利用平台随时随地管理课程、上传课件、自动生成课堂测验和布置课后作业以便加强与学生之间的交流协作。此外，作为学生，感受最明显的还是可以自由选择学习的时间、地点，随时随地向老师提出问题，通过便捷的渠道和同学进行交流。

（6）学习更有针对性。

通过制作Wiki，我们可以针对自己学习中的不足，根据自己的兴趣，广泛地涉猎课外的相关领域来提升学习的质量和效果，避免了传统教学中老师面向整体授课缺乏针对性的问题。由于避免了“大锅饭”，学生的学习效果就得到了提升。

4 Wiki模块的不足

（1）部分工具的设置不完善。

有一些功能的设置不完善，如：在文本编辑中的表格工具使用不便捷。改变行高、列宽不能在文字编辑时靠拖拽表格完成，而需要在插入表格前就通过磅数来预先设定行高、列宽。这就导致预先设置表格格式时，由于不能预见到页面的大小和插入表格在页面中所占的比例而造成不便。

（2）插入文件格式限制。

在插入文件的时候需要预先选择插入文件的类型，而不能直接插入文件，且对文件的种类有限制，需要分门别类地选择上传类型，而且视频文件插入仅有特定的几种格式。

5 结语

Blackboard平台具有强大的网络教学功能，具有其他平台所不具备的优势，可以多种渠道帮助学生自主学习。其中的Wiki模块给师生提供了自主学习的有力工具。在利用Wiki模块进行学习时，学生可以充分借助自己已有的知识和经验来认知和掌握新的知识，对新的知识有更加充分的理解，同时对新旧知识加以融会贯通，记忆更加深刻。虽然Wiki模块自身存在一些瑕疵，但是也可以在提升学生学习自主性上起到很大的作用。在解决各种技术问题的同时，我们将已有知识运用到解决问题中，也提升了我们解决问题的能力。

参考文献

[1] 何克抗. E-learning的本质——信息技术与学科课程的整合[J]. 电化教育研究,2002(1):3-6.

[2] 何克抗. 运用“新三论”的系统方法促进教学设计理论与运用的深入发展[J]. 中国电化教育,2010(1):7-18.

[3] 刘娟. 多媒体教学在俄语精读课上的使用[J]. 俄罗斯文艺,2006(2):66-70.

开发与研制多套难度相似的思辨技能量具
——拉丁方测试前期准备

李英杰

摘　要：要研究大学生思辨能力的发展，必须研制多套量具。量具中单个题目的难易度和区分度必须达到一定指标，以确保多套量具的等效性。而题目从形成、修改到最后成熟是一个漫长的过程。经过长达一年半的开发与研制，最后形成了三套平行量具，用于后续拉丁方测试。本文报告了三套平行量具的研制过程。

关键词：思辨能力；发展研究；量具研制

1 引言

本研究是上一项已经完成的国家社科项目（批准号12BYY051）的延伸，上一项目经过2008年先导研究和2009年正式研究和两次大规模测试，开发出一套成熟的客观量具，经全国18917名受试检测，该量具的平均难易度0.53，区分度0.33，内部一致性Alpha值.71。我们认为，已有量具从整体上说可以用于测量大学生的思辨能力，但仍有部分题目区分度不够理想，难易度偏容易。根据研究计划，本期研究要跟踪研究大学生思辨能力的发展过程，总共需要三套平行量具，用于测量大学生思辨能力的发展过程。从上套量具的开发过程中得到的启示是，依据题型设计量具题目的做法可操作性

项目/基金：本文是国家社科基金项目“我国大学生思辨能力发展差异的比较：跟踪研究”（批准号：12BYY051）的阶段性成果。

作者简介：李英杰，女，北京工商大学外国语学院讲师，主要研究方向为第二语言习得、语用学。

强，我们继续沿用这种作法。本次研究中，我们以前套量具为参照，一方面按照前套量具的分类甄选构成新量具的题目，另一方面我们删除和修改了前套量具的部分不达标题目，并把修改后的题目按照题型归入新开发的量具中一起参与测试。经过五轮测试（见表1），历时一年半，最后确定下来的题目构成三套平行量具，进行拉丁方测试。

表1 前五次测试说明

测试轮次	时间	人数	说明
一	2010年12月	65	京内某二类院校31人；京内某一类院校34人
二	2011年6月	78	京外某二类院校
三	2011年9月	189	京内两所一类院校
四	2011年10月	66	京内某二类院校
五	2012年4月	174	京内某二类院校36人；京内某一类院校42人；京外两所二类院校96人

这五次测试检测单个题目的难易度和区分度，拉丁方测试则检测整套量具难易度和区分度，确保三套平行量具整体相当。也就是说，三套量具能够同样有效地测量出大学生思辨能力。因篇幅所限，本文只报告前五次研究。

2 题目说明

我们继承原有量具根据题型分类的做法，但对原有量具的分类和各类题目的数量略作调整（见表2）。

前七类题型主要来源于国内外各类考试、国外思辨能力测试网站和国内外教科书上的练习题。所有题目都经过了研究人员的修改，使之在表达方面更为简洁明了，国外题目通过翻译润色使之本土化。后三类题型没有现成的题目，由研究人员自行搜集材料拟题。

表2 题目说明

题型	数量	说明及示例
① 识别假设/论点	6	给出一个陈述，要求被试就给出的与陈述相关的四个预设，或四个论点做出恰当的选择。 以上结论基于/暗含了下列哪一项预设？ 下面哪句话可作为上述言论的结论？ 以上论述想要说明的观点是……
② 推论/形式推理	5	给出一个包含推理过程的陈述，要求被试在陈述为真的前提下，在给出的四个结论或推理结果中做出恰当的选择。 以上如果为真，则以下哪项一定为真/为假？ 由此可以得出以下哪一项推论？
③ 匹配相似推理/运用潜在规则	5	给出一个包含推理过程的陈述，再给出四个包含推理过程的选项，要求被试从中选出与题干推理过程最为相似的一个选项，或与题干的潜在推理规则相同的选项。 以下哪一项和上述推理最相似？ 下面哪个例子最符合上述论证的潜在原则？
④ 辨别推理错误/评价推理	4	给出一个包含推理错误的陈述，要求被试指出四个选项中哪个选项是陈述所包含的推理错误；给出一个包含推理过程的陈述，要求被试根据四个选项对推理的正确性及其理由进行判断。 下面哪句话指出了上述言论的推理错误/推理中的漏洞？ 对上述推理的最佳评价是……
⑤ 评价附加证据对结论的影响	4	给出一个含有结论的陈述，再给出四个附加证据。要求被试对附加证据是削弱还是加强了陈述的结论加以判断。以下哪项最能加强/削弱上述论断？
⑥ 数字题	2	给出涉及数字的推理陈述，要求被试经过逻辑运算，从四个选项中选出正确答案。
⑦ 图表题	2	给出图表、数字和简单描述，要求被试根据所给信息从四个选项中选出正确答案。
⑧ 根据争论内容评价结论	4	简单介绍两人争论的议题，然后给出5个单人发言，这5个发言之间没有联系。要求被试就单个发言的内容和逻辑做出判断： 若结论是所给论据的必然结果，选A； 若结论与所给论据相矛盾，选B； 若结论既不是所给论据的必然结果，也不与所给论据相矛盾，选C。

续表

题型	数量	说明及示例
⑨ 根据实验报告评价陈述	4	给出一项实验的简介和实验数据,然后列出3道题,每题含有两个陈述。要求被试根据所给信息对题目中的两个陈述做出判断并选择: 如果你认为第一个陈述更可信,选A; 如果你认为第二个陈述更可信,选B; 如果你无法判断哪个陈述更可信,选C。
⑩ 根据案例评价推论	4	描述一个案例,并给出3个推论。要求被试对3个推论做出判断: A. 推论正确; B. 推论缺乏足够信息依据; C. 推论错误。

3 题目的形成过程

前七类题目的形成经过四个阶段：淘题—测试—数据分析—修改。在淘题阶段研究组成员先淘出质量较好的题目，同时修改题目的措词，使语言简洁明了，接下来按照题型归为七类。然后同后3类题目一起，组成一套待测试量具。在测试阶段，我们一般选择项目组成员自己所带的自然班学生作受试，这样做一是方便操作，二是研究人员同时是受试的老师，可以保证大部分受试能认真完成题目。测试完毕后，由各研究人员分别录入自己所负责的班级的原始数据。在数据分析阶段，为了保证计算的准确无误，每次都有至少两名研究人员同时处理分析原始数据，然后根据区分度（D），把题目分为达标题目（$D \geqslant 0.3$）、待改进题目（$0.3 > D \geqslant 0.2$）和淘汰题目（$D < 0.2$）。区分度的分析主要以效标为依据，即把受试在整个测验上所得的总分当成考生的实有水平，考察被试在每个试题上的反应与其在效标上的表现之间的相关程度。这样做有利于让每个题目为整套量具作贡献，增强测验试题间的同质性，从而提高整个测验的信度。在修改阶段，先挖出区分度达标的题目放入成题库，删掉淘汰题目并淘出新题来替换这些题目，最后项目组成员共同讨

论是要保留还是淘汰待修改题目，如果要淘汰，则补入新题；如果要保留，则继续讨论如何修改（修改示例见下文）。修改完毕的题目和补入的新题都进入下一轮测试（见表3）。

表3　前五次测试数据

轮次	难易度区间组	频数	实际比例	理想比例	区分度分组	频数	评价区分度标准
第一次	<0.19	1	3%	10%	<0.19	20	删除
	0.20~0.39	4	10%	20%	0.20~0.24	5	不太好，但可修改
	0.40~0.59	11	28%	40%	0.25~0.29	5	
	0.60~0.79	14	35%	20%	0.30~0.39	5	较好
	>0.80	10	25%	10%	>0.40	5	很好
第二次	<0.19	3	8%	10%	<0.19	16	删除
	0.20~0.39	10	25%	20%	0.20~0.24	5	不太好，但可修改
	0.40~0.59	11	28%	40%	0.25~0.29	6	
	0.60~0.79	11	28%	20%	0.30~0.39	5	较好
	>0.80	5	13%	10%	>0.40	1	很好
第三次	<0.19	4	10%	10%	<0.19	16	删除
	0.20~0.39	9	23%	20%	0.20~0.24	6	不太好，但可修改
	0.40~0.59	12	30%	40%	0.25~0.29	3	
	0.60~0.79	9	23%	20%	0.30~0.39	8	较好
	>0.80	6	15%	10%	>0.40	7	很好
第四次	<0.19	3	5%	10%	<0.19	12	删除
	0.20~0.39	7	11%	20%	0.20~0.24	9	不太好，但可修改
	0.40~0.59	13	20%	40%	0.25~0.29	6	
	0.60~0.79	12	18%	20%	0.30~0.39	6	较好
	>0.80	5	8%	10%	>0.40	7	很好

续表

轮次	难易度区间组	频数	实际比例	理想比例	区分度分组	频数	评价区分度标准
第五次	<0.19	3	6%	10%	<0.19	16	删除
	0.20~0.39	8	17%	20%	0.20~0.24	7	不太好，但可修改
	0.40~0.59	12	25%	40%	0.25~0.29	5	
	0.60~0.79	22	46%	20%	0.30~0.39	6	较好
	>0.80	3	6%	10%	>0.40	14	很好

后3类题目由项目组研究人员自行研发，整个过程也分为四步：出题—测试—数据分析—修改。在出题阶段，项目组成员从各自不同专业的亲朋好友处索要材料，或者从网上寻找话题，搜集材料，考虑到大学生的认知特点和专业各不相同的实际情况，我们在选择材料的时候一是要避免因过于专业而增加题目难度，因为这样就无法准确测出受试的思辨能力；二是尽量选择有争议的话题，以引起受试的阅读兴趣，活跃他们的思维。选好材料之后再润色材料文字，使其尽量言简意赅。然后采出出题点，设计题目。测试、数据分析和修改阶段同上述前七类题目相同，不再赘述。不同的是，新出题的修改阶段不再重新选择材料，只修改已有材料和已测试过的题目（见表3）。

以上四个步骤我们总共重复了五轮。

凡是区分度不达标的题目，一方面我们逐题检查，从内容的充实到文字的润色，不断修改。另一方面考虑到整套量具需要不同难易度指数的题目分布均衡，我们增大难易度小于0.39的题目的比例，尽量减少难易度大于0.60的题目的比例。以下是我们修改和新出题目的示例。

3.1 修改题目示例

下题是修改前后的题目和统计数据对比：原题P=0.84，D=0.18，说明有84%的受试选出了正确答案，题目偏易；区分度为0.18，也没有达到0.20的要求。四个选项分布显示：A、D两个干扰项的干扰度太低（3%和4%）。研究人员经过讨论，分析该题目可能存在的问题是：题干的语言不够精炼，四个选项长短不一。经过修改题干和选项后再次测试，P=0.4，D=0.4，四个选项的分布也基本均匀了（见表4）。

表4　修改题目示例

	修改前	统计数据	修改后	统计数据
题干	因为未成年人不应该吸烟，所以制定禁止向未成年人销售香烟的法律是合理的。然而禁止设立售烟机的立法提案就如同设置路障拦截概率为1%的无照驾驶。路障阻挡了所有的驾驶者，而不仅仅是那些违法的人。下列哪项陈述包含着与上述反对意见相似的推理？	P=0.84 D=0.18	“禁止向未成年人销售香烟的法律是合理的，然而禁止设立售烟机的立法提案如果通过，将给许多买烟的成年人带来不便，因此不应支持该提案。”下列哪项陈述包含着与上述意见相似的推理？	P=0.4 D=0.4
选项	A.无须禁止设立禁烟机，目前已有法律禁止把香烟出售给未成年人。	6/3%	A.为防止盗窃，有超市不允许顾客带包购物，但购物前排队存包将给顾客造成不便。	66/38%
	B.即使把香烟销售税再提高1%，也无法有效阻止未成年人购买香烟。	17/9%	B.公共场所不应禁烟，因为这样的法律规定严重妨碍了吸烟者作为公民的行动自由。	19/11%
	C.禁止设置自动售烟机给许多购买香烟的成年人带来不便。	158/84%	C.打击无照驾驶的一个有效途径是设置路障拦截，但这种方法增加了交通事故隐患。	76/44%
	D.虽然自动售烟机比零售店价格更贵，也无法有效阻止未成年人购买香烟。	8/4%	D.没有必要实行电影分级制度，家长们的认真监督就能避免对未成年人的不良影响。	10/6%

3.2 新出题目示例

以下新出题原题材料来源于课题组成员曾做过的一项研究，题目由研究者拟定。以下是原题和修改后的题干、题目及统计数据（见表5）。修改后题目的难易度降低，说明题目难度加大，区分度增加：难易度从0.9到0.3，区分度从-0.3到0.4。修改前，选项A和B没有什么干扰力，受试的选择集中在D上，修改后除去未作答人数，四个选项分布基本均匀。

这仅仅是两次测试中的数据，一般题目都要经过多次修改，反复测试，最后才能达到要求。

表5　新出题示例

	原题	统计数据	修改后	统计数据
题干	某研究者根据采集到的300篇中国大学生所写的英语作文，进行了一项关于“写作主题词与作者身份认同”的研究（作文主题同为“Emotion Management”，即“情绪管理”）。数据统计显示，这些作文中某些词汇出现的频率呈显著性集中，具体情况见下边的表格（表略）。 下面是依据这项研究所得出的结论： 结论（1）：“中国外语专业大学生普遍具有女性特征的心理，比如爱哭。”	P=0.9 D=-0.3	某研究者根据采集到的300篇中国大学生题为“我的情绪管理”的英语作文，进行了一项关于“写作主题词与情绪管理”的研究（情绪管理，即“Emotion Management”，指调节情绪的方式和途径）。研究者提取出作文中的部分主题词，计算其出现频次，以此来整体描述和分析研究对象情绪管理的特点及相关影响因素。详细数据见下表（表略）。 下面是依据这项研究所得出的结论： 结论（1）：“中国外语专业大学生比较爱哭，具有女性倾向的心理特征。”	P=0.3 D=0.4
选项	A. 合理，因为外语专业女生多，男生少，女生又很少有不爱哭的。	0/0%	A. 合理，因为外语专业女生多，自然在作文中流露出女性心理特征。	56/32%
	B. 合理，哭是一种正常的情感宣泄方式。	1 0/0%	B. 合理，外语类大学生的焦虑程度高于非外语专业，哭可以缓解焦虑。	16/9%

续表

	原题	统计数据	修改后	统计数据
选项	C. 不合理，研究者忽视了外语类大学生中的男女比例。	1 6/9%	C. 不合理，研究者忽视了外语类大学生中的男性学生的存在。	39/22%
	D. 不合理，数据中“专业”与“哭泣”并无显著相关性。	60/91%	D. 不合理，与其他专业同学相比，外语类学生提及“哭泣”的频率并不高。	54/31%

说明：修改后，未作答9人/5%。

4 启发与反思

经过前期的反复测试与修改，我们得到如下启示：第一，虽说试题的区分度是检验其是否有效的重要指标，但当样本的同质性（homogeneity）太强或样本太小时，题目的取舍不能取决于区分度。因为同样的题目，如果受试同质性较强，无论受试整体水平高或低，试题区分度都会较低；而当受试异质性较强，即受试水平有高有低时，试题区分度会较高。第二，小样本的区分度也只能做参考数据，不能做决定性数据，因为样本人数相对较少时，往往一个或几个受试的数据就会对整个样本数据造成很大影响。我们的前五次研究因为过于看重区分度数据，导致走了很多弯路。其实在这两种情况下，比较可靠的做法是看选项分布的均匀程度，增加干扰程度不够的选项的干扰力。

由于国内可借鉴的此类研究较少，我们基本是摸着石头过河，一边开发，一边反思，希望我们的做法能够给日后开发思辨量具的研究者一些借鉴。

参考文献

[1] GCT逻辑精练365题及详解[EB/OL]. http://ishare.iask.sina.com.cn/f/20507683.html?from=like&sudaref=www.baidu.com&retcode=0.

[2] 谷振诣,刘壮虎. 批判性思维教程[M]. 北京:北京大学出版社,2006.

[3] 文秋芳,王建卿,赵彩然,等.构建我国外语类大学生思辨能力量具的理论框架[J]. 外语界,2009(1):37-43.

[4] 文秋芳,赵彩然,等. 我国外语类大学生思辨能力客观性量具构建的先导研究[J]. 外语教学,2010(1):55-58.

[5] 文秋芳,王海妹,等. 我国英语专业与其他文科类大学生思辨能力的对比研究[J]. 外语教学与研究,2010(9):350-355.

[6] 文秋芳,李英杰,等. 研制多套难度相似的思辨技能量具:实践与反思[J]. 外语电化教学,2014 (7):3-13.

牛津大学英语培训模式的借鉴与思考

刘 影

摘 要：北京工商大学自2005年至今，已连续10年派学生团组前往英国牛津大学赫特福德学院进行为期两周左右的商务英语培训。相对而言，两周的培训时间并不长，但是对学生的影响却很大。那么，牛津大学英语教学方面有哪些值得我们借鉴和学习的地方呢？本文围绕学习者学习动机的激发、激发策略的实施等方面，对牛津大学的培训方式进行了分析。文章指出，只有符合语言教学规律，激发学生主观能动性，帮助其建立并提升学习自信心，并创造合适的语言学习环境，才能更有效地促进英语教学。

关键词：牛津大学；英语培训；借鉴；思考

1 赴牛津培训团组情况、效果及影响

北京工商大学自2005年至今，已连续10年派学生团组前往英国牛津大学赫特福德学院进行为期两周左右的商务英语培训。每期培训团组人数从18人到45人不等，主要以我校在校本科生为主。项目属于学校公派自费短期境外培训项目，食宿和上课均在牛津大学学院内部，任课老师由学院语言培训中心老师担任，学生到达英国后日常生活和所有活动由牛津大学在校的大学生全程陪同。

本人对学校牛津培训团组进行了不完全统计和调查，并对自己所带的

作者简介：刘影，女，安徽亳州人，北京工商大学国际处副处长，讲师，研究方向为应用语言学。

两个团组成员进行深入访谈。调查发现，总体上来说，培训团成员对培训效果满意率较高，基本上在90%以上。根据对已毕业培训团组团员的跟踪调查显示，超过50%的学生毕业后选择了出国留学或到外企工作，而这种选择对他们中的一些同学来说是在参加培训团以前没想过的。第一期培训团带队老师一直与所带团员保持联系，她说很多团员表示牛津培训对他们的工作选择、出国留学等方面影响深远，有的甚至直接改变了其毕业后的选择。

那么培训项目究竟如何进行的？为什么会对学生产生那么大的影响？对我们的英语教学来说，又有那些可借鉴之处呢？

2 牛津培训模式、过程及要求

初到牛津，学生面对的第一件事就是进行分级考试。测试内容主要是读、写，没有听力和口语。根据学生成绩，对学生进行分级教学，每班8~15人，分别由不同的老师来执教。

本人曾多次深入教学课堂，观摩其教学过程。整体上感觉教学内容不难，在信息量方面也不大，但让学生自己去搜集信息，完成作业。牛津大学的老师在教学方法上，与自己接触过的中国老师相比，并无“过人”之处，交际教学思想和任务型教学法贯穿整个教学过程，教学设备甚至很“落后”，很少使用电子设备，大部分还停留在人与人之间的直接交流上。但是课堂上老师能最大限度地调动学生的积极性，让学生参与到每一个教学活动中，并且根据学生特点，把握学生发言的频率，确保每一位学生的发言机会和发言时间大致平衡，不会因为某个学生很积极，就一直让他发言，也不会因为某个学生性格内向等原因而使其错失了发言机会。关注和尊重让学生有被重视的感觉。

培训结束时的考核方式是要求学生分组做结业汇报（presentation）。所有团员包括带队老师、任课老师都要出席。评委老师由培训中心主任担任，负责给出评分和评语。这既是对学生的考核，也是学生学习成果的展示、交流和比赛，对学生和任课老师的压力都很大，往往在考核前学生会主动约老师对其进行多次单独指导。老师的点评会在汇报结束后给出，而学生的综合表现则是在结业仪式上合影时学生所在位置的参考。一般会让最优秀的学生站在中间位置紧挨着老师合影，这也是给他们的荣誉和奖励。

本人每次参加学生的汇报会，感触都很深。整体上来说，与刚开始上课时相比，学生的表现远超出预期！短短两周的时间，学生无论从语言方面还是知识方面，与在国内十几年的学习积累相比，都不可能学到太多的东西，但是在汇报会上，学生却能把自己的专业知识、语言技能和自身素质最佳地融合，充分展示出自己最优秀的一面。这是怎么做到的?

3 牛津模式的借鉴和思考

威廉姆斯（Williams）指出，学习动机使学习者一段时间内付诸努力以达成既定目标，是一种情感认知的唤醒状态。它是预测二语学习成功与否的重要因素，长期以来受到心理学家和二语习得研究的广泛关注。对牛津培训团教学感触最深的一点是牛津方面会尽最大努力，创造并利用各种条件，以有利于学生学习动机的培养和激发，充分发挥每一位学生的主观能动性，以达到最佳的教学效果。

3.1 明确的学习目标和考核方式

学习动机应当由三部分组成：实现目标的愿望，为实现目标所做出的努力，和对完成任务的满意度。牛津方面全面了解学生学习动机，并帮助学生完成学习目标。

牛津培训团在组团之初，会通过团员个人信息表和问卷调查，充分了解每一位培训团团员的个人情况和学习目的和要求。在课程设计时，在满足大部分团员培训要求的同时，尽量照顾到每一位团员的个性化要求。

教学过程中，在明确教学任务和最终考核方式的同时，要求学生最终的结业汇报必须体现出教学过程中所学到的和掌握的知识和方法。这种方式可避免学生事先准备好一份汇报内容，或者过度关注考核而忽略了学习过程。不少学生表示，本来抱着老师能“点石成金”的想法来学习的，现在发现还需自己一步步的努力才行。但是学习过程很愉快，很自信。对于经过自己精心准备的结业汇报的完美展示，很有一种成就感。

3.2 分级小班教学，保证学习者的学习小环境

“动机策略是实现个体目标有关行为的必要手段”。但动机激发策略并不总是能够有效发挥其实际作用，学生的英语水平参差不齐与差异性可能是影响动机激发策略的有效性的一个重要因素。牛津培训团团员来自学校各个学院，各个年级，英语水平参差不齐，尽量减小这种由于水平差异可能会带来的影响，分级小班教学是牛津方面采取的有效手段。

本人曾经和牛津语言教学中心的老师们讨论过班级人数问题。他们认为对于语言技能类的教学，若班上人数少于8人，上课气氛会受影响，若超过15人，那么老师就很难照顾到每一位同学的学习进展。一般来说，学生人数在这两者之间教学效果最好。2010年培训团组共18人，牛津方面并没有因为团组人数仅仅超过3个学生而“将就”成一个班。而是根据学生测试成绩分成两个班，每班9人。2015年团组学生共43人，这个团组有部分研究生加入，使得学生的英语水平差异更大。牛津方面并没有按照一般惯例分成三个班，而是根据实际测试情况分成了四个班进行教学。每增加一个班，就要增加教学成本。在经济利益和教学的效果之间，他们选择了把教学效果放在首位。

3.3 提升学生自信，尊重学生个性

培训老师对学生学习自信的培养和保护，是我感触最深的方面。学生发言时，老师很少打断他们去纠正一些语法等错误，但又会以正确的语言重复学生的意思，从而使之受益。不少学生表示，以前总是对自己的英语没有信心，现在到了牛津大学培训，感觉纯英语授课“不过如此”，“上课都能听懂”，以后自己也可以考虑出国留学了！也有学生表示，“上课都听懂了，太容易了，应该加大难度！”那么上课内容究竟是否太容易了姑且不论，毕竟对“能否听懂”和“是否掌握”的要求还是不一样的，但从另外的角度来看，对一些学生来说，英语学习的信心还是得以建立并提升。这对学习者来说是非常重要的。

老师们对学生个体的尊重也让我感触颇深。2011年的团组中有一个女学生，很任性，也很有个性，每次上课都非常“积极”要求发言，有一次课上甚至直接“威胁”老师：你若再不让我发言，我就不教你打麻将！大家都安

静下来，看着老师，气氛有点尴尬。老师走到她面前，很委婉地对她说，“课后打麻将时，你是老师，我听你的；现在我是老师，你听我的。我们先听听其他同学的想法，你来总结。”简单几句话，既维持了课堂教学秩序，也保护了学生的自尊。

3.4 有效的辅助教学手段

与我们平时所讲到的课后辅导、答疑等辅助教学手段不同，以下重点讲的是另外一个群体所起的作用，即被称为RA（Residential Advisor）的牛津大学的在校生们。每个牛津团都会有牛津大学的在校生全程陪同，负责学生除了课堂教学以外的几乎所有事项。他们与学生同吃同住，并负责组织各项课外活动，为学生提供各种咨询，并随时进行各方面的交流。2015团组的每一位团员在总结时都重点提到了RA们对他们的帮助和影响。他们的存在，一方面会随时创造一种英语交流的小环境，使得团员们养成即使是下课了在生活中也要用英语进行交流的习惯，使得英语的表达和使用很“接地气”，对于一些没有解决的争论性的话题，学生又会带到课堂上，请老师指导，形成学习良性循环。另一方面，他们组织的各项活动极大地调动了学生学习的兴趣，开阔了学生眼界。学生与RA之间的交流，有助于学生更直接地了解英国文化和风俗习惯，学习生活中“活”的英语。这对于我们如何充分利用中国高校英语国家的留学生辅助英语教学提供了很好的参考模式。

英语教学绝不仅仅是老师和学生的事情，它和学生学习的大环境、小环境都息息相关。如何充分激发学生学习积极性，帮助其建立并提升自信，实现个体的尊重，需要各方面的共同努力。通过近几期的调查发现，学生对牛津培训团的要求也越来越高，要求时间更长，要求内容更系统更专业。那么，作为母语为非英语的英语老师来说，也面临更加严峻的挑战。在老师不断学习提升自己的同时，学校也应该提供更多去英语国家学习进修的机会，同时创造更适合英语教学的环境，共同提高英语教学水平。

参考文献

[1] DORNYEI Z. Motivated strategies in the language classroom[M]. Cambridge: Cambridge University Press, 2001.

[2] GARDNERT R C, MACINTYRE P D. A student's contribution to a second language learning [M]. Rowley, MA: Newbery House, 1993.

[3] WILLIAMS M, BURDEN R. Psychology for language teachers[M]. Cambridge: Cambridge University Press, 1997.

[4] 文秋芳. 英语学习者动机、观念、策略的变化规律与特点[J]. 外语教学与研究, 2001(3): 105-110.

大学英语分级教学形式下分班及排课方法探讨

陈思伊

摘　要: 大学英语分级教学是当前高校在英语教学改革中越来越提倡和推崇的一种教学组织形式，在实际教学实践中收到了良好的教学效果。然而随着大学英语分级教学研究和实践的深入，问题和困难也不断显现。其中，科学分级与顺利排课之间矛盾尤为突出，学校规模越大、学生数量越多该矛盾就变得愈加尖锐。本文结合实践工作经验，以北京工商大学为例对高校大学英语分级教学分班排课方法进行一定的探讨。

关键词: 大学英语；分级教学；分班方法；排课方法

分级教学即分层次教学。大学英语分级教学已成为教学改革的大势，其理论基础是因材施教。科学合理地分级教学是因材施教的前提和保证，在提高教学质量、优化师资配置、促进学生个性发展方面有积极的作用。以上海交通大学为首创，我国高等院校的公共英语分级教学始于20世纪80年代。到2010年，我国高等院校的公共英语分级教学已经基本普及。然而随着大学英语分级教学研究和实践的深入，困难和问题也不断显现。其中，科学分级与顺利排课之间矛盾尤为突出，学校规模越大、学生数量越多该矛盾就变得愈加尖锐。许多学校不得不因此而放弃分级或降低分级的科学性以保证排课的顺利实施。北京工商大学于2010年开始实施大学英语分级教学改革实

作者简介: 陈思伊，女，英国曼彻斯特大学会议口译专业硕士，北京工商大学外国语学院本科教学秘书。

践，并根据自身实际总结出了一系列针对分级教学的具体的分班和排课经验，但仍面临诸多困难和挑战。本文以北京工商大学为例，试针对大学英语分级教学形式下的分班排课方法进行探讨。

当前诸多分级教学的高校普遍采取的分级方案即根据学生英语水平分级，学生分属不同级别的教学班级进行英语授课，这不可避免地要打破原来自然班的建制，造成同一自然班的学生可能被分到不同的英语教学班，同一英语教学班的学生可能分属于不同的自然班，甚至分属不同专业。这种同一学生的双重班级属性为排课带来很大难度。学生随英语教学班上英语课、随自然班上其他课。在排课上，为保证学生在同一时间英语课与其他课程不冲突，只能将英语上课时间固定，在这个时间除了英语课外不上任何其他课程。然而这样绝对预留时间的方法产生的问题是：首先，大学英语授课教师的人数是固定的，每位教师所带班级数量也是有限的，如果英语课上课时间预留少，意味着该时间段上英语课的班级数量多，即使暂时忽略教室资源的限制，教师人数也是肯定不够的；那么，必须优先考虑教师数量，根据教师数量和学生总人数，确定分班的班级数以及每位教师所带班级数，进而确定英语课的排课时间。以北京工商大学为例，每个年级修大学英语课程的学生大约为2700人，公共外语老师18位，故以平均每班50人分班的话，则将学生分为54个班，每位教师带3个班。若每个班每周大学英语为4课时，则每位老师每周上12课时，在排课时即需要至少为大学英语课预留12课时的时间。占用时间如此多势必会影响到其他课程排课，显然是不可行的。

针对这一困境，分级教学排课方法上采用一种分组排课法。在教师资源允许的情况下，为尽可能少占时间，只能将分班方式细化，分组预留排课时间，具体操作方式如下：① 将全体学生以自然班（或学院专业）进行分组，分组个数等于单位教师所带班级数。② 在每位老师承担教学任务一致的假设前提下，每一组的教学班级数量均等于教师数量。③ 分组定时间，每组班级上英语课的时间固定，且不同组英语上课时间互不交叉。④ 每位教师每组带一个班。这样做就保证了对于单一自然班的学生，虽然在不同教学班级上课，但是在同一分组，而同一分组上课时间是一致的，在其他组的班级上英语课的时间，该班级依然可以上其他课程，有效减少了英语课占时间段过多影响其他课程排课的问题。

然而，这种分组定时间的排课方式虽然解决了打乱自然班建制产生的占时间问题，在实际操作中依然存在诸多弊端。由于分组是按照自然班进行的，各个专业班级的英语水平有可能差异甚大，每组内学生英语水平分布各有千秋，这意味着每组内部分级情况将不可预估。在这里有三个变量：分级标准、班级人数和教师授课班级的级别。在统一分级标准的情况下，如果优先保证班级人数，则每个分组下不同级别的班级数量也不尽相同，而英语教师每组带一个班，势必会有教师所带的班级来自不同的级别，这是不利于老师们发挥自身特长和教学效果最优化的；如果优先保证教师所带班级的级别，以更好地有针对性的因材施教，则只能人为调整班级人数，造成个别班级人数过多或过少，影响授课效果；如果既要保证班级人数又要保证教师不跨级别授课，只能以调整分级标准牺牲分级科学性为代价。无论哪一种都将违背分级教学的初衷。

北京工商大学在探索大学英语分级教学排课方法上进行了多年的探索，2015年以前，北京工商大学大学英语分级采取两级法，英语成绩优秀的学生分在商务英语班，主修商务英语，其他学生为普通班，主修新标准。在分班和排课上，采取“分组定时间+局部分级”的方式，即按照上述分组方式分组后，在组内进行分级，按照一定比例，每组产生相同班级数量的学生进入商务英语班级，如2014年我校大二大学英语排课分为3大组，每组产生4个商务英语班级，由四位商务英语教师分带这12个班，每组带一个班，每人共3个班。这样优先保证每组内部每个级别班级数量相同，有效避免了老师跨级别授课的隐患，商务英语授课老师形成独立的研讨备课小组，专门教授商务英语，有利于教师更好发挥优势，提升教学质量。但是，正如前文提到，每个分组的学生英语水平有所不同，每组内部分级很可能造成分级不公平，降低了分级教学的科学性。以上方式是面对分级教学排课困难进行的妥协方案，对于两级法来说，由于级别少，分级不公平的因素可以通过微调班级人数等方式，尽可能降低到最少；如该组商务英语人数多，则可以增加该组商务英语单位班级人数，减少普通班人数，综合来讲利大于弊，在一定时间内起到了良好的教学效果，是一定条件下所能够实现的最优方案。但对多级别分级模式将不适用，因为级别越多，局部分级造成的不科学性越强。

2015年北京工商大学英语分级改革正式启动，将分级数增加到5层10

级，分级面扩大到全校范围，将不再采取之前的局部分级。这种情况下，还要在预留时间段、教师跨级别授课、分级班级人数等因素中达成妥协实现最优化，给排课带来了巨大挑战。最终，为保证教学质量，避免老师跨级别授课，北京工商大学采取的方案是进行局部分组，在占时间段上做出让步。与前文所说的绝对的分组法相比，虽然2015级每位教师带3个班，上英语课有三个不同时间，但分组时分2个大组，而每组占两个时间，如果是周4课时的英语课，每个班级占用时间由绝对分组的4课时，增加到6~8课时，但是依然优于不分组时候的12课时。具体来说，假设每位教师上英语课的时间有a、b、c，则第一组占时间a、c，第二组占时间b、c，分班时，可将第一个班固定第一组，第二个班固定第二组，第三个班为两组学生都有。这样做，在占用时间上取了中间值，但是留出一个机动班级，方便在分班的时候进行调整，以保证三个时间段内每个级别的班级数一致。假设第一组第一级80人，时间为a和c，第二组第一级50人，时间为b和c，即可以取第一组40人作为第一级老师的第一个班级，上课时间为a，取第二组40人作为第一级老师的第二个班，上课时间为b，第一组剩下的30人和第二组剩下的10人，一起组成该老师的第三个班，上课时间为c。这种排课方法在占时间和跨级别授课上达成了妥协，但其最大的隐患就是过于复杂容易造成混乱，严重增加了排课人员的工作量。随着我校2015级改革的推进，其可行性还有待进一步考证。

大学英语分级教学为大势所趋，顺应教学改革的要求，保证改革质量，寻求与之适应的排课方法势在必行。作为教学运行关键环节，如果无法顺利排课，再好的改革方案也很难实施。解决科学分级与顺利排课之间的矛盾，找到一条合理可行排课方案，也是大学英语分级教学改革亟需解决的问题。

参考文献

[1] 朱再春. 高校大学英语分级教学分级方法与排课方法探讨[J]. 时代经贸,2010(6):240.
[2] 张国辉. 分组分级法和分组定时间段排课法[J]. 湖北广播电视大学学报,2009(2).